GRILL

W9-BFZ-358

HOOVER'S

MATT MOORE

PHOTOGRAPHS BY

Andrea Behrends
and Helene Dujardin

HOUGHTON MIFFLIN HARCOURT
BOSTON · NEW YORK 2020

SERIAL GRILLER

Grillmaster Secrets for Flame-Cooked Perfection

For information about permission to reproduce selections
from this book, write to trade.permissions@hmhco.com or to
Permissions, Houghton Mifflin Harcourt Publishing Company,
3 Park Avenue, 19th Floor, New York, New York 10016.

hmhbooks.com

Library of Congress Cataloging-in-Publication Data

Names: Moore, Matt (Matt R.), author.
Title: Serial griller : grillmaster secrets for flame-cooked
perfection / Matt Moore.
Description: Boston : Houghton Mifflin Harcourt, 2020. |
Includes bibliographical references and index.
Identifiers: LCCN 2019042991 (print) | LCCN 2019042992
(ebook) | ISBN 9780358187264 | ISBN 9780358182696 (ebook)
Subjects: LCSH: Barbecuing. | Outdoor cooking. | Cooking. |
LCGFT: Cookbooks.
Classification: LCC TX840.B3 M664 2020 (print) | LCC TX840.B3
(ebook) | DDC 641.7/6—dc23
LC record available at https://lccn.loc.gov/2019042991
LC ebook record available at https://lccn.loc.gov/2019042992

Book design by Kara Plikaitis

Food styling by Anna Hampton

Prop styling by Angie Mosier

Printed in China

TOP 10 9 8 7 6 5 4 3 2 1

To Persistence.
Nothing in the world can take
the place of persistence.

acknowledgments

To the Grillmasters. Though most of us started as strangers, we are now one family bound by our love for Serial Grilling! I cannot thank you enough for entrusting me with your stories, recipes, and time. Thank you for your patience. I'm eternally grateful and humbled by all of you.

To my agent, Stacey Glick. Through the thick and the thin—you are a constant. Your enthusiasm, motivation, and transparency has always been my literary compass, especially in guiding me through this endeavor—I'm incredibly blessed to have you in my corner.

To Andrea Behrends. Your lifestyle photography continues to capture our journeys beyond my most vivid memories. You are a true pro, a great traveler (so long as you get PreCheck), and a true friend. Thank you for being you. You are such an incredible woman who believes and fights for the very best in this world.

To Helene Dujardin, Angie Mosier, and Anna Hampton. Wow. You ladies sure rocked and rolled on some of the most beautiful grilled food and photography these eyes have ever seen. *Merci beaucoup!*

To Katherine Cobbs. You are strong beyond strong—keep being a light. Thank you for all of the support. And also to Sid Evans, Anja Schmidt, Margot Schupf, Kourtney Sokmen, Hunter Lewis, Robbie Melvin, Christi Crowley, Lyda Burnette, Martha Foose, and Danielle Costa.

A very special thanks to the incredible team at Houghton Mifflin Harcourt and everyone else who brought this book to life. For believing in me and this project, especially Sarah Kwak and Deb Brody. Cheers to this book—and to the many more to come. And because it takes an army: Jamie Selzer, Tai Blanche, Kara Plikaitis, Brianna Yamashita, Breanne Sommers, Tom Hyland, and Deri Reed.

And finally, to my family. There are a lot of us! To Mom and Dad for your leadership and love, best exhibited through your actions. To Ashley and Daniel for your enthusiasm and encouragement. To my greater family of in-laws, cousins, and more—your promotion always means more than you know.

And of course, to my lovely wife, Callie, and our daughters, Vivienne and Everly. My selfish gains of gallivanting for gluttony is only tempered by your sacrifice of having me always be somewhere other than home. Thank you for letting me do what I do without fear or regret. I love you girls.

And to the rest of y'all—the Serial Grillers reading this book. Crack open a cold beer and get to work.

INTRODUCTION

`I must confess: I'm a Serial Griller.`

It's a messy job—but I take pride in my work. Truth be told, I'm not the only one who finds pleasure in standing among the smoke and the flames to pursue one's craft. You see, for us Serial Grillers—no matter the season, the occasion, the meal, or the course—you can catch us all toiling over fire.

And since I'm coming clean, I'll say that I come from a family of Serial Grillers.

My grandfather Giddy spent his days butchering at our family store in Valdosta, Georgia. Though his chickens were always destined for my grandmother's cast-iron skillet filled deep with bubbly, caramel'd oil, his "butcher cuts," as he called them, were always skewered and grilled. Nothing beats my Sitty's fried chicken, but the delicious tastes of those grilled cuts certainly survive.

My other grandfather, Papa, a cattleman in Enterprise, Mississippi, lived larger and longer than most—always enjoying a supper of butter beans and a grilled Angus steak—a habit I fostered in favor, especially in his later years, despite the fact he readily demanded his meat be cooked well-done. I suppose each Serial Griller has their own signature way of doing things.

But my real experience in Serial Grilling came from both my father and my mother. Rarely a day would pass that Mama and Daddy wouldn't fire up the grill at our home in Lilburn, Georgia, stepping out on the brick patio they had laid by hand to cook our family supper. To the tunes of James Taylor and the Allmans, a veritable slew of grilled meats, sides, veggies, and desserts would make their way onto our table—though

it was rarely just our family gathering for the meal. The truth is, Serial Grilling might be personal work, but it benefits many.

Many say, including me, that cooking is love—and it's Old Smokey that my father partially credits to landing and keeping his wife, my mother, of over forty years.

Long before the white sandy beaches of Florida and Alabama earned the "30A" moniker, my family enjoyed our annual summer respite of sun and discovery there. But my father, ever persistent, could never let a vacation be a vacation. Fearing I would forget the mechanics of throwing a circle changeup after a few days on the beach, he would always schedule an extracurricular athletic day, far away from the emerald water and sandy beaches. But this particular year, I had my own game plan.

On that day, I ensured that I would cut our workout short, after I busted my father's catcher's mitt with a two-seam fastball. What can I say? Anger, or lack of vacation, gets the best of us. Dismayed, my father stopped into an old-timey hardware store, the kind that smells of oil and fertilizer, in hopes of finding some leather to mend up our mess. Going about our separate ways, aisle by aisle, I heard my father let out a scream…

I was perplexed. I found my father, a man stronger than any, literally hugging, hat tilted from pressing his face into the corrugated cardboard, a box that pictured what looked to be a small tin spaceship displaying two iconic words: "Old Smokey." No explanation was given to me, and we were out the door, Old Smokey in hand, in less than two minutes flat.

When we arrived back to our beach condo, Daddy proudly brought his find to Mama. Her eyes rolled, but it renewed the spark that was first lit with the pork chops grilled during their first dates in South Georgia. I took notice, and apparently that Old Smokey would light a spark in me too.

Up until that moment, I never realized our family's Serial Grilling was more out of convenience—and not for the art, as we might say. Better said, we were grilling with gas. Though such tools as gas certainly have their benefits when it comes to Serial Grilling, Old Smokey provided my father, and mom, too, with an opportunity to teach us kiddos about the purity of cooking with wood and charcoal. Soon, everything that was once old, became new. Hamburgers, chicken thighs, corn, ribs, and okra—all items we'd grilled before—came back to life on the grates of Old Smokey. Since then, I've devoted my life to Serial Grilling.

Over the years, I've come to learn that Serial Grillers come from all walks of life. No matter gender, race, or religion—Serial Grillers are all united by a passion for great taste. I'm proud to be a Serial Griller.

So I'm doing what I do—traveling by whatever means necessary, in the friendly skies in my '76 Piper Cherokee or on the road, to meet and convene with more Serial Grillers. As always, I'm inviting you to come along with me, to the smoke-filled, dark, secret places where these folks—some recognized, others soon to be—do their work. But I will caution you. This is a journey that will change your life—in the most delicious way possible…

...So be warned—you might, yourself, become a Serial Griller.

Part One

THE GRILLING

GUIDE

Whether you are a Serial Grilling enthusiast or a true pro, it's a good idea to take in the basics to help understand and expand upon our craft. After all, Serial Grilling is meant to be communal—it's fun to gather with other like-minded folks to enjoy not only the fruits of our labor (the food!), but also the science, tools, techniques, tricks, and hacks that help all of us stay on top of our grilling game.

MAILLARD REACTION

Put simply, browned food is good food. Put scientifically, browned food receives its distinctive look, smell, and taste from a process known as the Maillard reaction.

Yes, the grill marks on a steak or that golden char of crispy chicken skin that produces that rich, umami flavor is all the result of … science. We can all thank French chemist Louis-Camille Maillard, who discovered and detailed this process back in 1912.

While studying amino acid and sugar reactions at increased temperatures, Maillard noticed elevated levels of browning that occurred when temperatures began to reach, and exceed, 300°F. These complex flavors are not just limited to grilled foods, as toasted bread, roasted coffee, and my favorite beer (from malted barley) are all the result of this important reaction.

Here's the good news—you do not need to be a scientist in order to benefit from this technique. At its basic level, you simply need to grasp how the process works. Remember this: Foods will produce enhanced flavors, aromas, and colors when the natural proteins and sugars are exposed to heat. Got it? Good.

So when I tell you to preheat your grill, I'm doing it on purpose. I want it to reach the right temperature so that cut of rib eye, or that Brussels sprout, meets the grill at the right time and heat level to ensure that the Maillard reaction can occur.

When I tell you to not overcrowd your grill, again I'm doing it for a purpose. I want your food to react to the heat—to brown—and not steam (not brown). Putting too much food on the grill throws off the heat and moisture ratio—a double whammy of no-no.

For those paying attention, heat is your friend; moisture, from a grilling standpoint, is not. Most grillmasters will tell you to pat your meats or vegetables dry prior to cooking, as you don't want to throw a "wet" steak on a grill—no sear, *no bueno*. Sometimes, salt is added hours in advance to cooking, known as dry-brining, to draw out the moisture, or simply added à la minute to reduce the loss of moisture during the process.

Typically, foods that are billed as boiled, poached, or steamed do not produce the same flavor as those that are grilled, roasted, or otherwise cooked at high surface temperatures. Of course, there are exceptions to every rule—but for grilling purposes, we are largely always seeking to create an opportunity for the Maillard reaction to occur.

Whatever your approach, all of these techniques are done in an effort to cook more delicious food.

So, that's your *Jeopardy!* answer and cooking lesson all at once. Browned food is good food.

THE THRILL OF THE GRILL

It is widely noted that 75 percent of Americans own some form of a grill or smoker. But what type of grill or smoker is best to own is a hot debate. I realize most folks are not like me, with a trove of nearly every type of grill sitting in their backyard (or my 'cue cave, as my wife calls it). Rather than debate which grill, design, or brand is best, I have a question for you:

What is your grilling goal?
Better said, what are you willing to sacrifice
if you can only choose one type of grill?

The truth is, it really all comes down to *your* preferred balance of expense, time, convenience, cooking style, and, perhaps most important, flavor.

Most grills are built based on how they will be fueled. So let's examine some of the most accessible fuel types and designs.

Wood

The OG: From open pit to campfire, wood is the original fuel for fire. As such, most purists will state that using dried, natural hardwoods is still the superior form for authentic grilling.

In practice, typical woods like hickory, mesquite, oak, and even fruit woods are often burned away from the grill, with the resulting hot coals then placed underneath the cooking area. With a bit of sweat equity, you can create an open pit or grill on any budget. Modern-day versions, featuring custom sizes and grates that can be raised and lowered based on the desired temperature (i.e., proximity to the coals), can be built for those for whom money is no object.

The main drawback to using natural hardwoods as a fuel source is that it's normally a two-step, time-consuming process to cook food. Wood must be readily accessible and kept dry, and a fire must be started, followed by a period of burndown to produce coals for grilling. Though not convenient, it's hard to argue with the authentic flavor and atmosphere of a true wood-fired grill.

Wood Pellets

There is a camp of folks who believe they can have their cake, and eat it too. I'm eyeing all of you pellet grillers out there. A relative newcomer on the scene, a pellet grill utilizes food-grade wood pellets as both a source of fuel and flavor. That's right—you can get all of that delicious, authentic wood-fired flavor without the effort of maintaining a traditional wood-fired setup. But it comes at a cost—and I don't just mean the initial purchase price of a pellet grill, which is usually quite high.

Typically, a power outlet is required to light and fuel the pellets, and also to maintain an internal fan to keep the pellets burning at the desired temperature. In other words, you won't find many pellet grills at tailgates, unless a power generator is nearby. In my experience, while pellet grills are a fantastic design for those seeking unmatched reliability for low and slow smoking, they fall a bit short when it comes to producing high heat temperatures for searing.

Nonetheless, for those seeking a sustainable, relatively convenient source of authentic wood flavor, a pellet grill is a veritable option, widely growing in popularity.

Charcoal

Lump

An accessible alternative to actual hardwood, charcoal is formed when wood (or another natural substance) is heated in an environment absent of oxygen, producing what we refer to as lump charcoal. With water and other components removed, lump charcoal can be lit quickly and reliably and reach high temperatures, producing very little ash. Though charcoal is composed of wood, it typically provides much less smoke compared to natural hardwoods. For that reason, lumps or chips of hardwood are often added to the lit coals to produce a more natural, wood-fired flavor. Grilling purists almost always prefer lump charcoal over the cheaper alternative, briquettes.

Briquettes

Like a good slice of bologna, sometimes knowing less about the content of your consumption is ignorant bliss. Most briquettes are manufactured with wood by-products and other additives to allow for easier lighting and a more consistent burn. It's the lengthy list of "additives" in most briquettes that causes concern for so many. While readily accessible and affordable, briquettes also have the disadvantage of producing a significant amount of ash, compared to lump charcoal.

That said, there are many folks, including some featured in this book, who find briquettes superior to lump charcoal. Briquettes are formed in a consistent size, unlike lump charcoal, which can come in large chunks or small pieces, meaning they provide a reliable, consistent amount of energy, which can translate to superior temperature control.

Gas

It is estimated that 62 percent of grill owners own a grill fueled by gas. Why the majority? We are creatures of convenience. Gas provides an open flame environment with unrivaled ease and consistency. Virtually available in every shape and size, open and closed, gas grills utilize propane or natural gas, either by tank or fixed line as a heat source. Higher-end (more expensive) versions support well-insulated exteriors with high-quality, cast-iron grates, or infrared technology to conduct heat more evenly. Additional features might include side gas burners for stovetop-style cooking. Temperature control is precise and simple, used by dialing the knobs to the preferred settings. When cared for properly, these grills can last for decades.

While ease of use, affordability, and convenience might be king, flavor from a gas grill is certainly lacking. Some versions support grates designed to vaporize drippings to enhance flavor, but such elements seem more like a sales gimmick to this guy. Wood chips, usually contained within a foil packet, can be used over direct heat to produce a smoke effect, again to a varying degree of success. Daddy always taught me that if you want something, you need to work hard for it. In other words, do not expect foods cooked expediently on gas to have the same flavor as those made over hardwood or charcoal.

Electricity

This form is used most in urban environments where open flame is prohibited, like condos or small apartment communities. Flat top grills (usually referred to as griddles) or grill pans can also be used for indoor environments on stovetops (electric or gas). These setups provide a veritable source of consistent, reliable heat to deliver a grill-like look and flavor. Recently, infrared smokeless grills have also been gaining in popularity.

GRILLING DESIGNS AND SETUPS

Let's examine some of the most common types of grilling setups.

OPEN: Hardwood, lump, or briquette coals are typically positioned close to the cooking surface, and no lid or cover is utilized. Examples include flat top grills, hibachis, and Spanish-style *parrillas*. Open grills are most effective for high-heat, direct grilling due to the inability to trap heat for convection cooking, and are typically utilized for cooking smaller cuts of food that have been skewered, such as kebabs, satay, or yakitori. A main advantage of these grills is affordability and portability. I have a trusty open cast-iron setup that basically always sits in the back of my truck— meaning I can grill up anything, anywhere, if and when the mood strikes.

CLOSED: This is the most common of all setups, with the ability to burn nearly every type of wood or charcoal. Closed setups (i.e., with a lid) allow for direct-heat grilling, indirect grilling, and convection cooking (see page 11) by trapping the heat and maintaining a controlled airflow. The most popular designs are kettle, drum, or barrel—which all provide a large range of affordability and versatility.

KAMADO: Often referred to as egg-style smokers or grills, these setups serve as a great dual-purpose grill and smoker. Lump charcoal, and not briquettes, are typically encouraged for this design. More expensive versions are made of thick ceramic to provide an elevated source of insulation and allow the grill to maintain extremely precise temperature control for very low and high heat temperatures. A main drawback of this setup is that it can take 30 to 60 minutes for the grill to reach its desired setting, which often relegates its use to weekend cooking. Care must also be exercised to prevent the ceramic from cracking, which can occur in certain regions, especially those based in areas susceptible to cold temperatures with high humidity. Less expensive versions, featuring cheaper steel or porcelain insulators, have also gained in popularity. Although the temperature holding and control is less precise, to a degree, on these cheaper models, the start-up time to achieve a desired temperature, whether low or high, is typically 10 to 15 minutes, making them nearly as convenient as a gas grill.

HYBRID: A setup that most often can use both gas and charcoal, a hybrid is ideal for folks who want the convenience of gas cooking along with a charcoal-driven alternative for enhanced flavor when time permits.

LIGHTING THE FIRE

First and foremost, lighter fluids or other toxic flammable compounds should always be avoided for wood and charcoal setups.

WOOD: Always remove any ash or debris from the area supporting a controlled fire (which could be a patch of earth, a rockbed, or a large area of concrete free of other flammable items). Tightly ball or twist together sheets of newspaper to serve at the base. Nontoxic fire starters can also serve as kindling. Stack smaller pieces of kindling on top of the paper, each layer perpendicularly opposed, until you have at least two layers. Light the papers and allow the smaller wood to catch and burn. It is important to ensure oxygen reaches the fire; fanning the flames can help drive more oxygen to the fire, especially in the early stages. Avoid adding more wood until the smaller pieces have completely started to burn. Within 45 to 60 minutes, coals from the smaller pieces should be ready to transfer for use, depending on the setup. More wood can be added to the fire after it is established to provide further coals when required.

CHARCOAL: I prefer using a chimney starter with charcoal, especially when setting up a direct heat fire. Place crumpled newspapers in the bottom of the chimney and fill it with charcoal. Light the paper and place the chimney on a surface that can support a controlled fire (a concrete pad works great). I typically avoid placing the chimney on my grill, as I do not want the paper ash to collect. Once the lump charcoal or briquettes have completely turned to gray ash, add to the grill, then use the top and bottom vent openings to control airflow, which allows you to master temperature control. Keeping the vents fully open provides more airflow for high-heat direct grilling. Varying how much the top and bottom vents are open will let you restrict airflow and therefore reduce temperature. Every grill is different, as is your charcoal. I always tell folks that it's a good idea to do a "dry run" on a new grill—especially if you are planning on a lower, slower cook on an expensive piece of meat like brisket. You can simply light your fire and adjust the vent settings (without anything on the grill) to get a good idea of temperature and airflow control.

Another convenient method is to use an electric charcoal starter, assuming you have access to electricity. Simply place the metal prongs into a pile of charcoal, with the grill lid open and the bottom vents open. Plug the starter into a power outlet and allow the metal to heat, thereby catching the coals on fire. Once the surrounding coals have caught fire, carefully unplug and remove the starter, placing it in a safe area to cool until ready for storage. This device is especially helpful when only a portion of the coals are desired to be lit for low and slow grilling.

GAS: Gas grills should always be lit according to the manufacturer's instructions. In general, ensure that your fuel line is open and that the tank, or fixed line, is providing fuel.

If multiple burners exist, turn on the side that's indicated for lighting. Igniters are commonplace on grills these days, but they are also frequently the first item on a grill to go bunk! In any instance, a match or long lead lighter can be used to light the burner. If you are unsuccessful at lighting the burner after 30 to 45 seconds with the gas on, shut everything down, and turn off the gas from the tank or line. Retry the process after waiting 5 to 10 minutes.

Once the burner is lit, turn the knobs, if multiple burners exist, to light the other areas. Preheat the grill, then adjust the knobs to the desired cooking temperature.

ELECTRIC GRILLS AND SMOKERS: These can be turned on and off per the recommended instructions on each select device. Ensure power outlets are properly equipped to handle the standard 120v or 220v settings.

CONTROLLING THE FIRE

No matter your type of grill, or heat source, I primarily recommend setting up both a direct and indirect zone for proper cooking and temperature control. This is commonly referred to as a two-zone setup. First, let's grasp what I mean by direct and indirect grilling.

DIRECT GRILLING (RADIANT): This is the "hot" zone, as food is cooked close to the heat source, used for searing or for foods that cook rather quickly, such as kebabs and seafood. Using a gas grill, the direct zone would be the area where the burner or sets of burners are turned to the higher heat setting. For charcoal setups, I recommend placing all of the lit, and even unlit (for longer cooking periods), coals toward one side of the setup. Sometimes I see folks setting up multiple areas of charcoal—which is nonsense if you ask me. Keep it simple, stupid, and put it all to one side.

Assess your gas situation first!

Nothing is worse than firing up a grill, getting halfway through the cooking process, and realizing you are out of propane. Most tanks do not have a gauge, so it's often hard to tell just how much you have left. When in doubt, pick it up. If it's light, you are getting close to empty. Take it a step further by pouring near-boiling water up and down the sides of a tank (NOT on top) tilted on its side. Wait a few seconds and touch the tank—where it's cool, that's where your propane level lies.

INDIRECT GRILLING (CONVECTION): This is when food is cooked offset, either horizontally or vertically, from the heat source. On gas grills, this would be the area where the burners are at a lower, or completely off setting. For charcoal setups, this would be the area away from the lit coals.

CONDUCTION: Note that food also cooks through a process known as conduction, most commonly by the heat retained by metal surfaces like the grates on a grill or a cast-iron skillet.

For me, it's always easier to learn by example, so let's put all these ideas into action.

Let's pretend it's a summer day in Savannah, Georgia. In other words, it's as hot as Hades. Waiting for the bus, you decide to stand out in the middle of the sun. Bad idea. Pretty soon, you'll be "burning up" as you are under the direct, radiant heat of the sun. You smarten up and decide to move under a shade tree—though it's still hot outside, you feel some relief as you are indirectly away from the sun. Spotting a park bench back out in the sun, you decide to go sit down, a lazy mistake. Ouch! Not only are you back under the radiant heat, but your skin is nearly burned to a crisp due to the conduction of the sun on the metal surfaces. It's too bad there isn't a park bench under a shady tree!

Now that you're catching on, here's a cooking example. I might start out by searing some thick, juicy hamburgers over my direct, radiant zone to produce that rich crust and flavor (Maillard reaction). Once I've achieved the perfect sear, I want to move the burgers away from the direct heat to prevent them from burning—no hockey pucks! So I move the burgers to an indirect zone, and if I'm working on a closed setup, I cover the grill to allow the convection airflow to gently cook the burger up to my desired internal temperature, with no fear of flare-ups.

The reverse might be starting some beer-brined chicken wings on the indirect zone to slowly cook the meat until just done—making them fall-off-the-bone tender. Because I want that crispy, golden-brown skin, I move the nearly fully cooked wings over to the direct zone to render the fat and crisp up the skin.

And lastly, in terms of conduction, a hot dog roasted on a skewer over fire is likely to take longer to cook, and taste differently, than one that I place on the grill grates, which will benefit from conduction (sear).

Man, I'm getting hungry.

Setting Up a Two-Zone Grill

Setting up different zones will allow you to work within different temperature ranges.

ON GAS AND ELECTRIC GRILLS: Controlling the temperature is as simple as dialing a knob. You can set up the direct zone with a higher heat setting, and the indirect zone with a lower heat, or no heat setting.

FOR CHARCOAL AND WOOD SETUPS: It's all about airflow. Most wood and charcoal grills have both a top and bottom vent to control the airflow, and thereby the temperature. Want a roaring fire to cook a pizza with a crispy crust on the grill? Open up those vents all the way. Cooking ribs low and slow? You will want to just barely open the vents, allowing you to keep just enough airflow to keep the fire at a steady, slow state.

When using a charcoal setup for a very long cooking time, I always recommend the Minion Method. This setup works best on kettle or Kamado-style grills. Essentially, you fill the lower grill chamber with charcoal, creating a reverse volcano of sorts, piling the outer coals around the perimeter, while the center of the grill is absent of coals and in direct contact with the bottom grate, or airflow. Imagine inverting a traffic cone into your grill—pile coals around it and when you pull the cone out, you'll have the previously mentioned reverse volcano. Now that you're set up, you'll want to add just a few lit coals into the empty center (bottom) of the setup—this is where an electric charcoal starter is superior to a chimney starter, provided its ability to light just a few coals. Make sure these lit coals are just adjacent to, and slightly in contact with, the outer formed perimeter of coals. From there, you control the airflow so that the initial coals burn in a slow, outward manner, lighting the perimeter coals as the fire burns. This method can provide up to 20 hours of reliable burn, without having to ever open the grill (loss of moisture, smoke, and flavor) or add more coals.

For further refined control, you can add water pans or physical dividers like smoking stones, either between the food and heat source to protect the food, or directly under the food to add moisture, which is typically more relevant to smoking than grilling.

Indoor Grilling

Sometimes it rains, snows, or is just too darned cold or hot to stand out in the elements to grill. (Note: None of those things prevent a true Serial Griller from manning the fire!) Or, you live in a place where an association prevents you from enjoying the thrill of the grill. In such instances, you can utilize a grill pan on the stovetop, or even an electric or infrared grill indoors to get your fix. If you are using a grill pan on the stovetop, think of it as your direct zone—getting those delicious and beautiful grill marks on a thick, juicy pork chop. Your indirect/convection zone can be a heated oven, to allow you to trap the heat and cook the meat up to your desired temperature. I always try to avoid covering foods on the stovetop, as it traps moisture, which deglazes the pan, thereby undoing my hard work of searing in the first place. If, by default, your grilling will be limited to indoors, a good hood or ventilation system is recommended. If you are stuck without such measures, make sure to open a window or two—nobody wants to create an indoor rainstorm set off by the fire alarm!

ACCESSORIES

I tend to be a minimalist when it comes to equipment and ingredients. In fact, I take pride in grilling great food without relying on too much "extra stuff." With that in mind, I put together a list of go-to items that I, along with many of the grillmasters from this book, rely on to make sure we are masters of the craft.

DIGITAL THERMOMETERS: Most stock thermometers on grills and smokers are terribly inaccurate, so I recommend a separate thermometer clipped or suspended near the cooking surface to get a true cooking temperature from your grill—this is especially helpful when low and slow temperatures are a must. A second digital meat thermometer can be used for checking internal temps of cooked items. Sure, there are the old-school rules about the touch test, looking at the color of juices, so on and so forth. But there's no need to guess when you can make a minimal investment in this piece of technology to make sure you are always 100 percent certain.

CHIMNEY STARTER OR ELECTRIC CHARCOAL STARTER: These items make your life a lot easier when building a wood- or charcoal-based fire, without any additional chemicals or additives.

GRILL COVER: Protect your investment when you're not using it, especially if your grill sits outside. Don't go for a cheap plastic cover either—it will melt if you place it on the grill while still warm and typically it will crack or fall apart in less than a year. Invest in a good-quality laminate, or treated heavy-duty canvas-style cover that will protect your grill and its components over the long haul, so you can keep calm, and keep on grillin'.

STAINLESS TONGS, SPATULAS, AND OTHER GIFT BOX ACCESSORIES: These are the cliché, monogrammed gifts we receive on holidays or birthdays, but truth be told, you don't need your name on a tool to make you cool. Some quality stainless tools will serve you well while working the grill. I typically get by with a good set of tongs and a spatula—the rest is, well, not necessary if you ask an old fart like me.

GRILL SCRAPER: It's important to keep your grill and grates clean. A good-quality scraper will allow you to remove any stubborn items stuck to the surface. I typically avoid the wire bristle brushes, especially the cheapo ones, as those wire bristles have been known to break off and potentially get stuck into your food—seriously not good.

GRILL PANS, BASKETS, AND MATS: These are all great tools when cooking select items such as fish, vegetables, or small and delicate ingredients when you want to impart great grill flavor without too much fuss. You won't have to worry about losing items into the fire when you use these.

HEAVY-DUTY ALUMINUM FOIL: Foil is a Serial Griller's best friend. It serves as a great surface that can be placed directly on the grill grates to prevent items from sticking or falling through. In terms of staging and timing, using foil provides an invaluable solution to hold cooked items for long periods of time. I can't tell you how often I've cooked for larger groups and needed to use foil to hold the first batch of food until I finished grilling off the rest of the food. Last but not least, to create smoke flavor on a gas grill, add some wood chips into a handmade foil "packet." Make a few punctures into the packet to allow the smoke to penetrate and flavor the food when cooked over direct heat. Personally, heavy-duty foil is worth the extra investment—nothing is worse than cheap foil.

TIPS FOR GRILLING

OIL YOUR GRATES: To prevent sticking, dip a folded towel (an old terry cloth towel works best) in canola or vegetable oil and use tongs to rub the oil on the grates prior to adding your food.

TWO SKEWERS ARE BETTER THAN ONE: One skewer is often not enough—it's usually too flimsy to get a hold of when trying to turn kebabs or other skewered items. Instead, use two skewers for better control. On that note, do not overcrowd your skewers. The idea is to leave enough space in between each item to allow the heat to do its magic—remember the Maillard reaction. Items that are bunched too close together will steam, not brown.

GRAB A SIDEKICK: Hopefully you've got a friend around to chew the fat when grilling—and also for the extra set of hands. Most grills nowadays also come with a side table or foldable trays, which really help when prepping or holding items—and also give you a place to put down that frosty beverage when it's time to work the grill.

STOP POKING AND PRODDING: Most folks have trouble with items sticking to the grill because their grill temperature is not hot enough, or they have not allowed sufficient time for the food to cook prior to flipping. Be patient, folks.

Extinguishing the Fire

TO SAFELY EXTINGUISH WOOD AND CHARCOAL FIRES: Remove the oxygen. Open pits can be allowed to smolder and naturally expire. Water can be used, carefully, in instances where the fire needs to be extinguished quickly. For most closed grills, simply close the top and bottom vents to prevent oxygen from fueling the fire.

WHEN SHUTTING DOWN GAS GRILLS: Turn the gas off from the tank or fuel valve first to burn the gas from the fuel lines. Once the burners are no longer lit, due to fuel starvation, turn the knobs to the closed or off setting.

FOR ELECTRIC GRILLS: Set to the closed or off setting and remove the power cord from the outlet.

Cleanup

TURN THE HEAT UP: After you've finished grilling, turn the heat up (or open all the vents on a charcoal grill to drive up the temperature). After 5 minutes, the grates and surfaces will be super hot, making it easy to clean the grates with a brush.

NO GRILL BRUSH? How about an onion? Cut an onion in half and place the cut side down on the grill. Stick a fork in the onion and rub it up and down the grates—the natural oils from the vegetable will help clean and season the grill.

AGAIN, FOIL IS YOUR FRIEND: Crumpled-up foil can also be a great cleaning tool. Make small tight balls of foil and use some elbow grease to rub over the grates to remove any stuck-on grease or grime. If the grates are still hot, it's a good idea to grasp the foil ball with a towel first—to prevent the convection heat from causing any burns.

DEEP CLEAN: It's a good idea to occasionally do a "deep clean" on the grill, disassembling major items and giving them a through scrub. Personally, I love firing up a pressure washer, and cleaning my grill gives me an excuse to do so. If you do not have a pressure washer, soak the grates in warm water and, depending on the manufacturer's instructions, possibly include a dash of a nonreactive cleaning agent.

Part Two

THE GRILLMASTERS

As the saying goes, success is a journey—not a destination. And the doing is often more important than the outcome. Fortunately for you, the outcome of following these delicious recipes and stories will be worth the doing!

Truth be told, I relish—I survive—in the journey. The following pages are the amalgamation of an honest pursuit to hunt down some of the best Serial Grillers across America. By whatever means necessary, I traveled over 10,000 miles to meet folks wherever they would have me—in homes, in restaurants, on street corners, or in the wide-open Texas plains. There's never been a rhyme or reason to my madness. I prefer to go where the wind blows, literally. Some of these folks are acquaintances, others were recommended through friends of friends, and some I just put in my crosshairs and sought to meet. We are all friends now.

Grilling is practiced in nearly every culture throughout the world. And because we are blessed with so much diversity in America, my goal is to feature as many types of cuisines, philosophies, techniques, and recipes as possible. This is not an end-all-be-all format—rather it is a template. My hope is that you will relish these stories and recipes with the same enthusiasm with which I share them. Cheers.

BILL & TONY DARSINOS,
owners of Greko

scarfed down a pita, overstuffed with tender pork souvlaki as an afternoon "snack"!

I get a good rise out of Greko's owners, cousins Bill and Tony Darsinos, when I share my tales of gluttony and subterfuge. But when I try to blame them for my transgressions, they simply laugh and tell me that my family business is my family business.

Such is the case with these two gentlemen—and the entire Darsinos family. Bill's and Tony's fathers, Spiros and Evangelos, respectively, immigrated to America from Greece in the '60s and '70s. Seeking opportunity and a better life for their families, the elder Darsinos built several successful pizzerias after settling into life in Middle Tennessee. As kids, Bill and Tony spent their days working in the family restaurants as servers, busboys, and cooks. From an early age, they learned that hard work and sacrifice are the building blocks of good character that lead to success.

"Back then, if Dad couldn't make it to a movie on a Friday night, we all knew why," Tony tells me. It was what it was...the Darsinos family was focused on fueling their American dream through their love of food and hospitality.

But every summer there was a respite, a reconnection to the old country. Bill's and Tony's tone and demeanor soften as they speak of summers spent in their native Nemea, a town roughly a hundred kilometers southwest of the capital of Athens. This is a town that is steeped in mythology. It's where Hercules is credited for his heroic slaying of the Nemean lion. A mural of the lion lies just within the entrance of Greko—a symbol of pride and homage to Bill and Tony's deep Greek roots.

After achieving the American dream, the Darsinos family felt the siren call of their native Greece

MOST FOLKS will tell you that transparency, communication, and honesty are all keys to a good marriage. With that in mind, I have to come clean.

Greko Greek Street Food sits just a mere mile from my home in East Nashville. I can make it there and back in less than 20 minutes riding my bike. So, honey, when I claim to not be hungry for dinner, it's not due to my quick workout—it's because I snuck out to Greko and beckoning them home—so they sold their homes and businesses. Bill and Tony tell me that such an abrupt change was common practice for most first-generation immigrants—the short-term goal was to build stability abroad, with the dream of returning to live out the golden years back in their parents' homeland. But soon after returning to Greece, the family realized that the opportunities for them in America were like no place else. The majority of the family returned to the States in the late '80s.

While Bill continued in his family's footsteps as a successful restaurateur, Tony became an architect. Over the years—decades—the two talked often about opening a spot that would honor their memories of Greece and the street food there that they continue to enjoy during their travels back to visit friends and relatives—the inspiration for Greko.

Their restaurant is a departure from the traditional blue-checked tableclothed Greek diners familiar to most Americans. Situated on Main Street between Nashville's glitz and glam of downtown and its edgier east side, Greko's location was chosen with purpose. It is for the people. Eccentric graffiti-style murals appear on walls inside and out, Greek hip-hop serves as a tonal soundtrack, and the campfire smell of a wood-fired grill all provide a sensory overload in the best way possible. Despite the hip interior and trendy patio scene, the environment is welcoming and comfortable with a focus on food and family.

And like the location, everything on the menu at Greko is intentional; Bill and Tony spent ten years perfecting each dish. You can taste the inspiration and, perhaps most importantly, the authenticity of the cuisine in every single bite.

Bill, Tony, and their team effortlessly put out classics like tender grilled octopus, savory souvlaki, and the most delicious fall-off-the-bone chicken, which is served with a more modern spin on a honey-lemon sauce. And let's not forget about the house-made pita, grilled to order over the fire—unreal!

Bill and Tony reveal to me their main goal is not just to create a successful restaurant. Rather, it's all about respect. Respect for their culture, its cuisine, and their roots.

"If we opened this restaurant in Athens, Greece, and not Nashville, Tennessee, would we succeed?"... "Absolutely, brother!"

It is then that Bill tells me that the constant barometer for Greko is simple. "If we opened this restaurant in Athens, Greece, and not Nashville, Tennessee, would we succeed?"

Before I can speak (my mouth was full), Tony looks at Bill—it's a look that only another family member can give. He answers the question without hesitation: "Absolutely, brother!"

It's that kind of family support and love—unconditional—that earns plenty of respect in my book.

Forgive me, honey?

It is with a heavy heart that I share that Antonio (Tony) Darsinos passed away on August 18, 2019. It was an honor to enjoy his company and food. May he rest forever in peace.

PORK SOUVLAKI

SERVES 10 TO 12

Hands-On: 35 minutes | Total: 25 hours, including 24 hours marinating

Souvlaki (literally "skewers") is the quintessential street food of Greece. Typically ordered by the dozen, they are highly addictive. Bill and Tony spent years searching for the perfect domestic cut of pork to suit their tastes, finally settling on the pork collar for its mix of rich flavor, fat, and tenderness. In a pinch, you could substitute boneless pork shoulder (butt) or boneless, country-style ribs. To get the right amount of char, tenderness, and flavor, you need to grill the pork hot and fast over direct heat until just cooked through.

1 pork collar (4 to 6 pounds)

½ cup extra-virgin olive oil

2 tablespoons dried oregano

2 tablespoons kosher salt

1½ tablespoons freshly ground black pepper

Lemon wedges, to serve

1   Using a sharp knife, butterfly the pork collar until you have a large, flat layer about 1 inch thick. Cut the meat into 1-inch cubes and place in a large mixing bowl. Add the olive oil, oregano, salt, and pepper and toss everything together with your hands until evenly incorporated. Cover and marinate in the fridge for at least 24 hours.

2   Open the bottom vent of a charcoal grill completely. Light a charcoal chimney starter filled with charcoal. When the coals are covered with gray ash, pour them onto the bottom grate of the grill. Adjust the vents as needed to maintain an internal temperature of 400° to 450°F. Coat the top grate with oil; place on the grill. (If using a gas grill, preheat to medium-high [400° to 450°F].)

3   Carefully thread the marinated pork onto skewers, portioning about 6 ounces for each and being careful to leave about ¼ inch between the pieces to avoid overcrowding. Place on the grill and cook, uncovered and turning occasionally, for 8 to 10 minutes, until the internal temperature reaches 145°F. If flare-ups occur, cover with a grill lid to quell flames as necessary. Serve the souvlaki with lemon wedges.

OCTOPUS SOUVLAKI

SERVES 4

**Hands-On: 1 hour 25 minutes | Total: 26 hours
30 minutes, including 24 hours chilling**

Bill and Tony had their fears that this dish, a Greek favorite, would be less than welcomed by most landlocked Nashvillians. To their surprise and joy, it became one of their bestsellers. Tender, savory, and still sweet—this is a staple dish found throughout their homeland. Preparing this dish at home couldn't be easier, and finding fresh or frozen octopus at your local market is becoming more the norm than the exception.

Kosher salt

1 whole octopus (about 3 pounds), cleaned and dressed

Freshly ground black pepper

½ cup extra-virgin olive oil

¼ cup lemon juice

½ teaspoon dried oregano

1   Bring a large stockpot of heavily salted water to a boil over medium-high heat. Add the octopus, reduce the heat to medium, and cook for 50 minutes, until you can easily pierce the meat with a fork. Remove the octopus and place as flat as possible on a baking sheet. Pat dry and refrigerate, uncovered, for 24 hours or overnight.

2   Remove the head from the octopus and cut the tentacles into 1-inch pieces. Thread the octopus onto skewers, portioning about 3 ounces for each, and season with salt and pepper.

3   In a small serving bowl, mix together the oil, lemon juice, and oregano. Set the dipping sauce aside.

4   Open the bottom vent of a charcoal grill completely. Light a charcoal chimney starter filled with charcoal. When the coals are covered with gray ash, pour them onto the bottom grate of the grill. Adjust the vents as needed to maintain an internal temperature of 400° to 450°F. Coat the top grate with oil; place on the grill. (If using a gas grill, preheat to medium-high [400° to 450°F].)

5   Grill the octopus skewers for approximately 4 minutes on each side, or until just firm to the touch. Remove from the heat and serve with the dipping sauce.

LAMB PITA

SERVES 8

Hands-On: 40 minutes | Total: 25 hours 25 minutes, including 24 hours marinating

Although pork is the more traditional ingredient in Greece, most Americans associate either lamb or beef as the protein of any good wrap or gyro. To please as many palates as possible, Bill and Tony crafted their lamb in a style similar to what you find in the Corinthian region of Greece. The recipe and technique is built on their memories of their grandparents and experiences living and traveling in the old country.

1 (5-pound) boneless lamb shoulder

¼ cup extra-virgin olive oil

1 tablespoon minced garlic

5 tablespoons kosher salt

3 tablespoons dried oregano

1 tablespoon freshly ground black pepper

1 teaspoon dried thyme

1 teaspoon dried spearmint

For serving: grilled pita bread, Greek yogurt, thinly sliced tomatoes, minced fresh parsley, thinly sliced red onion, paprika

1 Trim any excess fat from the exterior of the lamb shoulder. In a small bowl, mix together the olive oil, garlic, salt, oregano, pepper, thyme, and spearmint. Using your hands, carefully rub the spice mixture over the entire lamb shoulder. Cover and marinate in the refrigerator for 24 hours or overnight.

2 Open the bottom vent of a charcoal grill completely. Light a charcoal chimney starter filled with charcoal. When the coals are covered with gray ash, pour them onto the bottom grate of the grill, and then push to one side of the grill. Adjust the vents as needed to maintain an internal temperature of 400° to 450°F. Coat the top grate with oil; place on the grill. (If using a gas grill, preheat to medium-high [400° to 450°F] on one side.)

3 Place the shoulder on the open grill over direct heat and grill, uncovered, for about 5 minutes on every side, creating a dark, seared crust. Move the shoulder to indirect heat and cook, grill covered, for an additional 45 to 50 minutes, until a thermometer inserted into the center of the shoulder reads 140°F. Remove the shoulder from the heat and rest on a cutting board for 10 minutes.

4 Using a sharp knife, thinly slice 4 to 6 ounces of lamb from the shoulder and arrange on a grilled pita. Top with a dollop or two of Greek yogurt, a few slices of tomato, a sprinkle of parsley, some thinly sliced red onion, and dash of paprika. Wrap partially in foil to hold. Repeat to make eight pitas.

ATHENIAN CHICKEN

SERVES 4

Hands-On: 50 minutes | **Total:** 26 hours, including 24 hours marinating

One of the first things you notice when walking into Greko is the slew of whole chickens slowly roasting, rotisserie-style, over the open fire. The sight and smell literally makes your mouth water, so it's hard not to order a quarter or a half when standing at the register. Nowadays, many consumer grills boast rotisserie attachments to mimic this cooking method at home. You can also get a great result by cooking the chicken on a rack, or even using a beer can–style setup over indirect heat.

Bill and Tony did not stop at great roasted, moist chicken, and you shouldn't either. In the past 10 or 15 years, they noticed several of their favorite spots in Athens started to serve up a honey-lemon sauce to accompany the bird. While the sauce might be a relatively new addition, it makes the dish.

CHICHEN

1 (3- to 4-pound) whole chicken

1 tablespoon dried oregano

1½ teaspoons paprika

½ teaspoon ground cumin

2 teaspoons kosher salt

1 teaspoon freshly ground black pepper

HONEY-LEMON SAUCE

⅓ cup lemon juice

¼ cup yellow mustard

¼ cup honey

¼ cup extra-virgin olive oil

1½ teaspoons dried oregano

1 teaspoon fresh cracked pepper

1 teaspoon kosher salt

Minced fresh parsley

1 **For the chicken:** Remove and discard the giblets from the chicken. Wash the chicken thoroughly and pat dry. In a small bowl, mix the oregano, paprika, cumin, salt, and pepper together. Using your hands, rub the spice mixture all over the bird, including inside the cavity. Place the chicken in a shallow dish, cover, and marinate in the refrigerator for 24 hours or overnight.

2 Open the bottom vent of a charcoal grill completely. Light a charcoal chimney starter filled with charcoal. When the coals are covered with gray ash, pour them onto the bottom grate of the grill, and then push to one side of the grill. Adjust the vents as needed to maintain an internal temperature of 300° to 350°F. Coat the top grate with oil; place on the grill. (If using a gas grill, preheat to medium-high [300° to 350°F] on one side.)

3 Place the chicken, preferably on a rotisserie or rack, over indirect heat and cook, grill covered, for about 1 hour, until the internal temperature reaches 165°F. The chicken can be served whole, or you can remove the backbone and serve in halves, or quarter it by removing the thighs from the breasts.

4 **For the sauce:** Mix together all the sauce ingredients in a small bowl. Generously drizzle the sauce over the cooked chicken and garnish with parsley.

Note: The sauce can be made in advance and kept for up to 2 weeks in the fridge, covered. Bring to room temperature and shake vigorously prior to serving.

CARLTON "CADILLAC" BRANDON,
chef/owner of Lillian's BBQ

"DON'T WALK BY, STOP BY."

If you are within earshot of Carlton Elliot Brandon, you are likely to hear those words, in his deep baritone drawl, over and over again. It's not just the sound of his voice that will catch your attention. Most likely, you'll be close enough to pick up the scent of smoke and spareribs wafting through the air. One sniff pretty much guarantees that not only will you stop by, but you will eat too.

A few minutes into my visit, I quickly gather that Mr. Brandon is better known throughout Atlanta as Cadillac, a nickname he inherited from his grandfather, yet also earned because he coincidentally happened to paint Cadillacs to make a living for a time.

"I suppose I worked over thirty jobs by the time I was thirty," Cadillac tells me while toiling over a large grill fueled with lump charcoal and red oak—the latter of which he harvests by hand. From driving trucks to working at the zoo, Cadillac credits his vast, varied resume as an asset that has allowed him to become "well-rounded, and able to work and deal with every-one no matter their background or experience."

But it was his grandmother, Annie Lillian Stodghill, who bestowed upon him the inspiration and passion to dedicate the second half of his life to cooking. Lillian, as she was known, shared her knowledge and recipes whenever called upon.

In his early thirties, after his thirty jobs, Cadillac decided it was time to enroll in the Culinary Arts program at Atlanta Technical College. Cadillac still proudly recalls sporting a crisp, white chef's coat. It was "a defining moment in his life" where, for the first time ever, he knew he was doing what he was

"This is what I love, man—that sound of the sizzle, the smoke, the atmosphere—and the food."

meant to do. "This is what I love, man—that sound of the sizzle, the smoke, the atmosphere—and the food," he told me with a big, candid smile.

A love for doing what you do is infectious, and the love bug soon bit Cadillac in more ways than one. While attending a school-sponsored culinary competition in Louisville, Kentucky, Cadillac was about to step into an elevator, unaware his life was soon to change. A beautiful gal crossed his path, and he thought, "Wouldn't it be crazy if she became my wife?" Apparently wild, spontaneous thoughts can become a reality—Deborah and Cadillac have been married a decade now and have two beautiful daughters, Kelsey and Sarah. Ain't it amazing how food brings us all together!

The journey continued. Most chefs will tell you that owning and operating their own restaurant is a career goal. So after working a stint at Atlanta's Café Intermezzo, Cadillac took an opportunity to strike out on his own—putting a pause on culinary school to gain real-life experience and chase the restaurant dream. Though that restaurant still survives, Cadillac stepped away from the endeavor after just a year. What some might view as a setback was just a growing pain for a man who felt he still had not yet found his true calling.

"I needed to get back to my roots," he says as he hands me a sliced sparerib that has been on the grill for only a few hours. It's as tender and fall-off-the-bone delicious as any I've tasted that required twice the time and effort. Mouths full, we bob our heads up and down, with childlike giggles. Without saying a word, our reactions and unspoken gestures make it perfectly clear we agree that this food is that good.

Apparently, Cadillac has cooked and sold a lot of ribs. After walking away from the restaurant and completing school, Cadillac bought a grill, put it on a trailer, and drove around the city of Atlanta selling his food. It seemed like a crazy endeavor, until I heard his sales pitch. Tapping quarter beats on the grill grate with his tongs, he sings, "five dollar, five dollar, five dollar rib sandwiches," to the tune of the footlong Subway jingle.

And the customers came.

After months on the go, a friend invited Cadillac to set up permanent shop outside the famed Clermont Lounge, a late-night Atlanta institution. The rowdy crowds came to realize that they were not just indulging in standard "drunk fare," as Cadillac shunned the processed nonsense of most street-food stands to cook things his way, without any shortcuts.

Before long, Cadillac and the creation of his chili-slaw dogs, pulled pork sandwiches, and smoked sausages were delivering just as much entertainment outside the lounge as the inside shenanigans. Seriously, watching this man work solo behind the grill is truly astonishing. Tongs and other utensils are shunned entirely. He uses his hands to quickly move items on and off the direct heat—a feat that would scorch most fingertips. Like a true pro, he preps and artfully finishes each item impeccably to order. On busy nights, Cadillac serves up to 600 hungry patrons, and always with a smile.

As a way to honor and carry on the legacy of his grandmother, Cadillac operates his cooking and catering outfit under the name Lillian's BBQ. Though he's found a steady home and reputation in his current gig, something tells me that bigger and better things are on the horizon. I tell him that my own grandmother regularly impressed upon me that "good things happen to good people." Cadillac laughs, telling me that Lillian always drove home that "if you can't do anything, you can always feed somebody."

And in that moment, bellies full and with endless grins, it occurs to both of us—grandmothers always know best.

GRILLED SPARERIBS

SERVES 6

Hands-On: 1 hour 5 minutes | Total: 1 hour 50 minutes

Most BBQ pitmasters will tell you that a low and slow technique turns out the best rib, but one bite of Cadillac's spareribs have me on the fence—this rather hot technique yields a smoky flavor with plenty of tenderness. Though this method takes less time, the actual hands-on time required is a bit more than the "set it and forget it" mentality. The key is to keep the ribs working, flipping them over direct heat for just under an hour, and then letting them slowly work their way up to temp over indirect heat for an additional hour or so.

Although I was able to learn the technique, Cadillac's Zone 1 (named for his neighborhood) dry rub and sauce remain under lock and key. But the fire and flavor of this grilled rib recipe is good enough, even without any extra secrets.

2 racks pork spareribs (about 6½ pounds), membranes removed

Kosher salt

Freshly ground pepper

Granulated garlic, or garlic powder

Preferred BBQ sauce (optional)

1 teaspoon fresh cracked pepper

1 teaspoon kosher salt

1 Open the bottom vent of a charcoal grill completely. Light a charcoal chimney starter filled with charcoal. When the coals are covered with gray ash, pour them onto the bottom grate of the grill, and then push to one side of the grill. Adjust the vents as needed to maintain an internal temperature of 350° to 450°F. Coat the top grate with oil; place on the grill. (If using a gas grill, preheat to medium-high [350° to 450°F] on one side.)

2 Rinse the ribs and pat dry. Season the ribs liberally on both sides with equal parts salt, pepper, and garlic.

3 Grill the ribs over direct heat, covered, for 10 minutes. Open the lid, flip the ribs, and continue in this manner for 30 to 40 minutes, flipping every 10 minutes, or often enough to prevent the ribs from burning on either side.

4 Move the ribs to indirect heat and continue to cook, covered and flipping halfway through the process, until an internal temperature of 170°F, up to an additional 30 to 40 minutes.

5 Slice the ribs and serve as is, or with your favorite BBQ sauce on the side.

GRILLED QUAIL

SERVES 3 AS A MAIN DISH OR 6 AS AN APPETIZER

Hands-On: 30 minutes | Total: 25 hours, including 24 hours marinating

It turns out that when Cadillac is not cooking, he's either hunting or fishing. A favorite of most sportsmen, especially in Georgia, is the ever-elusive yet delicious quail. Marinated for 24 hours and grilled, this game bird is an absolute showstopper. You can find whole, dressed quail by befriending a sportsman, or through any specialty retailer or online store. Cadillac does not suggest trying to substitute Cornish hen, as the fatty skin will not render in the same manner as wild game.

6 whole quail (about 4 ounces each), cleaned and dressed

½ cup orange juice

½ cup mojo criollo marinade (such as Goya; see Resources, page 299)

1 tablespoon Tajín Clásico seasoning (see Resources, page 299), plus more for seasoning

2 garlic cloves, minced

1　Combine the quail, orange juice, mojo criollo, Tajín seasoning, and garlic in a large freezer bag, seal, and marinate in the refrigerator for 24 hours.

2　Open the bottom vent of a charcoal grill completely. Light a charcoal chimney starter filled with charcoal. When the coals are covered with gray ash, pour them onto the bottom grate of the grill, and then push to one side of the grill. Adjust the vents as needed to maintain an internal temperature of 350° to 450°F. Coat the top grate with oil; place on the grill. (If using a gas grill, preheat to medium-high [350° to 450°F] on one side.)

3　Meanwhile, remove the quail from the marinade and pat dry; discard the marinade. Lightly season the quail, inside and out, with additional Tajín seasoning.

4　Add the quail to the grates over direct heat, breast up. Grill, uncovered, for 5 minutes. Flip the quail, breast-side down, and move to indirect heat. Cook, covered, until an internal temperature of 165°F, about 20 minutes.

GRILLED FLANKEN RIBS: MEXICAN AND KOREAN STYLE

SERVES 6 TO 8

Hands-On: 1 hour | Total: 25 hours 30 minutes, including 24 hours marinating

You really start to see Cadillac's mastery of flavor with these preparations of flanken ribs. Truth be told, I was relatively unfamiliar with his reference to this cut, until I saw the actual meat. To make your life easy, you can think of flanken as essentially thinly sliced short ribs. The finger-friendly bites are highly addictive and also a unique preparation for entertaining. The best part is that they cook up quickly on the grill.

To truly enjoy the Mexican-style ribs, Cadillac recommends you take a bite of a grilled jalapeño first, then chase it with a bite of rib. It's seriously one of the best one-two combos I've ever tasted. Also, Cadillac is adamant that you don't get too heavy-handed on the pear for the Korean ribs—just a bit will do. It's best to let the ribs marinate overnight to take on as much flavor as possible.

MEXICAN MARINADE

½ cup orange juice

½ cup mojo criollo marinade, preferably Goya brand (see Resources, page 299)

1 tablespoon Tajín Clásico seasoning (see Resources, page 299), plus more for seasoning

2 garlic cloves, minced

KOREAN MARINADE

½ cup soy sauce

½ cup brown sugar

1 tablespoon minced garlic

1 tablespoon minced fresh ginger

¼ ripe Korean or Bartlett pear, mashed

1½ teaspoons sesame oil

4 pounds flanken ribs

6 baby bok choy

6 jalapeño chiles, cut lengthwise with seeds and ribs removed

Kosher salt

1 Combine the marinade ingredients for each style in separate ziplock freezer bags. Divide the ribs evenly and add to the marinades. Seal and refrigerate for 24 hours.

2 Open the bottom vent of a charcoal grill completely. Light a charcoal chimney starter filled with charcoal. When the coals are covered with gray ash, pour them onto the bottom grate of the grill, and then push to one side of the grill. Adjust the vents as needed to maintain an internal temperature of 350° to 450°F. Coat the top grate with oil; place on the grill. (If using a gas grill, preheat to medium-high [350° to 450°F] on one side.)

3 Working in batches if necessary, grill the ribs on one side over direct heat, uncovered and undisturbed, for 5 to 7 minutes. Flip the ribs, and cook an additional 5 minutes. Move the ribs to indirect heat and place the bok choy alongside. Close the lid and cook the ribs for 20 minutes and the bok choy, seasoning lightly with salt while grilling, for 15 to 20 minutes, until tender.

4 While the ribs and bok choy are cooking over indirect heat, place the jalapeños over direct heat and grill, turning on occasion, for 10 to 12 minutes, until slightly charred and tender.

5 Remove the ribs, jalapeños, and bok choy from the grill. Dip the charred jalapeños into kosher salt and serve with the Mexican ribs.

New Orleans, LA

MARCUS JACOBS &
CAITLIN CARNEY

co-owners of
Marjie's Grill

It's this sort of back-and forth ribbing that I catch all day long while hanging with the two. Though Caitlin and Marcus both possess plenty of deft when it comes to witty banter, it's their artistry with food and hospitality that earns my deepest admiration.

Heat and New Orleans go hand in hand. Standing over embers and flames of a live oak fire borders on unbearable for me. But the heat doesn't seem to bother Marcus, a chef who has spent years tending fires—and it's these fires that serve as the necessary backdrop to his mélange of Asian and American cuisine. As I wait for Marcus to finish up on the grill, I peruse the eclectic dining area styled by Caitlin. "It's all about thrifting in Picayune, Mississippi," she says with a laugh as I admire the mismatched glassware and melamine plates. Caitlin's knack for design and attention to detail plays a vital, equally important role in setting the stage for the refreshingly inventive food coming from Marcus's kitchen.

Marcus's early life was spent in Eureka, California. Learning from his "own version of high school," he moved to cut his teeth working the grill station at the famed Zuni Café in San Francisco. There he learned the discipline of a professional kitchen in a city that blends cultures and cuisines. He spent weekends grilling with staff, and weekdays reading and learning from cookbooks in the free reading room of City Lights Bookstore.

After a year and a half, he traveled farther west—a lot farther...to join a three-month farming exchange program in Japan, where he worked on an organic farm in exchange for room and board. The simply prepared, straight from the farm meals made a lasting impression on Marcus—he credits the experience for the inspiration behind his constantly changing menus inspired by what is freshest and in season.

"IF WE WEREN'T doing this together, we'd never see each other. Anyways, there's nobody in the world, besides Marcus, that I would want to do this with," Caitlin Carney, co-owner and front-of-house wonder woman of Marjie's Grill, says. Without hesitation, and with a bit of sarcasm, Caitlin's partner, Marcus Jacobs, lets me know, "She owns 51 percent, and I've got 49 percent." "What can I say?" replies Caitlin. "He's the talent, and I'm his handler."

Upon returning to the States, Marcus made his way to the foodie jewel that is New Orleans, joining famed chef Donald Link and team at the renowned Creole-inspired Herbsaint. A few years in, life changed when Marcus met a new server, Caitlin Carney.

After a childhood in Paris, Caitlin moved stateside, where she went on to earn a graphic design degree from the Pratt Institute in Brooklyn. She headed to New Orleans, to take a "transitional" serving job at

✕ SERIAL GRILLER

Herbsaint. "We bonded over our mutual love for the same types of food," Caitlin told me of first meeting Marcus, "not to mention he is the most passionate, eloquent chef I had ever encountered." It's evident the two are smitten with each other.

While turning beef short ribs, spareribs, and crawfish-boil-soaked pig's tails on the large, oak-fired grill, Marcus turns the discussion back to cookbooks, specifically about one that changed his life forever. "Had I not picked up this book, we would not have this restaurant," Marcus says. I ask Marcus the name of the book, to which he replies *Traditional Recipes of Laos*. Perhaps some of Marcus and Caitlin's sarcasm wore off on me—we burst into laughter over the anticlimactic moment, expecting a much more dramatic title. Nevertheless, shortly after this book, Marcus and Caitlin decided to spend their Sundays dragging their grill around and cooking up their unique creations for their pop-up, Sparklehorse. It was a hit, and a dream was born. Saving money, purchasing a building, and embarking on a restaurant is no easy venture, yet it's exactly what Marcus and Caitlin did to go from pop-up to permanent.

In an effort to build on their success, the two took a three-month sojourn (and subsequent others) through Vietnam, Thailand, and Laos, where the pair say their best meals came from village women who cooked up everything from steaming bowls of pho to grilled everything at roadside stands. It's these types of simple preparations and meals that inspire Marjie's menu. "We like to keep one foot in Louisiana and one foot in the Mekong Delta," Marcus says.

To a soundtrack of Dolly Parton, I hastily devour the perfectly grilled shrimp, sucking the heads for good measure. In between bites, I meander like the Mekong through fatty, gelatinous pig tails and perfectly grilled chicken finished with a smoked, Thai-style barbecue sauce. Creole and Cajun cooking may reign in NOLA, but it's this sort of stuff—foreign to many yet still comforting—that will bring me, and others, back to the Big Easy.

I realize that there can be, in fact, too much of a good thing. I'd been distracted by such splendid food and conversation, I failed to ask the most basic of questions.

Why the name Marjie's?

As the smoke rose and the oak fire crackled, almost prophetically and on cue, Marcus tells me they named the restaurant after Caitlin's late mother, Ms. Marjorie Marks. "We remember and honor her every day...it is a pleasure hearing people say her name, and having her old friends stop by for a meal," Marcus tells me.

It occurs to me that food this good is only the result of divine providence. Cheers to you, Marjie.

"We like to keep one foot in Louisiana and one foot in the Mekong Delta."

CAJUN-GRILLED PIG TAILS

SERVES 2

Hands-On: 30 minutes | Total: 27 hours 50 minutes, including 2½ hours simmering and overnight chilling

Try this, seriously. Believe it or not, pig tail is something you can readily source. Marcus tells me the convenience store across the street even sells a few. A humble cut, it's readily found throughout Southeast Asia and the South—making it an even more appropriate item to feature at Marjie's. The tails are traditionally cooked very low and slow; Marcus nods to his Louisiana setting and first boils the tails in a crawfish boil mixture, imparting plenty of tenderness and gelatinous flavor to get them ready for the grill. Served with a simple dipping sauce, this dish might seem unconventional, but it's certainly one of my favorites to replace the Frito dip at my next cookout.

PIG TAILS

4 whole pig tails (about 2½ pounds), washed and patted dry

2 (3-ounce) crawfish boil packets

1 large lemon, halved

1 large orange, halved

2 heads garlic

DIPPING SAUCE

¼ cup Tiparos brand fish sauce, or your favorite brand

¼ cup lime juice

1 tablespoon cane syrup

¾ teaspoon red chili flakes

¾ teaspoon finely minced lemongrass

1 For the tails: In a large stockpot on a stovetop over high heat (or on a grill over direct heat), combine 5 quarts water and all the pig tail ingredients. Bring to a slow boil and simmer for 2½ to 3 hours, until the tails just bend on their own when picked up with tongs—the meat should not fall off the bone. Remove the tails from the pot and let cool. Air dry the tails in the refrigerator, uncovered, overnight.

2 Open the bottom vent of a charcoal grill completely. Light a charcoal chimney starter filled with charcoal. When the coals are covered with gray ash, pour them onto the bottom grate of the grill, and then push to one side of the grill. Adjust the vents as needed to maintain an internal temperature of 350° to 450°F. Coat the top grate with oil; place on the grill. (If using a gas grill, preheat to medium-high [350° to 450°F] on one side.)

3 Grill the tails over direct heat, uncovered and turning every 2 minutes, for 15 to 20 minutes, until the skin is crisp and charred. Remove the tails from the heat and cut into chunks.

4 Meanwhile, combine the dipping sauce ingredients. Serve the pig tails with sauce on the side.

HEAD-ON GULF SHRIMP WITH NAAM JIM SAUCE

SERVES 2 TO 4 AS AN APPETIZER OR SIDE
Hands-On: 45 minutes | Total: 1 hour 5 minutes

Perfectly grilled shrimp is difficult to master. The tender, delicate meat cooks so quickly that it often becomes overcooked and tough. But not these little guys. Marcus's technique of leaving the heads and tails on allows him to cook them gently up to temperature—while still getting a bit of char and plenty of great, smoky grilled flavor. Paired with the acidic and spicy naam jim sauce, this is a fantastic dish to serve as an appetizer, or with some hearty sides to round out a main.

NAAM JIM SAUCE

4 jalapeño chiles

1 head garlic

¼ cup fish sauce, preferably Tiparos brand

¼ cup lime juice

2 tablespoons cane syrup

½ teaspoon kosher salt

½ teaspoon freshly ground black pepper

SHRIMP

1½ pounds jumbo (21/25 count) whole Gulf shrimp (heads and tails still on), peeled

Vegetable oil

Kosher salt

Freshly ground black pepper

1   Open the bottom vent of a charcoal grill completely. Light a charcoal chimney starter filled with charcoal. When the coals are covered with gray ash, pour them onto the bottom grate of the grill, and then push to one side of the grill. Adjust the vents as needed to maintain an internal temperature of 400° to 450°F. Coat the top grate with oil; place on the grill. (If using a gas grill, preheat to medium-high [400° to 450°F] on one side.)

2   **For the sauce:** Grill the jalapeños and garlic over direct heat, uncovered, charring their skins entirely on all sides, about 15 minutes. Transfer to a heavy-duty ziplock freezer bag and let cool. Remove and discard the skins from the jalapeños, cut in half lengthwise, and remove the seeds. Place the peppers in a food processor. Remove the outer skin from the garlic and peel the cloves, adding 10 to 12 cloves to the pepper mixture (set aside any remaining cloves for another use). Add the remaining sauce ingredients to the processor and pulse until the mixture just comes together. Some pepper and garlic chunks will remain.

3   **For the shrimp:** Thread 5 or 6 shrimp onto two skewers—one skewer near the heads and the other near the tails. Repeat to skewer all the shrimp. Lightly coat the shrimp with vegetable oil and season lightly on both sides with salt and pepper.

4   Grill the shrimp over direct heat, uncovered, for 3 minutes on one side. Flip the shrimp and grill for an additional 2 minutes—the shrimp should be slightly charred and opaque. Remove the shrimp from the grill and slide them off the skewers. Serve with the naam jim sauce on the side.

HONEY-BUTTER YARDBIRD WITH THAI BARBECUE SAUCE

SERVES 4 TO 6

Hands-On: 45 minutes | Total: 2 hours 30 minutes

This darn bird is delicious, especially with the smoky Thai-style sauce. Be forewarned, this spicy and tangy sauce takes a bit of effort and an hour over the fire to prepare, but it's a total game changer worth the challenge—it also yields enough for more than a few birds. The key to this recipe, and any great chicken really, is to source the finest, pasture-raised birds you can find. Trust me, this recipe will become your new weekend ritual.

THAI BBQ SAUCE

1 head garlic

2 small shallots

1 small habanero chile

3 dried guajillo chiles

1 whole large tomato

¼ cup soy sauce

¼ cup apple cider vinegar

1 teaspoon lime juice

CHICKEN RUB

¼ cup paprika

¼ cup freshly ground black pepper

¼ cup kosher salt

2 tablespoons white pepper

2 tablespoons ground coriander

¼ teaspoon garlic powder

¼ teaspoon onion powder

CHICHEN

1 (3- to 4-pound) whole chicken, preferably pasture-raised, split in half and backbone removed

¼ cup honey

4 tablespoons unsalted butter

1   Open the bottom vent of a charcoal grill completely. Light a charcoal chimney starter filled with charcoal. When the coals are covered with gray ash, pour them onto the bottom grate of the grill, and then push to one side of the grill. Adjust the vents as needed to maintain an internal temperature of 400° to 450°F. Coat the top grate with oil; place on the grill. (If using a gas grill, preheat to medium-high [400° to 450°F] on one side.)

2   **For the sauce:** Grill the garlic, shallots, habanero, dried guajillos, and tomato over direct heat, charring on all sides until tender, 15 to 20 minutes. Remove from the heat, place in a heavy-duty ziplock freezer bag, and let cool (the steam will loosen the skins).

3   Using gloves, remove the skins from the habanero, then cut in half lengthwise and remove the seeds. Place the habanero in the bowl of a food processor. Remove the outer skin from the shallots and garlic. Peel the garlic cloves and add 7 to 10 cloves and the peeled shallots to the pepper. Place the grilled guajillo chiles in a small mixing bowl and cover with hot water to rehydrate; let stand for 5 minutes. Cut and remove the seeds from the guajillos and add to the food processor.

4   Peel and roughly chop the tomato, then add to the food processor along with the soy sauce and cider vinegar. Pulse until the mixture just comes together (chunks will remain). Place the processed mixture in an uncovered saucepan. Cook on the grates over indirect heat, covered, for 1 hour, or until slightly reduced. Remove from the heat and stir in the lime juice. Use immediately, or store covered in a refrigerator for up to 1 week.

5   **Meanwhile, for the rub:** In a small bowl, mix the rub ingredients together, reserving 4 to 5 tablespoons for immediate use. Store the remaining rub in an airtight container for up to 6 months.

6   **For the chicken:** Liberally coat each chicken half all over with 2 to 3 tablespoons of the rub. Grill the chicken, bone-side down, over direct heat, covered, for 15 minutes. Flip the chicken and cook, skin-side down, for 5 minutes. Continue to grill for about 30 minutes, moving the chicken from direct to indirect heat over an open grill and flipping often to keep the chicken from burning. The chicken is done when it develops a charred, crispy skin and the internal temperature reaches 155° to 160°F.

7   Meanwhile, melt together the honey, butter, and 2 tablespoons of the remaining reserved rub together in a saucepan over direct heat on the grill.

8   Coat the chicken with the honey mixture and continue to grill the chicken until the skin firms, about 5 more minutes. Remove the chicken from the heat once the internal temperature taken from the thigh reaches 165°F.

9   Let the chicken rest for 10 minutes. Using a cleaver, remove the breast from leg, cutting each into thirds. Serve with the Thai barbecue sauce.

GRILLED SPRING VEGETABLES

SERVES 6 AS A SIDE

Hands-On: 30 minutes | Total: 40 minutes

The ingredient list might call for spring vegetables, but truth be told, this recipe evolves through the seasons—and the day, for that matter—based on what is fresh and what is on hand. The key element to grilling any vegetable is to maintain its integrity, meaning just enough heat and smoke on the vegetable to allow it to let up its goodness to the heat. From there, toss the vegetables in Marcus's unique dressing for the right acidity and savory balance to allow the vegetables to really shine.

VEGETABLES

1 pound broccoli florets

½ pound Dragon tongue beans (or substitute Romano beans or green beans)

1 tablespoon vegetable oil

1 teaspoon kosher salt

1 teaspoon freshly ground black pepper

DRESSING

2 tablespoons unsalted butter, melted

½ lime, juiced (about 1 tablespoon)

1 teaspoon Creole seasoning

1½ tablespoons fresh green peas, blanched

1½ tablespoons thinly sliced scallion

1 tablespoon torn fresh mint

2 torn shiso leaves (or substitute fresh basil leaves)

1 tablespoon torn fresh dill

1 Open the bottom vent of a charcoal grill completely. Light a charcoal chimney starter filled with charcoal. When the coals are covered with gray ash, pour them onto the bottom grate of the grill, and then push to one side of the grill. Adjust the vents as needed to maintain an internal temperature of 400° to 450°F. Coat the top grate with oil; place on the grill. (If using a gas grill, preheat to medium-high [400° to 450°F] on one side.)

2 **For the vegetables:** In a large mixing bowl, toss the broccoli and beans in the oil, salt, and pepper until evenly incorporated. Place the vegetables in a grill wok or metal basket. Grill over direct heat, uncovered and tossing occasionally, for 8 to 10 minutes, until the vegetables are just charred and slightly give. Remove the broccoli and beans to a cutting board and cut into bite-size pieces.

3 **For the dressing:** In a large mixing bowl, stir all the dressing ingredients together. Stir in the grilled vegetables, toss to coat, and serve immediately.

LA RABBIT LEGS

SERVES 2 TO 3

Hands-On: 1 hour | Total: 5 hours, including
2 hours marinating

Sourced fresh from northern Louisiana purveyors, this dish is a real treat. Marcus unwittingly showed off his pro-chef skills when I was visiting by effortlessly deboning a rabbit leg in less than a minute flat. For the rest of us, local butchers known to source rabbit are more than happy to oblige; otherwise online purveyors of game can provide this cut in the appropriate manner. The rich, gamey flavor of the rabbit is complemented by a quick marinade.

In true Laos fashion, the rabbit is accompanied by whatever is "on hand," meaning an assortment of greens and herbs supplement the dish, and are literally consumed by hand.

RABBIT AND MARINADE

4 (6-ounce) rabbit legs, deboned

½ cup soy sauce

2 tablespoons honey

2 tablespoons fish sauce, preferably Tiparos brand

1½ teaspoons freshly ground black pepper

1 teaspoon white pepper

½ teaspoon chili flakes

ROASTED HABANERO SAUCE

1 habanero chile

1 head garlic

1 shallot, unpeeled

½ cup lime juice

¼ cup fish sauce, preferably Tiparos brand

2 tablespoons cane syrup

¼ teaspoon kosher salt

⅛ teaspoon freshly ground black pepper

For garnish: trimmed Swiss chard, mustard, or collard greens; trimmed baby savoy cabbage leaves; sprigs of dill and cilantro; arugula leaves

1 **For the rabbit:** Combine the rabbit legs with all the marinade ingredients in a large ziplock bag and marinate for 2 to 4 hours in the refrigerator.

2 Open the bottom vent of a charcoal grill completely. Light a charcoal chimney starter filled with charcoal. When the coals are covered with gray ash, pour them onto the bottom grate of the grill, and then push to one side of the grill. Adjust the vents as needed to maintain an internal temperature of 350° to 450°F. Coat the top grate with oil; place on the grill. (If using a gas grill, preheat to medium-high [350° to 450°F] on one side.)

3 **For the sauce:** Grill the habanero, garlic, and shallot over direct heat, uncovered, charring their skins entirely on all sides, about 15 minutes. Transfer to a heavy-duty ziplock freezer bag and let cool (the steam will loosen the skins). With gloves on if desired, remove the skin from the habanero. Cut it lengthwise in half, remove the seeds, and place the pepper in a food processor. Remove the outer skins from the shallot and garlic, and peel the garlic cloves. Add 5 or 6 cloves and the peeled shallot to the pepper mixture. (Set aside any remaining garlic cloves for another use in other marinades, salad dressings, or desired preference.) Add the lime juice, fish sauce, cane syrup, salt, and pepper to the processor and pulse until the mixture is just smooth.

4 Remove the rabbit legs from the marinade and pat dry; discard the marinade. Grill skin-side down over direct heat, uncovered, for 5 to 6 minutes to develop a sear. Flip the rabbit legs and grill an additional 2 minutes, until the internal temperature reaches 155°F. Remove the rabbit from the grill and let rest for 5 minutes.

5 Slice the rabbit legs thinly on the bias. Serve with the assorted garnishes and roasted habanero sauce on the side.

MEATHEAD, founder and owner of AmazingRibs.com

Chicago, IL

"I'm a control freak. I'm all about control."

Although some might be put off by such a statement, I can tell you that Meathead's insatiable passion and dedication to control makes him one of the world's most trusted experts on all things related to barbecue and grilling.

Meathead may well qualify as one of the most interesting cats I've come across. His name is just the first clue. I got a rare glimpse of the man and the madness in his smoke-filled backyard in Brookfield, a suburb of Chicago. It was as we finished our first glass—a French Bordeaux—before noon that I realized that I've barely scratched the surface of Meathead's story—and we hadn't even touched on food yet.

His family journeyed out of cold and windy Chicago shortly after he was born to join the space-race–crazed legions of folks who settled in hot and humid southern Florida during the 1960s. Meathead fondly recalls the ground shaking as Titan III and Saturn V rockets launched just miles from his suburban backyard. A self-described science geek, he credits his upbringing there during this incredible time in history as the foundation for his approach to life, art, and business.

Meathead had decided to hone his love of science by pursuing premedical studies at the University of Florida, but he indulged a bit more in the college social scene than his academic studies. After refocusing and shifting majors to journalism, he went on to become the sports editor of the *Florida Alligator* student paper, even landing a momentary stint (as in one play) as middle linebacker while on assignment for the paper.

A semester shy of graduation, the winds of change blew again and pushed him in a new direction.

He had heard about an upcoming show at the Art Institute of Chicago featuring his former professor, renowned photographer Jerry Uelsmann. He had taken photography classes under Uelsmann's tutelage in Florida, and remembers him telling the class, "When you speak, make sure both the expert and the novice can follow you." It may be one of the most important lessons Meathead gleaned from his university studies.

SERIAL GRILLER

Attending Uelsmann's show inspired Meathead to move to Chicago and pursue an MFA. According to him, he became the first graduate student in the world to obtain a master's degree in art and technology.

A side effect of going to school is the need to pay for it. He took a job at a liquor store to cover his bases, but hit a home run when he met Mary Lou Tortorello at the store. Theirs is a union that is forty-plus years strong.

I trail Meathead all over his backyard, listening to him talk, dodging charcoal fires, and getting constant affection from his golden retriever, Reese, who is on alert for any delicious bits Meathead might share. Dry-aged rib eye, flank, and skirt steaks hit a myriad of grills fueled by charcoal and grapevines. Neighbors in the tight-knit community begin stopping by. Like Reese, they sense Meathead is up to his mastery. I feel lucky to nosh on a reverse-seared steak with a dark rich crust and velvety medium-rare center. It's like nothing I've ever tasted. As I settle into my meal, Meathead hands me another glass of wine—a perfect pairing for the uniquely grilled fare.

All those years of working at the wine and liquor store, combined with his journalistic talents, helped Meathead land a gig as critic for both the *Chicago Tribune* and the *Washington Post*, working as a wine critic for nearly a decade. His next move was to

pioneer the first magazine in the world that used desktop publishing, the *International Wine Review*.

Ever the innovator, he foresaw the inevitable transition from print to online, and capitalized on a meeting with AOL founder Steve Case, where he convinced Steve to allow him to create and edit the site's online food and drink section. It was in this new medium that Meathead brought the great Julia Child online for the first time, via a chat room Q&A. It seems Meathead has been the first at many things throughout his life.

We finally come full circle, to fulfill a destiny, if you will. In an effort to show off his skills as a writer, photographer, and webmaster, Meathead built AmazingRibs.com, named mainly for SEO (search engine optimization). Applying his knowledge of science, gift of writing and photography, and the sage advice from Professor Uelsmann, Meathead's advice satisfied the experts, but most importantly spoke to the novice, which allowed him to build the top barbecue and grilling website in the world. Today, the site contains nearly 3,000 pages worth of material, and boasts nearly 40 million page views annually.

Despite all of the adventures and accolades, including a *New York Times*–bestselling cookbook, *Meathead: The Science of Great Barbecue and Grilling*, he still finds joy and satisfaction in the simple things, like the positive feedback from his massive gang of followers. Whether it's for someone hosting a first backyard barbecue for friends, a guy wanting to impress his date by grilling dinner, or a busy mom who utilizes his recipes and techniques to feed her family, Meathead loves to provide advice and assistance at every step of the way.

When I ask what he's got up his sleeve next, he points at Reese and tells me about his earnest passion: training guide dogs for the blind (so far, five of his trainees have graduated). He chuckles as he notes that Reese failed school, which is why he kept her.

I savor the moment. Meathead might not realize it, but his greatest quality is his guidance. The man has done a lot in his life and I've learned a lot about him during our day together, but perhaps the most lasting lesson I've learned is that this guy is a great teacher in every sense of the word, someone who can enrich others' lives both inside and outside the kitchen.

AFTERBURNER SKIRT STEAK TACOS WITH CHIMICHURRI

SERVES 4 TO 6 (8 TO 12 TACOS)

Hands-On: 30 minutes | Total: 1 hour 45 minutes

Grilling anything is fun, but grilling a piece of steak over a charcoal chimney starter, reminiscent of an F-16 jet engine, is a thrill. It allows for intense, radiant direct heat to quickly do its magic on the thin cut of meat. On a regular grill, it's almost impossible to get skirt steak to be medium rare or medium in the center *and* get a dark exterior. This is a great technique for quickly cooking any ingredient, really. Heck, you don't even need a grill...just a chimney starter and some sort of grate, rack, or skewer to hold the food over the flame. Skirt steaks have long been a favorite among carnivores due to the cut's rich, beefy flavor and tenderness. Slice the steak and serve in tortillas with a tangy chimichurri and you've got a quick-cook meal that's just as much as an adventure to cook as it is to eat.

2 (8-ounce) skirt steaks, trimmed to fit the circumference of the charcoal chimney

1 teaspoon kosher salt

Flour tortillas

Chimichurri (recipe follows)

Diced tomato

Minced onion

1 At least 1 hour in advance of cooking, season both sides of the steak evenly with salt, then return the steak to the refrigerator.

2 On a safe and open grill surface, prepare a charcoal fire in a chimney starter and wait until the coals turn completely gray. Add a grill grate over the surface of the chimney. Working with one steak at a time, add the steak on top of the grate and cook, flipping the steak every 30 to 45 seconds to prevent burning, until the meat reaches an internal temperature of 130°F, 4 to 5 minutes. Remove from the grill and repeat with the remaining steak. After both steaks have been cooked, remove from the grill.

3 Meanwhile, quickly grill the tortillas for 15 to 20 seconds per side, until warmed and slightly charred.

4 Thinly slice the steak against the grain and serve on the grilled tortillas with the chimichurri, tomato, and onion.

CHIMICHURRI

Makes 1 cup

Combine 3 cups packed fresh flat-leaf parsley leaves, ½ cup extra-virgin olive oil, ⅓ cup distilled white vinegar, 3 peeled garlic cloves, 2 dried chiles de arbol, ¼ teaspoon kosher salt, and ¼ teaspoon freshly ground pepper in a food processor. Pulse until just combined, scraping down the sides as needed. Some small pieces and chunks can remain. Use the sauce immediately, or store in the refrigerator up to 24 hours.

FLANK STEAK VIGNERON WITH BLACK-GARLIC BOARD SAUCE

SERVES 8

Hands-On: 45 minutes | Total: 1 hour 45 minutes

As a wine critic, Meathead traveled to premier areas of the French wine country, enjoying purveyors' wines paired with fantastic food. Rough gig! One method of cooking in particular—grilling small game birds over dried grapevines—truly captured his attention. So much so, he now grows his own backyard grapes, cutting back the vines after the season to use as fuel and flavor in this incredible recipe. Of course, if you do not have dried grapevines, you can get a similar effect using dried twigs of other woods, preferably apple, peach, or other fruit woods.

As a nod to renowned grillmaster Adam Perry Lang, Meathead put together his own version of Lang's signature board sauce—a cutting-board technique of mixing the juices from the resting meat with herbs and aromatics to create an incredible accompaniment to the steak. The black garlic here has a sweet, balsamic quality. It can be found online and at specialty retailers.

1 (2-pound) flank steak

1 teaspoon kosher salt

5 large fresh sage leaves

2 tablespoons fresh thyme leaves, stripped from the stems

2 black garlic or regular garlic cloves, minced

½ fresh red jalapeño chile, stemmed and seeded

½ teaspoon freshly ground black pepper

6 tablespoons extra-virgin olive oil

1 At least 1 hour in advance of cooking, season both sides of the steak evenly with salt, then return the steak to the refrigerator.

2 In the base of a charcoal grill, pile cut dried grapevines on top of twisted newspaper. The vines should completely fill the base and sit just above the top of the grill, so don't pile them too high. Light the newspaper and allow the vines to burn until they turn gray (the fire will be very hot, 750° to 800°F). Alternatively, for charcoal, open the bottom vent of a charcoal grill completely. Light a charcoal chimney starter filled with charcoal. When the coals are covered with gray ash, pour them onto the bottom grate of the grill. Adjust the vents as needed to maintain an internal temperature of 500°F or more. Coat the top grate with oil; place on the grill. (If using a gas grill, preheat to high [500°F or more].)

3 While waiting for the vines to burn down, chop the sage, thyme, black garlic, and jalapeño together on a cutting board until minced. Season with the pepper and add the olive oil to create a sauce.

4 Add the steak to the open grill and cook, flipping every 60 to 90 seconds, until an internal temperature of 130°F, 5 to 7 minutes total cooking time.

5 Remove the steak from the grill and place on the cutting board, topping the sauce. Slice the steak thinly against the grain, allowing the meat juices to combine with the sauce. Portion the steak, adding more residual sauce as necessary, onto serving dishes, spoon board sauce over each portion, and serve immediately.

REDNECK SOUS VIDE RIB EYE WITH BEEF LOVE

SERVES 2

Hands-On: 30 minutes | Total: 2 hours 45 minutes

Take the way that most of us cook a steak, and do it in reverse. This reverse sear method is the gospel for Meathead when cooking thicker cuts of steak— or any other larger cuts of protein and vegetables, for that matter. The idea is partially taken from the French sous vide method, which uses a precisely temperature-controlled water bath to gently cook items. In Meathead's method, we use a grill to gently and slowly cook the entire cut up to the desired temperature over indirect heat, then finish with an even sear over direct heat. The technique creates a steak that is medium-rare from edge to edge, not just in the center. Personally, I'm a big believer in the reverse sear whenever I cook a steak that is at least 1½ inches thick—it is the best way to get a steakhouse-quality steak at home.

For even more indulgence, rendered beef fat (aka Beef Love) is brushed on the steak during the process to add more flavor, and also to help brown the meat.

2 (1½- to 2-inch-thick) well-marbled, aged boneless rib-eye steaks (USDA choice or better)

Morton kosher salt

Extra-virgin olive oil

Freshly ground black pepper

1 At least 2 to 4 hours prior to cooking, trim the external fat from the steaks and reserve. Season the steaks with ½ teaspoon salt per pound. In a small saucepan, slowly render the trimmed fat over medium heat until it is translucent and becomes liquid Beef Love. Reserve.

2 Open the bottom vent of a charcoal grill completely. Light a charcoal chimney starter filled with charcoal. When the coals are covered with gray ash, pour them onto the bottom grate of the grill, and then push to one side of the grill. Adjust the vents as needed to maintain an internal temperature of 225°F on the indirect heat side. (If using a gas grill, preheat to low [225°F] on one side.) If you have a removable top grate, do not put in place prior to setting up the grill as the steaks will cook more gently and evenly on a cold grate.

3 When the grill reaches 225°F, place the grate over the heat. Brush oil on the steaks and place them on the grill. Cook the steaks, keeping the lid partially closed and checking the steaks' internal temperature in several areas with a thermometer every 10 minutes, until the steaks reach 110° to 115°F, 15 to 29 minutes. When the steaks reach 100°F, it is important to monitor the internal temperature every few minutes.

4 When steaks reach 110° to 115°F, remove the lid and take the meat off the grill. Increase the heat to high on one side if using gas, or add more lit coals to one side from a chimney if using charcoal, to create a high heat (500°F) direct zone close to the cooking surface. Set the saucepan of Beef Love over the direct heat to warm through.

5 Brush the steaks with the Beef Love and season with black pepper. If possible, rotate "cold grates" (from the indirect zone) over the fire. (Using cold grates will prevent grill marks from conductive heating and provides a more even, uniform browned exterior.) Sear the steaks for 1 minute. Rotate the grates and flip the steaks, brushing on more Beef Love and seasoning with more pepper. Continue in this manner, rotating the grates and flipping the steaks for approximately 1 minute per side, until the steaks reach an internal temperature of 130°F. This should take a total of about 2 to 3 minutes. Remove the steaks from the grill, season with more salt if desired, and serve.

REVERSE SEARED BAKED POTATOES WITH MEATHEAD'S MEMPHIS DUST

SERVES 4

Hands-On: 25 minutes | Total: 2 hours 10 minutes

The reverse sear ain't just for steaks. We took the classic steak accompaniment, a baked potato, to the next level on the grill. The result is a fluffy, tender potato with a seared crust and edge that stands up well to any hearty fare.

2 large russet potatoes (1½ pounds total), scrubbed

Kosher salt

Memphis Dust (recipe follows)

Extra-virgin olive oil

1 Open the bottom vent of a charcoal grill completely. Light a charcoal chimney starter filled with charcoal. When the coals are covered with gray ash, pour them onto the bottom grate of the grill, and then push to one side of the grill. Adjust the vents as needed to maintain an internal temperature of 225°F on the indirect heat side. Place the top grate on the grill. (If using a gas grill, preheat to medium [225°F] on one side.)

2 Cut the potatoes lengthwise in half, get them wet with water, and season liberally on all sides with salt and a generous portion of the Memphis Dust. (You can microwave the whole potatoes for 5 minutes prior to cutting and seasoning to reduce the time on the grill by roughly half.)

3 Place the potatoes on the grill over indirect heat, cut-side up. Cover and cook for about 1½ hours, or until an internal temperature reads 190°F. If you like a little crunch, pull them off at 200°F. If you want them really fluffy, take them to 210°F.

4 Brush the potatoes with the olive oil and move over direct heat, cut-side down. Grill, uncovered, for about 2 minutes per side, until slightly browned.

5 Remove the potatoes from the grill, drizzle with more olive oil, and season with more Memphis Dust to taste. Serve.

MEMPHIS DUST

Makes ⅔ cup

Combine ¼ cup firmly packed dark brown sugar, ¼ cup granulated sugar, 2 tablespoons paprika, 1 tablespoon garlic powder, 1½ teaspoons freshly ground black pepper, 1½ teaspoons ground ginger, 1½ teaspoons onion powder, and ½ teaspoon ground dried rosemary in a jar, breaking up any clumps. Store in an airtight container in a cool, dark place for up to 6 months.

Athens, GA

MIKE BRADSHAW,
owner of The Grill

Truth be told, I've spent more time than I'd like to admit at The Grill during said hours during my college years, nursing a flat top-griddled burger and crinkle-cut French fries plunged one by one into creamy feta dressing. The neon lights and smells of this iconic greasy spoon draw hundreds of drunken college kids after last call in downtown Athens. You see, in Athens, last call never means the night is over. It lives on at The Grill.

In 1981, right around the time Herschel Walker brought a national football championship home to the University of Georgia, Bob Russo was busy building another kind of legacy, opening The Grill. A restaurateur celebrated throughout Athens, Bob wanted to create a 24-hour diner reminiscent of those he loved from the days of youth in the Northeast. In '89, Steve Sgarloto took over, moving The Grill to its current location on College Avenue, just steps away from the famous Arch of the University of Georgia.

The Grill's third owner, Jeff Weinberg, noticed the talent and ceaseless drive in his employee Mike Bradshaw. In 2008, when the time came to pass the torch, Jeff offered Mike and his wife, Emily, the option to "purchase" The Grill.

The term "purchase" has a different meaning in Athens. Athenians have always operated under a different code in music, business, and relationships. Mike tells me that The Grill is run like "a family business, but nobody is family." All three owners never in fact purchased The Grill with cash. Instead, they earned it through a handshake and sweat equity. Such deals are hard to come by these days, but I do believe it's exactly the reason why The Grill has survived for nearly forty years in a town where most restaurants cycle out with every graduating class.

IT'S 2 A.M. in Athens, Georgia.

While most folks are catching z's, Mike Bradshaw, owner and proprietor of The Grill, is just getting started. "When I started at The Grill in 1996, I worked for six years, five days a week from midnight to 8 a.m.," Mike said. He finishes by proclaiming, "I learned that if I can do that, I can do anything."

> "I worked for six years, five days a week from midnight to 8 a.m. I learned that if I can do that, I can do anything."

"I've worked every job in the restaurant, from busser, to cook, to manager," Mike tells me. Knowing the trials of every position, while also maintaining a certain level of pride and respect for quality and heritage, has been key to his success and the restaurant's longevity.

Mike and I are finishing up on the unique history of the restaurant as Emily, surely sensing my hunger, hands me a handspun chocolate milkshake. She tells me the secret to any great milkshake is the quality of the ice cream used.

Despite the name, The Grill does not boast an open flame, but a flat top grill. Now, I know some grilling purists might take aim, but I do believe it is the flat top griddling method that is essential to the taste and flavor of The Grill's most signature dish—the hamburger. "I love being in the kitchen with the cooks, 'squishing' burgers," Mike says with a smile. It's Mike's "squishing" technique that makes the most of the flat top method—allowing the burger to sear and cook in its own fat and juices.

Hamburgers are always made with fresh-ground—never frozen—beef. The signature crinkle-cut fries are cut and fried on demand, using up to 3,000 pounds of potatoes a week. Milkshakes are spun by hand and everything is cooked to order. It's a greasy spoon with a high-end restaurant mantra when it comes to quality and ingredients. There are no shortcuts when it comes to the food.

The Grill also serves up a delectable breakfast and lunch to the masses, too, including students, professors, and even superior court judges. And because the operation is 365 and 24/7, nothing ever stops.

After the milkshake, a bacon and Swiss burger, and feta fries for lunch, I thank Mike and Emily for the indulgence and taste of my college days. I decide it best to pass on their kind invitation to stop by later, convincing myself that this old dawg is likely to call it an early night. But nostalgia—and the siren song of Athens—gets the best of me. After catching up with old friends and enjoying a local band at the Georgia Theatre, I realize age is just a mind-set (perhaps tempered by an adult beverage or two). The clock strikes 2 a.m. and my feet shuffle that eerily familiar path down Clayton Street before I hang a right on College Street to find myself standing in line at The Grill. It's not long before I am again dunking fries in that feta dressing in one hand, growling down a burger in the other, and slurping down another milkshake. I suppose the more things change, the more they stay the same.

Long live The Grill. And glory, glory to Old Georgia.

BACON AND SWISS BURGERS

SERVES 6

Hands-On: 25 minutes | Total: 45 minutes

Cooking on a flat surface allows the beef patty to cook in its own juices, a key element to The Grill's signature burgers. The best way to emulate this process at home is to cook the burgers in a cast-iron skillet, resting the skillet right on top of the grill grates. (You could, of course, do the same thing on the stovetop.) Mike has a special term for cooking burgers, saying he "squishes" them using two large flat spatulas. One would never do such on a regular grill, as the juices would be lost to the fire, but this technique works perfectly on the flat surface, as the juices surround the burger throughout the cooking process, delivering unrivaled flavor and texture.

2 pounds 80/20 lean ground beef

12 strips bacon, cooked crisp

2 cups shredded Swiss-American cheese blend, or whatever you prefer

6 sesame seed buns

For garnish: mayonnaise, green leaf lettuce, tomato slices, dill pickle chips

1 Open the bottom vent of a charcoal grill completely. Light a charcoal chimney starter filled with charcoal. When the coals are covered with gray ash, pour them onto the bottom grate of the grill. Adjust the vents as needed to maintain an internal temperature of 350° to 400°F. (If using a gas grill, preheat to medium-high [350° to 400°F].)

2 Meanwhile, loosely form the beef into six ⅓-pound patties. (The cooks at The Grill use a standard size ice cream scoop to measure.)

3 Place a large, seasoned cast-iron skillet on the grill grate over direct heat and preheat the pan for 1 minute. Add three of the patties to the skillet and smash each once with a spatula. Cook undisturbed, uncovered, for 3½ minutes to develop a sear. Flip the patties, smash again, and then slide the spatula underneath each to free it from the surface. Cook the patties for an additional 3½ minutes, or until cooked to desired preference.

4 Evenly distribute the bacon and cheese blend among the patties, cover the grill, and cook just until the cheese has melted. Remove the patties. Repeat for the second batch.

5 Working in batches again, add the buns to the hot skillet, cut-sides down, and toast in the pan drippings until lightly browned, about 1 minute.

6 Evenly spread mayonnaise on the cut sides of each toasted bun, add the patties, and top with the garnishes. Serve.

Note: If your grill is large enough, cook all the burgers at once, with two skillets or a cast-iron flat top griddle placed directly on the grill.

MEDITERRANEAN SAUSAGE BURGERS

SERVES 4

Hands-On: 35 minutes | Total: 55 minutes

A lesser-known item on the menu at The Grill, this is an absolute standout. Fresh ground pork, instead of the typical all-beef recipe, is mixed with beef, fennel seed, and other spices to create a wonderful, unique flavor. This is definitely a go-to when looking to change things up from the standard hamburger. Borrowing a term from the Philly cheesesteak world, this burger is served "wit," meaning with griddled onions and peppers. Because of the pork, it's important to cook the burgers all the way up to temperature.

ONIONS AND PEPPERS

1 tablespoon vegetable oil

½ red bell pepper, seeded and thinly sliced

½ green bell pepper, seeded and thinly sliced

¼ Vidalia onion, thinly sliced

½ teaspoon garlic powder

BURGERS

1 pound ground pork

⅓ pound 80/20 lean ground beef

1 large egg

1 tablespoon fennel seed

1 teaspoon garlic powder

1 teaspoon kosher salt

1 teaspoon white pepper

1 cup shredded Swiss-American cheese blend or any mild cheese

4 onion rolls

Mayonnaise

Green leaf lettuce

1   Open the bottom vent of a charcoal grill completely. Light a charcoal chimney starter filled with charcoal. When the coals are covered with gray ash, pour them onto the bottom grate of the grill. Adjust the vents as needed to maintain an internal temperature of 350° to 400°F. (If using a gas grill, preheat to medium-high [350° to 400°F].)

2   **For the onions and peppers:** Place a seasoned cast-iron skillet over direct heat, preheating for 1 minute. Add the oil, followed by the peppers, onion, and garlic powder and cook, stirring occasionally, until the vegetables are softened and slightly caramelized, about 15 minutes. Remove from the skillet.

3   **Meanwhile, for the burgers:** Loosely combine all the burger ingredients together with your hands. Form into four patties about 5¾ ounces each.

4   Add the patties to the skillet and squish or smash once with a spatula. Cook undisturbed, uncovered, for 4½ minutes to develop a sear. Flip the patties, squish or smash again, and then slide the spatula underneath each to free it from the surface. Cook the patties for an additional 4 to 5 minutes, until the internal temperature reaches 165°F.

5   Evenly distribute the pepper and onion mixture, followed by the cheese blend, over the patties, cover, and cook until the cheese has melted, about 1 minute. Remove the patties from the skillet.

6   Add the rolls to the skillet, cut-side down, and toast in the drippings until lightly browned, about 1 minute. Spread mayonnaise evenly on each bun half, add a patty, and top with lettuce. Serve.

Note: Slather on the Feta Dressing (page 65) for an even more gluttonous and delicious burger.

CRINKLE-CUT FRIES WITH FETA DRESSING

SERVES 4 TO 6

Hands-On: 1 hour | Total: 1 hour 25 minutes

This recipe is inspired by the iconic dish at The Grill, one that was made most popular by the customers. The feta dressing was long a staple on the menu, but customers started to request it as a side for dunking their fries. A new legend was born. Truth be told, the exact recipe for the feta dressing remains a secret, but the team was kind enough to share a version to allow all of us to get our fix at home.

The team cuts the potatoes using a vintage "Coney fry" cutter, forming them into their signature crinkle shape. Mike says this cut, which provides quite a bit of surface area, is why the fries are so delicious, allowing them to cook up crispy using a one-batch frying method. You can buy a fry cutter from specialty cooking stores and online—avoid using frozen fries.

4 russet potatoes
(about 3 pounds)

FETA DRESSING

6 ounces crumbled feta

¼ cup buttermilk

¼ cup sour cream

¼ cup mayonnaise, preferably Duke's brand

1½ teaspoons minced garlic

¼ teaspoon celery seed

¼ teaspoon ground black pepper

1 (48-ounce) bottle vegetable oil, about 6 cups

Kosher salt

1   Cut the potatoes into ½-inch fries with a crinkle cutter. As you cut the fries, submerge them completely in water and soak while cutting. Drain the cut potatoes and allow to air dry.

2   **For the dressing:** Combine all the ingredients in a blender and puree until just emulsified (about 45 seconds); some chunks of feta will remain. Makes 1½ cups. The dressing can be refrigerated in an airtight container for up to 1 week.

3   Heat the oil in a Dutch oven on the grill or stovetop to 350°F. Working in batches, add the fries, being careful not to overcrowd, and fry until golden browned and crisp, about 5 minutes. Season to taste with salt, if desired, and serve with the feta dressing on the side.

CHOCOLATE MILKSHAKE

SERVES 1 (2 CUPS)

Hands-On: 5 minutes | Total: 5 minutes

The team at The Grill believes great ice cream makes a great milkshake. Rather than use a cheaper ice cream that's been cut with air, they use thick, premium Mayfield Creamery ice cream to produce a classic milkshake that goes great with a burger and fries. Served old school in a stainless container, this delicious staple is an absolute must at any meal at The Grill—including breakfast!

1 Combine all the ingredients in a large blending cup or a blender. Process until entirely smooth. Serve immediately.

4 large scoops premium vanilla ice cream, preferably Mayfield Creamery brand

½ cup whole milk

2 tablespoons chocolate syrup, preferably Hershey's

Comanche County, TX

JERRY BAIRD,
founder of the American Chuck Wagon Association

"Jerry's the cowboy version of Forrest Gump."

THOU SHALT NOT ENVY. I mutter this to myself time and time again, but with boots in pasture, gazing out on the wide-open vistas of the Texas plains, with wafts of beef-laden smoke and cowboy tales filling the air, I find it hard not to envy the life and man that is Jerry Baird.

Most will tell you that envy will eat you alive, but when harnessed properly it often leads to a deeper understanding of one's self. So, in this instance, I jump through the mental gymnastics of faith, deciding to choose the latter. My time with Jerry Baird reminds me that relishing a day of outside splendor, cooking, and sharing great food, while enjoying the company of good friends and strangers brings not only pleasure, but also a deep sense of satisfaction. This is what it's all about.

"Jerry's the cowboy version of Forrest Gump," says J.D. Barham, one of Jerry's best pals. Born in Graham, Texas, in 1939, Jerry grew up between the tiny towns of Iraan and Sheffield. At age fourteen, he got his first taste of ranching, but it was the meals served up by the wagon cooks that captivated his attention. In West Texas, the chuck wagon remains a veritable fixture of the brushy plains and hill country just as much as the steer and the cowboy. That's due in large part to the efforts of Mr. Baird.

After high school, Jerry went on to Alpine, Texas, to pursue his education at Sul Ross State University. It was there that he met a girl he thought "was pretty shiny" after first spotting her down at the cow hall. Though the lovely Mickey was seeing another guy at the time, it did not deter a man as persistent as Jerry.

"We put bees in that guy's car," Jerry tells me, referring to Mickey's boyfriend at the time. When the two jumped out in a panic, Jerry was miraculously there to save her...and that's how they met. They were married 49 years until Mickey passed from God's country to somewhere greater.

At this point I realize Jerry's "cowtales," as he calls them, might be even better than his food. And that's a compliment, as Jerry's first dish—grilled whole okra, seasoned with his own proprietary blend of spices, is addictive as popcorn.

Jerry spent most of his life in education. He racked up several advanced degrees and then he and Mickey spent decades mentoring youth through teaching, coaching, and helping found and build Western Texas College in Snyder, Texas.

As fate would have it, on November 22nd, 1963, Jerry wound up in Dallas after pursuing some school-related business for the state. Seeing as though he had never been to a ticker tape parade, he climbed a grassy knoll to watch the president make his way through town. The world changed that day, and for the record, Jerry claims to have never heard a shot from his spot. "See what I mean about the Forrest Gump stuff—this man has lived nine lives," J.D. says, adding some much-needed levity to the moment.

After retiring from the college in 1996, Jerry began to crank things back up by spending a few weeks at a time cooking on chuck wagons at ranches throughout the vast expanse of West Texas. But to Jerry's dismay, much had changed since the early days, and the chuck wagon seemed to be a dying art.

Always a doer, Jerry decided to take action, forming the American Chuck Wagon Association in the late '90s. The association now boasts over 400 active wagons, with members throughout the United States, Canada, and Europe.

Jerry's cooked everywhere from bigtime cook-offs and competitions to the Olympics. He even developed his own signature line of seasonings. "When people quit spitting it out, I knew I was getting close," Jerry tells me, an unlit cigar constantly hanging from his mouth. When I ask if he is ever going light that cigar he flat out tells me no. "When momma weaned me, she gave me a cigar, and I've been chewing on 'em ever since."

Like a good politician, Jerry has a quick answer for any question, though some are more serious than others. But speaking of politics and sincerity, Jerry is very proud to have played a hand in convincing the Texas state legislators to designate the chuck wagon as the official vehicle of Texas.

When I ask him how he was able to pull off such a feat, he points to his signature rib-eye steak, seasoned with his own blend of spices, which he had just pulled off the live oak fire. "On the day of the vote, we circled the chuck wagons on the lawn of the state capitol, cooking up hundreds of steaks to feed the legislators." It took just one bite of his delicious, tender steak to understand why those folks overwhelmingly voted yea. "We got 'er done," Jerry says with a smile, both of us knowing the accomplishment will leave a legacy that will outlive the man.

Nowadays, Jerry passes the majority of his time serving as ranch manager on the Resley Creek Ranch. When he's not ranching, you will find him cooking. With plenty of encouragement from Mickey, and as a way to honor their story, Jerry published a cookbook, appropriately titled *Ribeyes & Cowtales*.

After a day of eating and listening to plenty of yarns, I ask Jerry if he'll take me on a tour of the ranch. I'm just not ready to leave. "Whatever you wanna do, pard," Jerry tells me. It's a sentence he repeats throughout the day.

Though my meal has barely settled, we wind our way, up and down, twisting through the oak and mesquite trees for miles and miles, finally finding ourselves sitting atop a hill country view as the sun peeks through the afternoon clouds. Stopping, and taking in the moment, I turn to Jerry, my envy now turned to gratefulness. "Ain't life grand?" I ask.

"Indeed, ole pard, indeed," says Jerry.

GRILLED OKRA

SERVES 4 TO 6

Hands-On: 15 minutes | Total: 1 hour 5 minutes

It doesn't get much easier than this, but the flavor and crunch of the okra, perfumed with the smoke from the live oak coals, will taste as though you've spent a lot of time and energy cooking up this dish. Try to find young okra pods, those that are small and tender, and be sure to grill and eat the whole thing— no need to trim the ends. This is a great side dish to accompany any grilled fare.

1 pound fresh young okra, washed

1 tablespoon vegetable oil

1½ teaspoons Jerry Baird's all-purpose seasoning (see Resources, page 299) or low-sodium Creole seasoning

1 Prepare a live oak fire (see page 9), burning split logs of oak until the wood burns down to medium-size coals. Carefully place the coals on a fire-safe surface, 6 to 8 inches beneath a cooking grate. Grill temperature should be 350° to 375°F. Alternatively, open the bottom vent of a charcoal grill completely. Light a charcoal chimney starter filled with charcoal. When the coals are covered with gray ash, pour them onto the bottom grate of the grill. Adjust the vents as needed to maintain an internal temperature of 350° to 375°F. Coat the top grate with oil; place on the grill. (If using a gas grill, preheat to medium [350° to 375°F].)

2 In a large mixing bowl, toss the okra with the oil and seasoning. Place the okra on the open grill over direct heat. Grill, carefully turning on occasion to prevent over-charring, until tender and cooked through, 15 to 20 minutes. Remove from the heat and serve.

SWEET-HEAT JALAPEÑO POPPERS

SERVES 6 AS AN APPETIZER

Hands-On: 35 minutes | Total: 1 hour

Sometimes good things happen when you least expect it. After arriving at a catering gig, both J.D. and Jerry realized they forgot to purchase cream cheese to make their beloved jalapeño poppers. Instead of panicking, the two improvised, stuffing the jalapeños with some sweet heat and inadvertently creating one of their now most requested dishes. J.D. tells me that they are called Act of Desperation Poppers. Truthfully, I'm thankful for their desperate act, as I ate about five of these guys right as they came off the fire—the heat of the jalapeño is balanced by sweet peach slices and the salty flavors of olive and bacon.

12 whole jalapeño chiles, ends removed, cored, and seeded

12 thin slices fresh peach (from 1 small peach)

12 small garlic-stuffed green olives (or large ones cut in half)

12 slices thick-cut bacon

1   Prepare a live oak fire (see page 9), burning split logs of oak wood until the wood burns down to medium-size coals. Carefully place the coals on a fire-safe surface 6 to 8 inches below a cooking grate. Grill temperature should be 350° to 375°F. Alternatively, open the bottom vent of a charcoal grill completely. Light a charcoal chimney starter filled with charcoal. When the coals are covered with gray ash, pour them onto the bottom grate of the grill. Adjust the vents as needed to maintain an internal temperature of 350° to 375°F. Coat the top grate with oil; place on the grill. (If using a gas grill, preheat to medium [350° to 375°F].)

2   Meanwhile, stuff each jalapeño with a peach slice, then an olive. Wrap a slice of bacon around the outside of each jalapeño and secure with a toothpick.

3   Grill the jalapeños over direct heat, uncovered and turning on occasion to prevent over-charring, until the bacon is crisp and the jalapeño is just softened, about 4 minutes per side, 16 to 20 minutes in total. Remove from the heat, remove and discard the toothpicks, and serve.

COWBOY RIB EYES

SERVES 2 OR 3

Hands-On: 30 minutes | Total: 1 hour

There's really no secret to this recipe, beyond finding a great cut of steak—the size of Texas of course—and grilling it up to your preferred temperature. Jerry's secret (besides his proprietary seasoning), I will say, is that while standing over the fire and watching him work these steaks with plenty of deft and skill, he was still able to keep me hunching over in laughter by feeding me a slew of great stories and one-liners. After a short rest, we couldn't wait any longer— Jerry used an old knife that resembled a machete to cut into these steaks—each cowboy and cowgirl was invited to dig in. I caught on quickly that the steak was best chased alongside Jerry's Dutch oven yeast rolls dunked in the drippings to create a steak sandwich that's out of this world.

2 (10- to 12-ounce) rib-eye steaks, approximately 1½ inches thick, at room temperature

1 tablespoon Jerry Baird's all-purpose seasoning (see Resources, page 299) or low-sodium Cajun seasoning

1 Prepare a live oak fire (see page 9), burning split logs of oak wood until the wood burns down to medium-size coals. Carefully place the coals on a fire-safe surface 6 to 8 inches below a cooking grate. Grill temperature should be 400° to 450°F. Alternatively, open the bottom vent of a charcoal grill completely. Light a charcoal chimney starter filled with charcoal. When the coals are covered with gray ash, pour them onto the bottom grate of the grill. Adjust the vents as needed to maintain an internal temperature of 400° to 450°F. Coat the top grate with oil; place on the grill. (If using a gas grill, preheat to medium-high [400° to 450°F].)

2 Liberally sprinkle both sides of the steaks with the seasoning. Add the steaks to the grill over direct heat and grill, uncovered, for 5 to 7 minutes. Flip the steaks and cook for an additional 5 minutes, or until an internal temperature reads 130°F for medium-rare.

3 Remove the steaks from the grill and let rest for 5 minutes. Serve.

DUTCH OVEN YEAST ROLLS

SERVES 12

Hands-On: 1 hour | Total: 3 hours 10 minutes

A fundamental part of chuck wagon cooking is preparing dishes in Dutch ovens. This beloved form of cookware lets cooks prepare dishes hours in advance, as it does its magic immersed in coals, safe from the weather and the elements. That said, one does not need to be on the wide-open Texas plains to put this recipe to good use. The Dutch oven can be placed on nearly any grill, or in the oven for that matter, to produce these highly addictive rolls. Don't forget to serve them alongside the rib-eye steaks.

1 cup warm water
(105° to 115°F)

1 (¼-ounce) package
active dry yeast

4 cups all-purpose flour

½ cup sweetened
condensed milk

1 large egg, at room
temperature, beaten

2 tablespoons sugar

1 teaspoon kosher salt

¼ cup vegetable oil

Note: The rolls may be baked in a 350°F oven for 20 minutes.

1   Combine the water and yeast in a 2-cup glass measuring cup and allow the yeast to react and form bubbles, about 30 minutes.

2   In a large mixing bowl, stir together the yeast mixture, flour, condensed milk, egg, sugar, and salt. Knead several times into an evenly formed dough ball. Add the oil and once again knead the mixture into a dough ball. Cover the ball with a wet dish towel, place in a warm, draft-free environment, and let the dough double in size, 1 to 2 hours.

3   Pinch off about 1⅛-ounce portions of dough (about the size of a golf ball) and place in an 11-inch round baking pan. Cover and allow the dough to rise until doubled in size, 1 to 2 hours. Set the baking pan inside an 8-quart Dutch oven and cover with the lid.

4   Meanwhile, prepare a live oak fire (see page 9), burning split logs of oak wood until the wood burns down to medium-size coals. Carefully pile the coals on a fire-safe surface. Place the Dutch oven on top of a pile of established coals and add several coals to the top of the closed pot. Ideally, the coals will maintain the temperature of 350°F, but if you see flames, the fire is too hot. Alternatively, light a charcoal chimney starter filled with charcoal. Use the coals in the place of live oak coals, and maintain the temperature of 350°F.

5   Bake the rolls, rotating the Dutch oven 15 degrees every 5 minutes to allow the bottoms to brown evenly, until browned and tender, about 20 minutes. Serve.

SUNDAY COBBLER

SERVES 10 TO 12

Hands-On: 1 hour 5 minutes | Total: 1 hour 55 minutes

The life of a chuck wagon cook is one of sleeplessness. Cooks are often up around 3 in the morning to start fires in order to prepare breakfast. Most stay awake long after dark, reveling in the tales of the cowboys and polishing off a dessert like this one, along with a few libations. The pecans and Amaretto really make this cobbler special and the recipe offers a nice respite for cooks by using shortcut ingredients to pull off a downright delicious dessert. In true cowboy fashion, Jerry pulls a personalized brand out of the hot fire, searing it on top of the cobbler to give it his signature look.

1 (28-ounce) can peaches plus 1 (15.25-ounce) can peaches, drained

¼ cup granulated sugar, plus 1 tablespoon for topping

¼ cup packed brown sugar

4 tablespoons unsalted butter

2 tablespoons Amaretto

½ teaspoon vanilla extract

½ teaspoon ground cinnamon, plus a dash for topping

½ cup Maraschino cherries, drained and rinsed

2 tablespoons cornstarch

2 tablespoons warm water

1 (15-ounce) package refrigerated piecrusts (two 9-inch crusts)

½ cup whole pecans

1 Prepare a live oak fire (see page 9), burning split logs of oak wood until the wood burns down to medium-size coals. Carefully pile the coals on a fire-safe surface and set an 8-quart Dutch oven on top. Alternatively, light a charcoal chimney starter filled with charcoal. Use the coals in the place of live oak coals to maintain the temperature of 350°F.

2 Combine the peaches, granulated sugar, brown sugar, butter, Amaretto, vanilla, and cinnamon in the Dutch oven. Cook over the coals, stirring occasionally, for 12 to 15 minutes, until the mixture is evenly combined and the ingredients are just beginning to soften and combine. Add the cherries.

3 Make a slurry by combining the cornstarch and warm water in a small bowl. Add the slurry to the peach mixture and continue to cook until the mixture comes to a slow simmer, about 15 minutes. Transfer the filling to a large mixing bowl. Wipe the Dutch oven clean and place back over the coals.

4 Lay one pie crust on the bottom of an 11-inch round baking pan and add the pan to the Dutch oven. Cook for 2 to 3 minutes to set the crust. Add the filling on top of the pie crust, then top with the remaining pie crust. Sprinkle the top crust with the remaining 1 tablespoon sugar and dash cinnamon and the pecans.

5 Cover the Dutch oven with the lid and keep the pot on top of a pile of the established coals, adding several coals to the top of the closed pot. Ideally, the coals will establish a temperature of 350°F. Cook the cobbler until the filling is bubbly and the crust is browned, 40 to 45 minutes, rotating 15 degrees every 5 minutes to allow the bottom to brown evenly. Remove from the heat and let the cobbler rest for 15 minutes. Serve.

Note: The peach filling may be prepared on the stovetop and the cobbler may be baked in a regular oven at 350°F for 45 minutes.

New Orleans, LA

EDGAR CARO,
chef/owner
of Brasa
Churrasqueria

STANDING OVER GLOWING BRASAS ("embers" in Spanish), I ask chef Edgar Caro how long the grilled lobster wrapped in kombu he is preparing has been on the menu. He smiles ear to ear, sweat rolling from his brow, enthusiastically replying, "Never...but it is going to be!"

Edgar tells me he's been up since 5 a.m., thinking through every aspect of the lobster dish we are now

grilling. Shortly thereafter, we are dunking the perfectly prepared crustacean in garlic butter, washed down with a few cold Colombian Aguilas. Edgar then breaks off a piece of the charred kombu. As he chews, I know it's good, just by the way he deadpans me in the eyes and exclaims, "Dude!"

Born and raised outside Cartagena, Colombia, Edgar got a head start in cooking and business. At fourteen years of age, he was frustrated with the processed, frozen selection of empanadas and pizzas served in his high school lunchroom. So Edgar went to work on providing for himself—and the rest of the school. He'd start his day off at the market, sourcing local deli meats, cheeses, fresh baked ciabatta bread, and his secret sauce—a garlic-based aioli. Borrowing a toaster press from his grandmother, Edgar would prepare sandwiches—easily a hundred or so—while all of the other kids were at recess. All was good until the principal called him into his office, informing Edgar that he was in fact putting the lunch lady out of business. He struck a deal with the administration, licensing the school to prepare and sell his sandwiches in exchange for a cut of the goods. That, my friends, is called Serious Hustle.

At seventeen, Edgar moved stateside to New Orleans. He lived with his uncle Hernán Caro, a famous local artist, and pursued a degree in graphic design. When he wasn't studying, he was learning the fine art of crafting po'boys at Cooter Brown's, a restaurant that helped foster his love for a great, locally sourced oyster from P&J Oyster Company. It was during this time that Edgar also learned the growing pains of independence. Thomas Carlyle once famously wrote of men chasing Blumina, a fictional character meant to represent ephemeral love—it's a literary lesson learned the hard way by Edgar.

"I quit school, taking a lot of heat from my family, and moved to Miami—only to realize she had another boyfriend once I got down there," he tells me laughing. "I was a broken man, and a broke man."

Edgar moved back to New Orleans, landing a job at the foregone Living Room. But the stint was short-lived when Hurricane Katrina hit in August 2005, disrupting the entire city and nation. When the city finally dried up, so did the hospitality jobs. Edgar was forced to

80 ✕ SERIAL GRILLER

learn a new vocation, working as a sales rep to source roofing jobs to help rebuild the city. The momentary gig might not have been his passion, but it provided him with the funds to open his first restaurant, Baru Bistro, at the age of twenty-four.

Fast-forward a decade: The success of Baru led to Basin Seafood and Spirits, which led Edgar to the city of Metairie, Louisiana, where he created his prized possession, Brasa Churrasqueria.

"The wood-burning grill is the heart and soul of the restaurant," Edgar relays as he showcases the custom grill he helped design and build with his uncle Hernán. The red oak–fueled fire quickly gives up its brasas, which are then shoveled beneath a grate as the fuel to cook nearly every item on the menu. "I wanted to showcase the great flavors of South America, along with the incredible ingredients we are able to source right here in Louisiana. And honestly, man, I sometimes feel like I'm cheating. Seriously, put anything on that grill, cook it the right way, and it's going to be good."

Edgar might feel like he's taking the easy way out, but standing over the fire, constantly feeding the flames with oak pieces to create more embers is by no means cheating. It's an art. It's proof that great ingredients, in skilled hands, grilled over a live wood fire, can be transformed into undeniable, primal goodness.

> **"Seriously, put anything on that grill, cook it the right way, and it's going to be good."**

Brasa's menu is full of steakhouse classics, but I've come for the picanha, a back-of-house offering that's a humbler cut of top sirloin with a hefty fat cap. After cutting a few steaks, we head to the grill. Edgar cooks the fat cap first, to let it crisp while the rendered fat drips on the brasas. It's that sizzle and sound that makes my mouth water in anticipation. Soon after, the meat leaves the grill, and after a brief rest it's sliced thinly and topped with Edgar's take on chimichurri, which he refers to as chimi de la mesa.

I dive right into the picanha, forgetting about the lobster, whole red snapper, and sweet potatoes I'd already consumed. It's everything I've ever wanted in a steak: big beef flavor gently kissed with smoke, with plenty of tenderness but still some chew. The acidic chimi de la mesa, with its tinge of pleasing bitterness, provides just enough balance to bring out the best in the meat.

In my full-on meat coma, I realize Edgar is living out a duo of dreams. The first is the American dream, as an immigrant who has built a sizable empire on a foundation of talent, hard work, and respect. The second is a personal dream. "Since I was fourteen, making those sandwiches, I knew I always wanted to be surrounded by food. I get to wake up and do what I love to do every day, man," Edgar says with a bit of awe.

After hours talking and tasting and with our bellies busting, Edgar abruptly tells me he has to get going. Sensing my confusion, he flashes his bright smile, telling me that he's got to head off to his "other" job— his favorite. His daughters, Genevieve and Eden, are expecting Daddy to come home for dinner.

On second thought, better call that a trio of dreams fulfilled.

GRILLED PICANHA WITH CHIMI DE LA MESA

SERVES 4

Hands-On: 50 minutes | Total: 1 hour 10 minutes

Picanha is the top cut of the sirloin. It's a staple of Brazilian cuisine, typically rolled, skewered, and roasted. Edgar prefers to use Wagyu for this recipe, for its tenderness and rich flavor; and instead of using the traditional method, Edgar simply portions the large cut into individual steaks. Most top sirloins in the States come with the fat cap removed—*no bueno.* Be sure to ask the butcher to keep the fat cap on. Sometimes you can get lucky and find the exact cut sold as a cullote steak.

The big key here is to first grill the steak fat-side down to render the fat, which also provides flavor as the rendered fat drips on the coals. This is a standout cut that's perfect for entertaining. The Chimi de la Mesa recipe makes enough sauce for the steak with enough remaining for both the snapper and the lobster recipes that follow.

4 (8-ounce) top sirloin or cullote steaks, fat cap on

Kosher salt

Fleur de sel

Chimi de la Mesa (recipe follows)

1 Prepare a two-zone fire using red oak coals. Alternatively, open the bottom vent of a charcoal grill completely. Light a charcoal chimney starter filled with charcoal. When the coals are covered with gray ash, pour them onto the bottom grate of the grill, and then push to one side of the grill. Adjust the vents as needed to maintain an internal temperature of 400° to 450°F. Coat the top grate with oil; place on the grill. (If using a gas grill, preheat to medium-high [400° to 450°F] on one side.)

2 Liberally season both sides of the steaks with salt. Add the steaks to the grill over direct heat, fat cap–side down, and cook, uncovered, for 8 minutes, or until the fat is well rendered, moving the steaks off direct heat from time to time if flare-ups occur.

3 Grill the steaks on the skinny side for 3 minutes, or until charred. Flip and grill an additional 2 minutes. Set the steaks with the unseared side down and cook an additional 3 minutes, until the internal temperature reaches 130°F. Remove the steaks from the grill and rest for 10 minutes.

4 Serve by slicing the steak against the grain into ¼-inch-thick slices. Season the slices with fleur de sel and top with chimi de la mesa.

CHIMI DE LA MESA

Makes 1½ cups

10 garlic cloves, peeled

¼ cup fresh oregano leaves

1 shallot, peeled, ends removed

2 bunches fresh flat-leaf parsley, stems removed

1 tablespoon red wine vinegar

1 cup vegetable oil

¾ teaspoon olive oil

Kosher salt

Freshly ground black pepper

Combine the garlic, oregano, and shallot in a food processor and pulse until combined. Remove from the processor. Add the parsley to the processor and pulse until roughly chopped. Return the garlic mixture to the processor and add the vinegar, vegetable oil, and olive oil. Process until the ingredients are thoroughly incorporated into a roughly chopped mixture. Season to taste with salt and pepper. Chimi de la mesa is best used immediately, but you can cover and refrigerate it for up to 1 day.

WHOLE GRILLED RED SNAPPER

SERVES 2 TO 3

Hands-On: 35 minutes | Total: 55 minutes

Whole cooked fish is one of my favorite dishes. Chef Edgar's technique is all about letting the fish and the live wood fire work in harmony to create a masterpiece. Red snapper and redfish are the preferred sport fish that Edgar likes to grill, depending on the catch and the season. His first rule is to always source the freshest catch you can find. The second rule is to catch your own fish when you can! Though I typically am a minimalist when it comes to extra equipment, it's super helpful to have a fish grill basket to work and flip the whole fish on the grill.

1 (3- to 4-pound) whole red snapper, gutted and scaled

4 sprigs fresh thyme

2 sprigs fresh rosemary

4 thin lemon slices

Extra-virgin olive oil

Garlic salt

Chimi de la Mesa (page 83), for topping

Microgreens

1 Prepare a two-zone fire using red oak coals. Alternatively, open the bottom vent of a charcoal grill completely. Light a charcoal chimney starter filled with charcoal. When the coals are covered with gray ash, pour them onto the bottom grate of the grill, and then push to one side of the grill. Adjust the vents as needed to maintain an internal temperature of 400° to 450°F. Coat the top grate with oil; place on the grill. (If using a gas grill, preheat to medium-high [400° to 450°F] on one side.)

2 Stuff the fish cavity with the thyme, rosemary, and lemon slices. Brush both sides of the fish with olive oil and lightly season with garlic salt. Add the fish to a grilling basket.

3 Grill the fish over direct heat, uncovered and turning every 4 to 5 minutes to prevent overcooking. Continue in this manner for 20 to 25 minutes, until the meat is just firm and flakes–the skin will be slightly charred and crispy.

4 Remove the fish from the grill and the grill basket and plate on a large serving platter. Drizzle the fish with chimi de la mesa, and top with microgreens.

  SERIAL GRILLER

GRILLED WHOLE LOBSTER WRAPPED IN KOMBU

SERVES 2

Hands-On: 1 hour 15 minutes | Total: 1 hour 45 minutes

A soon-to-be-signature dish on the menu at Brasa, this technique really showcases Edgar's creativity and desire to always push the envelope. Dried kombu, a form of kelp, is typically found in many East Asian dishes—it's readily available at farmers' markets and online. The key is to rehydrate the dried kombu in rice wine vinegar. Wrapping the lobsters in the kombu allows them to gently steam on the grill; they are then unwrapped for a slight char over direct heat to finish. Be sure to serve the grilled kombu with the lobster—it's crunchy, a bit bitter, but delicious.

Salmeura is a saltwater brine used to add even more moisture and flavor throughout the grilling process. This solution always sits by the grill at Brasa to mop onto steaks, fish, and anything else that might need an extra hit of love.

SALMEURA

1 cup water	1 teaspoon kosher salt
2 tablespoons Chimi de la Mesa (page 83)	

LOBSTER

2 (1½-pound) live whole lobsters	½ cup (4 ounces) butter, melted
4 large sheets dried kombu (enough to wrap the lobster, from a 5½-ounce package)	2 garlic cloves, finely minced
	2 lemons, halved
1 (12-ounce) bottle rice wine vinegar	

1 **For the salmeura:** Combine the water, chimi de la mesa, and salt in a small saucepan. Cook over low heat, stirring, just until salt dissolves, about 5 minutes. Set aside.

2 **For the lobster:** Place the lobsters in the freezer for 30 minutes. Submerge the kombu leaves in the vinegar and soak for at least 20 minutes.

3 Place a damp paper towel on a work surface. Top with a rimmed baking sheet and line the baking sheet with a damp paper towel. Fit a cutting board into the baking sheet. Place one lobster on the cutting board and straighten the tail. With the sharp side of a chef's knife facing the head, pierce the lobster straight down through the midline of the carapace (where the head connects to the body) until the knife tip reaches the cutting board. Repeat with the remaining lobster.

4 Prepare a two-zone fire using red oak coals. Alternatively, open the bottom vent of a charcoal grill completely. Light a charcoal chimney starter filled with charcoal. When the coals are covered with gray ash, pour them onto the bottom grate of the grill, and then push to one side of the grill. Adjust the vents as needed to maintain an internal temperature of 400° to 450°F. Coat the top grate with oil; place on the grill. (If using a gas grill, preheat to medium-high [400° to 450°F] on one side.)

5 Remove the sheets of kombu from the vinegar, shaking off excess. Carefully remove the bands from lobster claws and tightly wrap each lobster with two kombu leaves to completely enclose. Place the kombu-wrapped lobsters, bottom-side down, on an open grill over direct heat and cook for 10 minutes, mopping occasionally with the salmeura. Flip the lobsters onto their backs and cook an additional 10 minutes, mopping occasionally.

continued

GRILLED WHOLE LOBSTER WRAPPED IN KOMBU, CONTINUED

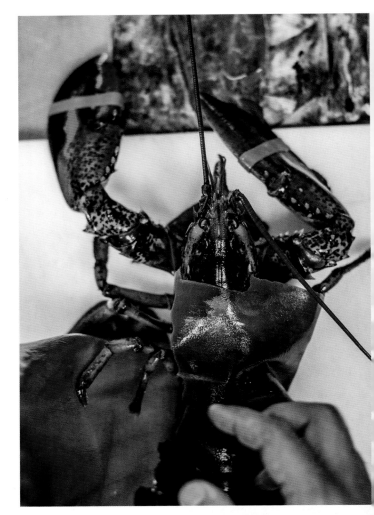

6 Carefully move the lobsters to indirect heat and unwrap from the kombu, leaving the kombu over indirect heat until ready to serve. Move the lobsters back over direct heat and grill for about 2 minutes on each side, mopping occasionally. The lobsters are done when brightly colored and the juices are just steaming through. Let rest for 5 minutes.

7 Meanwhile, combine the melted butter and garlic in a saucepan and place over indirect heat until warmed. Grill the lemon halves, cut-side down, over direct heat for 2 minutes, or until slightly charred.

8 Remove each lobster tail by twisting it apart from the body; cut the tails in half lengthwise. Remove the claws and carefully split using a cracker or sharp knife. Serve the entire lobsters on top of the charred kombu with the grilled lemons and garlic butter.

SWEET POTATOES AL RESCOLDO

SERVES 4

Hands-On: 25 minutes | Total: 1 hour 35 minutes

Honestly, these sweet potatoes are so good, I'd eat them for dinner...and dessert. The technique of cooking the potatoes in the dying *brasas*, or embers, is known as *al rescoldo* and is widely practiced throughout Argentina and South America. Potatoes are not the only thing buried in the coals at Brasa—peppers, onions, and squash regularly receive this charring treatment.

You'll need about two charcoal chimneys worth of coals to cover the potatoes. The flavors produced by this technique, combined with the sweet, spiced pecan butter, melds Louisiana and South America in one simple dish. Serve as a hearty side to a grilled steak or pork chop or, as I said earlier, for dessert.

4 sweet potatoes

4 tablespoons unsalted butter

1 cup packed light brown sugar

1 cup roughly chopped pecans

1 teaspoon Mexican cinnamon (canela)

½ teaspoon guajillo chile powder

Finely chopped fresh parsley

1 Prepare a fire of live red oak coals or two chimneys full of charcoal. If you do not have two chimneys, work in batches to produce enough coals. After the coals have gone from glowing red-hot to gray, pour the coals onto a grilling surface and use tongs to carefully submerge the sweet potatoes completely beneath the coals. Allow the potatoes to sit in the coals until completely cooked, about 1 hour. Remove the potatoes from the coals and let cool to the touch. Brush clean and cut in half.

2 Meanwhile, melt the butter in a saucepan over medium-high heat on the stovetop or over direct heat on the grill. Add the sugar, pecans, cinnamon, and chile powder and mix until thoroughly combined.

3 Generously spoon the butter on top of the cut potatoes. Place the potatoes, cut-side up, back on the grill over direct heat (500°F), cover, and cook for 5 minutes to allow the potatoes to firm. (You can also place the potatoes under a broiler for 2 to 3 minutes to set.)

4 Plate the potatoes and garnish with the parsley.

SHARON HAYNES, owner, & MALLORY BUFORD, chef, of Fajitas A Go Go

Houston, TX

attention. "I'm an artist at heart, but I got started as a bartender by default. It was the only way I could pay for my art habit," she relays as we discuss her early days in Houston. Sharon's interest in fine art and photography soon led to a different form of expression—welding. "Back then, I was certainly the only female welder in Houston, and likely the entire state of Texas."

The role of restaurateur has always followed Sharon. It's something she refers to as a love-hate relationship. In 1997, she opened her first concept, Solero, in the historic Henry Brashear Building in downtown Houston. "We literally had to beg, steal, and borrow," she said in reference to coming up with the funds to launch her first concept. The hard work and the risk paid off. Solero paved the way for reintroducing Houstonians to the idea of eating in an urban, downtown setting after years of chain eateries monopolizing the surrounding suburbs and dominating the dining scene.

Eventually Sharon sold Solero to focus on her most important role—motherhood. It proved to be a time that allowed her to get back to her artistic roots. She reenrolled at the University of Houston to pursue a masters in art education.

Though her tether to the hospitality business had slackened, Sharon, in time, wound up right back in the business of cooking and serving great food. The Continental Club, one of Austin's iconic music venues, was expanding to the Magnolia City. "Houstonians have an insatiable appetite for Tex-Mex," says Sharon, so when the 1,400-square-foot eatery adjacent to the club opened, she knew it was an opportune time to chase the noise.

That opportunity spawned Tacos A Go Go—which became the go-to place to find authentic street-style Tex-Mex tacos. She gave the place a retro 1950's vibe and had Johnny Cash in regular rotation over the loudspeakers. The artwork that adorned the walls was carefully curated or even created by Sharon. With the help of a team of investors, including famed DC restaurateur Jeff Black, there are now five Tacos A Go Go locations throughout greater Houston.

So when I ask what the difference between a taco and a fajita is, I get a puzzled look from both Sharon and Mallory Buford, the chef at her new sister restaurant,

"THE ONLY THING better than one margarita is two."

These are the words that greet me on a large sign as I walk into Fajitas A Go Go. Though I've yet to meet anyone, or try the food, I can already tell that I like this place.

Sharon Haynes, the creator of the Texas-based A Go Go empire, certainly knows a thing or two about capturing

Fajitas A Go Go. But soon, they start answering for each other, telling me that a taco is served to you already predefined by what is inside. The fajita, however, is deconstructed, allowing an individual to curate his or her own creation. True fajitas, they agree, are always grilled over a wood fire. Ah yes, the grill, I came here for the grill and not the margaritas, I remind myself.

"We opened Fajitas A Go Go to prove that there is a better way to cook and eat fajitas with no shortcuts," says Mallory as I bite into a flap steak he'd just pulled off the grill. "Just salt, pepper, and the flavor of the oak and mesquite," he exclaims proudly, recognizing that my taste buds were in full delight as I noshed on the thinly sliced meat. Between bites of steak and grilled Gulf shrimp, I dunk handmade tortillas into a rich, tangy white queso. Of course, before I can get the mess into my mouth half of the molten cheese dip drips on my shirt—chalk it all up to another casualty of Serial Grilling.

Mallory majored in zoology, but he tells me that his lackluster GPA wasn't going to take him far, so he became a chef instead. A true pro, Mallory has trained and cooked in dozens of kitchens throughout his career, including Eric Ripert's Le Bernadin in New York City. When I ask Mallory the most important lesson he's learned over the years, he says, "Being in the hospitality business is a reminder to be hospitable."

His answer reminds me of a recent event that gravely affected Houston. Hurricane Harvey hit hard on August 17th, 2017, bringing an immense amount of devastation and flooding and over $125 billion in damage. Sharon

> "It's moments like these where you realize the power of food. It brings all of us together."

told me that, miraculously, the flood affected none of her six locations.

Rather than sit back and count her blessings, Sharon and her team went to work and opened their doors. Employees who had been displaced took residence in the restaurants. Once the waters started to recede, they got busy cooking and serving the community.

"Everybody wanted to help," says Sharon. "It's moments like these where you realize the power of food. It brings all of us together. What we do on a daily basis literally gets distilled down to nourishing people, both physically and emotionally." For weeks, Sharon and her staff fed first responders, doctors and nurses, and neighbors. Houston has roared back stronger than ever.

The delectable food at Fajitas A Go Go is certainly worth the trip, but hearing about the actions and kindness of this team is what I left savoring most. Their story is a reminder of how important it is to take care of one another—friends, neighbors, and complete strangers. Grill up some fajitas and mix up a margarita.

Better yet, make it two!

FAJITAS A GO GO

With so many combinations of proteins, vegetables, and toppings, making a fajita is like reading a *Choose Your Own Adventure* book. The key to the delicious flavor starts with an open fire wood grill, fueled with a blend of mesquite and oak. The team at Fajitas A Go Go serves up a variety of proteins and veggies—here you'll find the signature steak, shrimp, and vegetables, as well as favorite accompaniments: homemade tortillas, guacamole, queso, pico de gallo, and the Fajitas A Go Go seasoning.

The key to great fajitas is to get creative. Making all the recipes is often a daylong affair, best fueled by a few margaritas and Roger Creager's music. I promise that the end result, a big ol' spread of grilled meats and veggies with all the accoutrements, is worth the effort.

GRILLED STEAK FOR FAJITAS
SERVES 8
Hands-On: 20 minutes | Total: 40 minutes

The flap steak here is cut from the bottom sirloin butt. Ask your butcher for it, or find it at Latin markets. It's tender, virtually gristle-free, and worth it. You can also sub in skirt steak or top sirloin.

1 (3-pound) flap steak

1 tablespoon kosher salt

1 tablespoon freshly ground black pepper

1 Remove most of the fat and silverskin from the steak with a sharp knife. Season the steak on both sides liberally with the kosher salt and pepper.

2 Prepare a direct heat fire using live oak coals. Alternatively, open the bottom vent of a charcoal grill completely. Light a charcoal chimney starter filled with charcoal. When the coals are covered with gray ash, pour them onto the bottom grate of the grill. Adjust the vents as needed to maintain an internal temperature of 400° to 450°F. Coat the top grate with oil; place on the grill. (If using a gas grill, preheat to medium-high [400° to 450°F].) Note: One cup of oak chips can be used to impart flavor when grilling with charcoal or gas. Soak the chips in water for 30 minutes prior to grilling, and drain. If using charcoal, add the chips to the lit coals just prior to grilling. If using gas, add the chips to a foil-styled packet, poke small holes in the foil, and place over direct heat.

3 Grill the steak over direct heat, uncovered and flipping once, for 4 to 5 minutes per side, until charred. Remove the steak from the heat and allow to rest for 5 minutes. Slice the steak thin, or as preferred, for serving.

GRILLED SHRIMP FOR FAJITAS

SERVES 8

Hands-On: 20 minutes | Total: 40 minutes

2 pounds large Gulf shrimp (tails on), peeled and deveined

¼ cup vegetable oil

2 tablespoons Fajitas A Go Go Seasoning (page 99)

1 Place the shrimp on a flat pan, drizzle with the oil, and generously sprinkle with the seasoning.

2 Prepare a direct heat fire using live oak coals. Alternatively, open the bottom vent of a charcoal grill completely. Light a charcoal chimney starter filled with charcoal. When the coals are covered with gray ash, pour them onto the bottom grate of the grill. Adjust the vents as needed to maintain an internal temperature of 400° to 450°F. Coat the top grate with oil; place on the grill. (If using a gas grill, preheat to medium-high [400° to 450°F].) Note: One cup of oak chips can be used to impart flavor when grilling with charcoal or gas. Soak the chips in water for 30 minutes prior to grilling, and drain. If using charcoal, add the chips to the lit coals just prior to grilling. If using gas, add the chips to a foil-styled packet, poke small holes in the foil, and place over direct heat.

3 Cook the shrimp over direct heat, uncovered, for 2 minutes. Flip, and cook for an additional minute, until the shrimp are pink and firm.

FAJITAS A GO GO GRILLED VEGETABLES FOR FAJITAS

SERVES 4

Hands-On: 25 minutes | Total: 50 minutes

This recipe proves that just a few quality ingredients, simply prepared, can equal one delicious dish. The trio of these grilled veggies packs a delicious punch when paired with the shrimp or steak fajitas.

1½ pounds asparagus, ends trimmed, cut into small pieces

2 large yellow squash (6 ounces each), ends trimmed, julienned

2 ears corn, kernels cut from cob

2 tablespoons Fajitas A Go Go Seasoning (page 99)

2 tablespoons vegetable oil

1 Prepare a direct heat fire using live oak coals. Alternatively, open the bottom vent of a charcoal grill completely. Light a charcoal chimney starter filled with charcoal. When the coals are covered with gray ash, pour them onto the bottom grate of the grill. Adjust the vents as needed to maintain an internal temperature of 400° to 450°F. Coat the top grate with oil; place on the grill. (If using a gas grill, preheat to medium-high [400° to 450°F].) Note: One cup of oak chips can be used to impart flavor when grilling with charcoal or gas. Soak the chips in water for 30 minutes prior to grilling, and drain. If using charcoal, add the chips to the lit coals just prior to grilling. If using gas, add the chips to a foil-styled packet, poke small holes in the foil, and place over direct heat.

2 Combine all ingredients in a large bowl. Transfer to a grill basket, place the basket over direct heat, and cook for 1 minute. Toss the ingredients in the basket, and continue to cook, tossing every minute, until the ingredients are just tender and slightly charred, 7 to 8 minutes total.

FLOUR TORTILLAS

MAKES 25 (6- TO 8-INCH) TORTILLAS

Hands-On: 1 hour 10 minutes | Total: 1 hour 40 minutes

With so few ingredients, it's very easy to create your own deliciously soft flour tortillas at home. If you don't have a tortilla press, you can roll them thin with a rolling pin, though a press makes it much easier. Griddle these up on a cast-iron pan right over the heat from the grill. Note: Any and all leftover tortillas freeze well.

4 cups Supreme brand bread flour

⅓ cup vegetable shortening

1½ teaspoons baking powder

¾ teaspoon kosher salt

1½ cups cold water

1   In the bowl of a stand mixer, combine the flour, shortening, baking powder, and salt. Beat at low speed with the paddle attachment until just evenly combined. Switch to the dough hook attachment and gradually beat in the water on low speed; beat 4 minutes. Let the dough rest in the mixing bowl, covered with a dish towel, for 30 minutes.

2   Divide the dough into 25 (1⅓-ounce) balls. Flatten each into 6- to 8-inch tortillas with a hand press. Or roll each portion with a rolling pin into an even 6- to 8-inch round, about ⅛ inch thick, or to your preference.

3   Griddle the tortillas in a cast-iron skillet over direct heat (400° to 450°F) on the open grill for 15 to 30 seconds per side, until slightly charred.

GUACAMOLE

MAKES 2½ CUPS

Hands-On: 30 minutes | Total: 1 hour

The heat of jalapeños gets tempered a bit on the grill and the touch of smokiness it adds to this guac is a nice change of pace. If you're making the queso (at right) too, go ahead and grill all the jalapeños you need at once.

1 jalapeño chile

3 large ripe avocados

¼ cup finely chopped red onion

¼ cup fresh lime juice (from 2 limes)

2 tablespoons chopped cilantro

½ teaspoon kosher salt

⅛ teaspoon white pepper

1 Open the bottom vent of a charcoal grill completely. Light a charcoal chimney starter filled with charcoal. When the coals are covered with gray ash, pour them onto the bottom grate of the grill, and then push to one side of the grill. Adjust the vents as needed to maintain an internal temperature of 350° to 400°F. Coat the top grate with oil; place on the grill. (If using a gas grill, preheat to medium-high [350° to 400°F] on one side.)

2 Grill the jalapeño over direct heat, turning occasionally, for 10 to 12 minutes, until charred. Transfer to a heavy-duty ziplock bag and let stand for 10 minutes to loosen the skin. Peel the chile, remove and discard the seeds, and chop.

3 Remove and discard the skin and seeds from the avocados. Place the avocado flesh in a large mixing bowl. Add 1½ tablespoons chopped jalapeño, the onion, lime juice, cilantro, salt, and pepper and mix properly with your hands. Cover the guac directly with plastic wrap and keep refrigerated until ready to serve, or up to 1 to 2 days.

QUESO

MAKES 3 CUPS

Hands-On: 30 minutes | Total: 1 hour

Quesadilla cheese is available in many grocery stores or Latin markets, but white American cheese is a worthy substitute. If you're making this recipe solo, follow the recipe as is, but if you're making the guacamole or grilling up fajitas, I suggest throwing in a few extra jalapeños for this recipe along with everything else on the grill to save time and effort.

2 jalapeño chiles

1 cup milk

12 ounces white extra-melt cheese, cut into ½-inch cubes

4 ounces quesadilla cheese, shredded (1 cup)

⅓ cup finely chopped white onion

2 tablespoons water

1 Open the bottom vent of a charcoal grill completely. Light a charcoal chimney starter filled with charcoal. When the coals are covered with gray ash, pour them onto the bottom grate of the grill, and then push to one side of the grill. Adjust the vents as needed to maintain an internal temperature of 350° to 400°F. Coat the top grate with oil; place on the grill. (If using a gas grill, preheat to medium-high [350° to 400°F] on one side.)

2 Grill the jalapeños over direct heat, turning occasionally, for 10 to 12 minutes, until charred. Transfer to a heavy-duty ziplock bag and let stand for 10 minutes to loosen the skin. Peel the chile, remove and discard the seeds, and chop.

3 Fill the base of a double boiler (or a 3½-quart saucepan) with 3 inches of water. Bring the water to a boil over medium-high heat.

4 Combine 6 tablespoons chopped jalapeño, the milk, cheeses, onion, and 2 tablespoons water in the top insert of the double boiler (or in a small metal mixing bowl that nestles in the saucepan without touching the water to improvise a double boiler). Whisking constantly, mix the ingredients until the queso is melted and smooth, about 10 minutes.

5 Serve immediately, or keep warm, stirring from time to time to keep a skin from forming on the surface. Store any leftovers in an airtight container in the refrigerator for up to a few days; reheat gently when ready to serve.

PICO DE GALLO

MAKES 2 CUPS

Hands-On: 15 minutes | Total: 15 minutes

Also called salsa fresca and salsa crudo, pico de gallo literally translates as "rooster's beak." An uncooked, fresh salsa that is a staple condiment in Mexican cooking, it's delicious in fajitas and tacos or as a dip for chips. Though I've just defined this as an uncooked fresh salsa, you could always play up the grilling theme by substituting some grilled jalapeños for the fresh ones for a nice smoky change of pace.

3 Roma tomatoes, seeded and diced (1½ cups)	**1 tablespoon fresh lime juice**
¼ cup diced red onion	**1 tablespoon finely chopped jalapeño chile**
3 tablespoons finely chopped fresh cilantro	**½ teaspoon kosher salt**

1 Place all the ingredients in a mixing bowl and mix well to combine. Cover and refrigerate until ready to serve. Keeps well for a day or so when covered in the refrigerator.

FAJITAS A GO GO SEASONING

MAKES 1 CUP

Hands-On: 10 minutes | Total: 10 minutes

The restaurant's signature seasoning blend is a great all-purpose taco seasoning. Stir any leftover seasoning into softened butter to serve over grilled steak or a baked potato.

¼ cup seasoned salt, preferably Lawry's brand (see Resources, page 299)	**3 tablespoons onion powder**
¼ cup smoked paprika	**3 tablespoons celery seed**
3 tablespoons garlic powder	**1 tablespoon cayenne pepper**
3 tablespoons freshly ground black pepper	**1 tablespoon dried thyme**
	1 tablespoon dried oregano

1 In a mixing bowl, mix all the ingredients thoroughly to combine. Cover and store in an airtight container in a dark, cool place for up to 6 months.

Raleigh, NC

ASHLEY CHRISTENSEN & LAUREN IVEY,
chef/owners of Death & Taxes

> "We do not have customers.
> We only have guests."

I LEARN ABOUT this philosophy within minutes of meeting chef Ashley Christensen. It's a practice she takes seriously—the word "guest" is tattooed on the underside of her left forearm.

After walking into Death & Taxes, one of Christensen's many concepts located in Raleigh, North Carolina, I see that she puts those words into action. "We're having pork chops for breakfast," she tells me. I already feel right at home.

As a Carolina girl from birth, cooking is in her blood. Her truck-driver father and real estate–agent mother maintained a vast garden, cooking what they could of its bounty and preserving the rest. Though the idea of cooking seasonally and locally is popular now, this ritual was a way of life for Ashley and her family at a time when most of the rest of the country feasted on processed convenience foods. At the Christensen's, the daily family meal was a tradition, as were regular gatherings of family, friends, and an array of others around the table. These traditions cultivated Ashley's belief in the importance of communal experiences around food.

After moving to Raleigh to attend NC State, Ashley began to replicate her family's traditions by hosting dinner parties as both a way to hone her skills and foster a sense of community. When she wasn't hitting textbooks, she was devouring cookbooks, which provided the foundation for her culinary self-education.

Ashley left college to pursue her passion for cooking by taking a first job at Raleigh's Humble Pie. After a few lean years there, made leaner by a hefty bar tab

she'd accumulated at Enoteca Vin, an industrious Ashley made a deal to barter down her tab in exchange for work and the tutelage of chef Andrea Reusing. Eventually, she followed Reusing to Chapel Hill, where she gained further expertise under chef Scott Howell.

A decade of long hours and backbreaking work was soon rewarded when Christensen took an opportunity to return to Raleigh to remake the menu as executive chef back at Enoteca Vin. In no time, she was recognized for her talents when *Food & Wine* magazine ran a fourteen-page spread praising Christensen's brilliance in creating simple, approachable dishes that allowed quality ingredients to shine.

Christensen went on to open her first restaurant in 2007, Poole's Diner, a no-reservations, hip, retro-style diner serving up comfort food with precision. Poole's put Raleigh on the national culinary destination map, and its success led to several more restaurants for Ashley. She now owns five concepts in Raleigh, including her latest, a pizza hall known as Poole'side Pies.

Let's get back to business...I've come for the fire. Ashley's concept Death & Taxes was sparked by a trip to Uruguay with the FatBack Collective, a group of chefs, writers, and entrepreneurs who travel to foster engagement and community. It was on this trip that Ashley began to appreciate the art of "shaping fire," a term she uses earnestly, as if simply learning to grill misses the point.

When an old building that housed a mortuary and a bank became available, the concept came to life as Death & Taxes, which opened in 2015. Ever humble, Christensen tells me that she is only one part of the story of Death & Taxes. To truly understand this place, I'm introduced to her business partner, chef Lauren Ivey.

Lauren got a late start in the world of cooking—though she has always been accustomed to serving others in her past role as a teacher. When the culinary calling rang loud in her late 20s, she soared to the top of her class in culinary school. Lauren eventually met Ashley during a yearlong stint cooking at Poole's—venturing westward to Denver to further her experience and skill set. After a few years, Lauren returned to Raleigh to take over the reins as executive chef at Death & Taxes.

Providing opportunity and accountability is key to the success of Christensen's empire. As a leader, Ashley is one of the first chefs to work toward a culture of less competition and more compassion. Her employees are not on a short track, rather they are groomed to further themselves—at her many restaurants or elsewhere. Food is not the only comfort, either, as Ashley and team devote much of their time towards philanthropic initiatives: favorites include the No Kid Hungry campaign and the Frankie Lemmon Foundation. Both organizations help to serve youth—or better said, the future leaders and decision makers who will lead the next generation. Ashley has been named Outstanding Chef by the James Beard Foundation, but I most admire the work she puts in outside the kitchen.

After stuffing myself full on pork chops and grilled corn, Ashley suggests we head back to her home to continue the meal. Truth be told, I'm like Hansel & Gretel—I'll follow the breadcrumb trail wherever it leads as long as Ashley and Lauren are cooking. But upon arriving at Ashley's home, I begin to feel guilty about this whole guest thing.

Rain poured down incessantly—it nearly quelled the flames of the fire rising out of an oak-filled barrel. Sporting a T-shirt with the words "Respect the Pig," Ashley is hard at work, standing in the soaking rain preparing even more food for everyone—her guests.

I bite into the soft-shell crab that Ashley had grilled over coals of oak and slathered with a garlic and herb butter. An explosion of brine and sweetness, tempered with just a bit of smoke, it is—no joke—one of the best bites of my life.

From her cooking, to her leadership, to her activism, Ashley is always thinking about how to make you feel at home. In the past few years, she's shared this outward action with a sign—the words "Don't Forget Kindness" are displayed outside all of her establishments.

Be kinder than necessary. Eat together. Love one another.

This, in my opinion, is the best recipe a chef can offer.

GRILLED SOFT-SHELL CRABS WITH WARM HERB BUTTER

SERVES 4
Hands-On: 40 minutes | Total: 1 hour

I was intrigued when Ashley told me that we'd be grilling soft-shell crabs—down south, these little guys are typically headed straight for the deep fryer. There are some bites in life that you'll never forget, and this was one of them. Briny, smoky, sweet, and crunchy—a taste of sea and smoke combined into something both familiar and entirely new. Soft-shell crab season is short, so take advantage of it while you can, and skip the fryer—these beauties are best grilled.

4 live jumbo soft-shell crabs

Warm Herb Butter (recipe follows)

Lemon wedges

1 Clean the crabs: With a pair of kitchen shears, snip off the front (face) of each crab, about ¼ inch behind the eyes and mouth (this is the move that kills them, so be bold and quick). Fold one of the pointy "wings" of the top shell back and snip out the gills (they look like little white fingers on either side). Repeat on the other side. Flip the crab over and pull off the apron (the darker-colored strip on the belly of the crab) as if you're pulling off the tab on a can. It is optional to remove the green tomalley, but this is a matter of preference…it's sweet and rich in flavor.

2 Open the bottom vent of a charcoal grill completely. Light a charcoal chimney starter filled with charcoal. When the coals are covered with gray ash, pour them onto the bottom grate of the grill. Adjust the vents as needed to maintain an internal temperature of 400° to 450°F. (If using a gas grill, preheat to medium-high [400° to 450°F].)

3 Place a perforated grilling basket or rack directly onto the bed of coals. Working in batches of two or three, place the crabs on their backs directly on the grilling basket and cook for 6 to 8 minutes. Flip the crabs every 60 seconds, making sure all of the surfaces of the crab are seared and flavored by the coals. You should see juices start to delicately simmer out of the crabs. This is the clue that the crabs are done.

4 Remove the crabs from the heat and place on a cooling rack to rest for 3 to 4 minutes before serving (this will let those simmering juices rest back into the crab, resulting in juicier bites). Drizzle with the warm herb butter and serve with lemon wedges.

WARM HERB BUTTER

Makes ½ cup

In a saucepan, melt ½ cup (4 ounces) unsalted butter over low heat on the stovetop, or over indirect heat of the fire. Add 4 sprigs fresh thyme, 1 fresh bay leaf, ½ head garlic (cut in half across the equator), and ½ lemon. Cook for at least 5 minutes to allow the flavors to marry. Remove from the heat and squeeze the juice from the warmed lemon half into the butter, and then drop the rind back into the butter so that the aromatic oils from the peel continue to infuse the sauce.

GRILLED ARTICHOKES

SERVES 4 AS A SIDE OR APPETIZER

Hands-On: 30 minutes | Total: 1 hour 15 minutes

Artichokes are meaty enough to stand up to the high heat and take on plenty of smoky flavor. Poach them the day ahead or in the morning to get a jump-start on the recipe.

POACHING LIQUID

6 quarts water

1 (750-mL) bottle dry white wine

1 cup kosher salt

2 fresh bay leaves, torn

20 sprigs fresh thyme

3 heads garlic, cut across the equator

2 tablespoons black peppercorns

1 lemon, thinly sliced

4 whole artichokes

Extra-virgin olive oil

Fine sea salt

Freshly ground black pepper

Warm Herb Butter (page 102) or your favorite seasoned mayo or aioli

1 **For the poaching liquid:** In a large stockpot, combine all of the poaching liquid ingredients and bring to a boil over high heat.

2 Add the artichokes, fully submerge (I weight them down with an upside-down glass pie pan), and return to a boil. Reduce to a simmer (with the liquid gently rolling) and poach the artichokes for 30 minutes. Transfer the artichokes to a baking sheet to cool. Once cooled, slice each artichoke in half and remove and discard the coarse red leaves and fibrous strings near the heart. The artichokes can be poached up to a day ahead and refrigerated, uncovered, until ready for use.

3 Open the bottom vent of a charcoal grill completely. Light a charcoal chimney starter filled with charcoal. When the coals are covered with gray ash, pour them onto the bottom grate of the grill. Adjust the vents as needed to maintain an internal temperature of 400° to 450°F. (If using a gas grill, preheat to medium-high [400° to 450°F].)

4 Place a perforated grilling basket or rack directly on the bed of coals (or on the gas grill's oiled grates). Season the artichoke halves with a drizzle of olive oil and salt and pepper. Place, cut-side down, on the grilling surface. Cook over the coals, rotating the grilling surface 45 degrees every minute or so, for about 5 minutes. The meat of the artichokes will caramelize and pick up smoky flavor from the coals. Grilling time on a gas grill will be 6 to 8 minutes. Serve with the warm herb butter.

HEIRLOOM TOMATO AND EMBERED OLIVE SALAD WITH CHARRED TOMATO VINAIGRETTE AND GRILLED BREADCRUMBS

SERVES 4 TO 6

Hands-On: 1 hour | Total: 2 hours 45 minutes

I'm a sucker for anything salty, so when Ashley told me she was combining heirloom tomatoes, sourced from local farms, with grilled olives, I knew I would love the dish. The olives take on a rich, smoky flavor from the coals, and pair as a nice warm contrast to the cool, meaty tomatoes.

12 Castelvetrano olives

3 heirloom tomatoes, preferably German Johnson, Cherokee Purple, or Carolina Gold

1 pint cherry or grape tomatoes

Fine sea salt

Freshly ground black pepper

1 cup Charred Tomato Vinaigrette (page 108)

1 cup fresh whole-milk ricotta

½ cup Grilled Breadcrumbs (page 108), or seasoned toasted breadcrumbs

Fresh basil

1   Open the bottom vent of a charcoal grill completely. Light a charcoal chimney starter filled with charcoal. When the coals are covered with gray ash, pour them onto the bottom grate of the grill. Adjust the vents as needed to maintain an internal temperature of 400° to 450°F. (If using a gas grill, preheat to medium-high [400° to 450°F].)

2   Add the olives to a grill basket and place directly over the coals (or on the gas grill's grates). Roast the olives, tossing on occasion, until slightly charred and tender, about 5 minutes. (Cooking time on a gas grill will be 8 to 10 minutes.) Let cool, and then slice each in half.

3   Dice the heirloom tomatoes into equal, 1- by 1-inch pieces. Slice the cherry tomatoes in half lengthwise. Place all the tomatoes in a large bowl and season generously with sea salt and pepper. Let stand for 5 minutes.

4   Toss the tomatoes with the vinaigrette and mix well. Divide the tomatoes and olives among four serving plates. Spoon a dollop of ricotta over the top of each salad and sprinkle with the breadcrumbs. Garnish with torn fresh basil.

continued

CHARRED TOMATO VINAIGRETTE

Makes 1½ cups

1 head garlic

1 (10-ounce) package
fresh cherry tomatoes

2 tablespoons white wine
vinegar

¼ cup canola oil

2 tablespoons extra-virgin
olive oil

Fine sea salt

Freshly ground black
pepper

1 Preheat the oven to 350°F. Slice off the root end of the garlic head so the cloves are slightly exposed. Wrap the head of garlic in foil. Roast in the oven for 35 to 45 minutes, until the cloves are very tender. Let cool. Squeeze four cloves from the skins and place in a blender. Discard the skins. (Cover and refrigerate the remaining roasted garlic for up to a week to save for another use.)

2 Open the bottom vent of a charcoal grill completely. Light a charcoal chimney starter filled with charcoal. When the coals are covered with gray ash, pour them onto the bottom grate of the grill. Adjust the vents as needed to maintain an internal temperature of 400° to 450°F. (If using a gas grill, preheat to medium-high [400° to 450°F].)

3 Place a grill basket with fine holes directly on the coals to preheat, about 3 minutes. Add the cherry tomatoes to the grill basket in an even layer (you may have to cook in batches, depending on the size of your basket) and cook over the coals, stirring occasionally until the skins are charred and blistered, a few minutes. Remove from the heat and let cool.

4 Add the tomatoes and vinegar to the garlic cloves in the blender and puree until smooth. With the machine running, slowly drizzle in the oils to emulsify. Season well with salt and pepper to taste and use immediately.

GRILLED BREADCRUMBS

Makes 1 cup

3 slices (about 4 ounces)
hearty whole grain bread

Extra-virgin olive oil

1 garlic clove, peeled

1 Open the bottom vent of a charcoal grill completely. Light a charcoal chimney starter filled with charcoal. When the coals are covered with gray ash, pour them onto the bottom grate of the grill. Adjust the vents as needed to maintain an internal temperature of 400° to 450°F. Coat the top grate with oil; place on the grill. (If using a gas grill, preheat to medium-high [400° to 450°F].)

2 Preheat the oven to 275°F.

3 Remove and discard the crust from the bread. Slice into ¼- to ½-inch slices; drizzle with olive oil. Grill the bread on both sides until browned but not burnt (about 1 minute). Remove from the grill and, while the bread is still very hot, rub each side with the garlic clove.

4 Transfer the bread to a baking sheet and bake until crisp, about 10 minutes.

5 Let the bread cool completely. Pulse in a food processor until crumbled, but not a powder (with crumbs about the size of panko).

EMBERED SWEET CORN WITH LIME-BASIL BUTTER

SERVES 4 TO 6
Hands-On: 25 minutes | **Total:** 45 minutes

There's something about this dish that's lingered on my taste buds since my visit. Ashley cuts the corn off the cob prior to grilling, as the cut kernels' starches and natural sweetness are maximized when they meet the high heat of the grill. The corn sits in a grill basket and is tossed, on occasion, right over the coals until the corn is slightly charred and almost smells of caramel. Honestly, this is a great side dish to a main, but it would be just as good for me as a dessert. The key is to buy fresh corn, in the peak of the season.

6 ears fresh shucked corn, kernels cut from cobs

8 to 12 large fresh basil leaves, torn

Fine sea salt

4 tablespoons unsalted butter, softened

2 teaspoons grated lime zest plus 2 tablespoons lime juice (from 2 limes)

1 Open the bottom vent of a charcoal grill completely. Light a charcoal chimney starter filled with charcoal. When the coals are covered with gray ash, pour them onto the bottom grate of the grill. Adjust the vents as needed to maintain an internal temperature of 450° to 500°F. (If using a gas grill, preheat to high [450° to 500°F].)

2 Place a grill basket with fine holes directly on the coals to preheat for about 3 minutes. Add the corn kernels and half of the torn basil to the hot basket and season with salt. Roast directly on the coals until the kernels start to char, 3 to 5 minutes. Be careful not to overcook, especially with fresh sweet corn. For a gas grill, cook in the basket on the grates over high heat for 8 to 10 minutes.

3 Transfer the corn to a large metal mixing bowl. Toss with the butter (it will melt from the residual heat of the corn), remaining torn basil, and the lime zest and juice. Add more sea salt to taste.

GRILLED PORK CHOPS WITH GRILLED FIGS AND SABA

SERVES 4

Hands-On: 45 minutes | Total: 21 hours, including 20 hours brining

I started my morning with these grilled pork chops for breakfast—a perfectly acceptable way to start any day. The bone-in pork chops at Death & Taxes are sourced locally and bathed in a brine to maximize flavor and tenderness. Ashley and Lauren cook them quickly over the fire, combining them with sweet grilled figs and tart saba (grape must reduction, for those wondering). In a pinch, substitute a quality balsamic vinegar for the saba. If you're looking for a main dish (or breakfast) to impress, you've found it.

1 gallon water

1 cup kosher salt, plus more to taste

4 bone-in pork chops, about 12 ounces each

2 tablespoons canola oil

Freshly ground black pepper

8 fresh figs

3 tablespoons saba or quality balsamic vinegar

1 **Make the brine:** In a large stockpot over medium heat, combine half the water and the salt, stirring until it dissolves. Remove from the heat, stir in the remaining water, and let cool completely (about 2 hours). Add the pork chops to the brine, making sure they are fully submerged (you can use a plate to weight them down if necessary). Refrigerate for 18 to 24 hours.

2 Open the bottom vent of a charcoal grill completely. Light a charcoal chimney starter filled with charcoal. When the coals are covered with gray ash, pour them onto the bottom grate of the grill. Adjust the vents as needed to maintain an internal temperature of 400° to 450°F. Coat the top grate with oil; place on the grill. (If using a gas grill, preheat to medium-high [400° to 450°F].)

3 Remove the pork chops from the brine and pat completely dry with paper towels. Drizzle the chops with some of the canola oil and season with pepper. Cook the chops on the hot grill for 4 to 6 minutes per side, until an internal thermometer reads 135° to 140°F. Remove from the heat and rest for at least 5 minutes.

4 Slice the figs in half and drizzle with canola oil. Grill the figs, cut-side down, over high heat until caramelized, about 6 minutes. Carefully remove the figs, being careful as they may stick to the grates.

5 To serve, slice the pork, drizzle lightly with saba, and garnish with grilled figs.

Philadelphia, PA

MICHAEL SOLOMONOV,
chef/co-owner of Zahav

> "Honestly, bro, you are either moving forward, or backward— there is no middle ground."

THIS IS THE REALITY and day-to-day mantra of chef Michael Solomonov. Humble yet firm, he quickly admits that he spent much of his early life treading water, perhaps even ebbing backward. "Things rarely go the right way, and if there is one absolute, things will always change," he says. Eventually, the tides of change swelled in Mike's favor—and he's been riding an endlessly cresting wave built on perseverance, transparency, and hard work.

The first time I met Mike, things were certainly not going my way. I was trying to catch a connecting flight through Philadelphia, but it got grounded due to thunderstorms. On the advice of a friend, I was told to go relish a meal at Zahav, the Hebrew word for gold.

Walking into Zahav was like walking into a savory version of Willy Wonka's chocolate factory—scents of burning charcoal and exotic spice teemed through the chatter and noise of the packed dining room. Snagging a seat at the bar was kismet and I was soon plowing through every mezze on the menu: stewed okra and tomatoes, hummus as fluffy as a cumulus cloud, and the satiny raw meat of kibbe naya. All were ordered in reprise. Stomach fully packed, I was certain I could not eat another bite, but the tastes, smells, and familiar foods prepared so uniquely beckoned like sirens. Eventually, I made it home, but the experience stuck with me. That meal remains one of the very best of my life.

Though Mike was born in Israel, his family moved stateside, settling in Pittsburgh. His younger brother, David, was soon born and a very American existence followed suit. At fifteen, Mike moved back to Israel with his family, yet he soon returned to the States to finish up high school, followed by a stint at the University of Vermont.

"I decided to move back to Israel, and I can remember pacing up and down this alleyway outside our house searching for work," Mike says. A bakery was in need of extra hands, so Mike started to grind. "I was literally an immigrant worker, learning Hebrew, Russian, and Arabic and baking—on the fly—breaking my back making borekas for two bucks an hour. But I was participating in society in a way I had never done before. It gave me a sense of purpose," he says.

The bakery gig led to a job working as a short-order cook at a nearby coffee shop. "Israelis never stop eating, bro. At all hours, they are always eating."

Mike committed himself to a life in the world of gastronomy. After snagging a culinary degree, he made the move to Philadelphia, a place he originally thought would be a stepping-stone to the Big Apple. Mike cut his teeth first at Striped Bass, then went to work with Mark Vetri at his eponymous Italian restaurant. His career was on the rise.

Returning to Israel for a much-needed break, Mike arrived to find out his mom had volunteered him to cook up dinner parties for friends. But all the cooking was tempered, with days spent on nearby beaches with his brother David and friends, who all were on leave from their duties in the Israeli Defense Forces.

Fresh off this sojourn and back at work in the States, Mike received news that can break even the strongest of souls. Three days away from completing his military service, and on Yom Kippur, David was killed by a sniper on the Israel border with Lebanon. He was just twenty-one years old. I'm certainly not the first to print this story, nor is this the last time Mike will tell it, but the moment left us both hauntingly silent.

Months after, Mike returned to northern Israel, along with Mark Vetri, to cook for David's soldier comrades. He saw the young soldiers, fatigued, covered in mud, yet still driven to protect their country. Something inside Mike changed. "I just cooked the food I wanted to cook, giving something of myself, and my life's work started to take shape," he says.

But first, some real, personal work needed to tran-spire. Depression and addiction had engulfed Mike, and the timing could not have been worse. He and his business partner, Steve Cook, were in the process of opening Zahav in 2008. Intervention and rehab were a struggle, but a necessity to save Mike's life.

Mike came back on course, but Zahav was still on shaky ground. "I remember Steve telling me one day

to just cook," Mike says. Instead of being bound by the roots of one idea of Israeli cuisine, Mike was free to represent Israel as a whole, pulling from a rich tapestry of ingredients, methods, and influences.

The imperative to "just cook" paid off. Fast-forward a decade, with nearly a dozen or so restaurants under his belt, Mike has won some of the industry's highest awards and accolades. I tell him he is like "the Michael Jordan of cooking." He shrugs off the compliment unpretentiously.

My papa used to say that if you hang around greatness long enough, it would spread like a Mississippi wildfire. And so it is with the staff of Mike's kitchens. Take ener-getic pastry chef Camille Cogswell. She credits Mike's leadership and camaraderie as critical to her landing a rising chef award from the James Beard Foundation. It's clear that legacies are being created, fostered, and honored inside Zahav.

After overcoming personal hurdles and reaching the pinnacles of success in one's industry while giving back and mentoring others, I have to ask the question, "What's next?"

In all sincerity, I expect Mike to tell me it is time to dial back a bit, to relish and savor the moment. Instead, he tells me of a new undisclosed project, something near and dear to him that will get him back to his roots. "Bro, there is always another story to tell," he says.

I can't agree with you more, Chef.

CHICKEN SHISHLIK WITH GREEN GARBANZO MASABACHA AND GRIBENES

SERVES 4 TO 6
Hands-On: 1 hour 5 minutes | Total: 2 hours 25 minutes

Mikes's goal is to cook food that reminds us of other places and times, and one bite of this chicken transports me to Sunday mornings in my grandmother's kitchen in Valdosta, Georgia.

The chicken sits in a puree of onion for an hour before cooking—a simple technique that yields amazing flavor. The creamy *masabacha* (a heartier hummus) is a great complement that keeps dairy and meat off the same plate—though Zahav does not keep kosher. I was unaware of the Jewish specialty *gribenes*, but one taste of the crispy fried chicken skin made my "Southernality" come out. "They taste like pork rinds," I exclaimed. "They do, sorta." Mike laughed. No matter your connections to the flavors, this dish hits on all cylinders.

½ **Spanish onion, chopped**

2 **tablespoons sumac, plus 1 teaspoon for gribenes**

1½ **tablespoons salt, plus 1 teaspoon for gribenes**

1 **tablespoon ground black pepper**

1½ **teaspoons ground coriander**

½ **cup canola oil**

4 **pounds bone-in, skin-on chicken thighs**

Green Chickpea Masabacha (recipe follows)

1. Puree the onion, sumac, salt, black pepper, and coriander in a blender, then stream in the canola oil until smooth.

2. Remove the skin from the chicken and set aside to make the gribenes. Remove the bones and cut the chicken into 1-inch chunks. Transfer to a ziplock bag and add the onion puree. Seal and marinate in the refrigerator for at least 1 hour, or up to overnight.

3. Meanwhile, make the gribenes: Add the reserved chicken skin to a 3½-quart saucepan and cover with 1 quart water. Bring to a boil, reduce the heat to medium, and cook until the water evaporates and the skins fry in their own fat, about 1 hour. When the skins are crispy, remove from the fat and cool on a plate lined with paper towels. Chop the skins. In a small bowl, combine the skins with the 1 teaspoon sumac and 1 teaspoon salt.

4. Open the bottom vent of a charcoal grill completely. Light a charcoal chimney starter filled with charcoal. When the coals are covered with gray ash, pour them onto the bottom grate of the grill. Adjust the vents as needed to maintain an internal temperature of 400° to 450°F. Coat the top grate with oil; place on the grill. (If using a gas grill, preheat to medium-high [400° to 450°F].)

5. Thread the chicken pieces onto skewers and grill directly over the hot coals, turning every few minutes, until the chicken is nicely charred on the exterior and cooked through, about 8 minutes.

6. To serve, spread masabacha on a plate, top with the grilled chicken skewers, and sprinkle the crispy gribenes on top.

GREEN CHICKPEA MASABACHA

Makes 2½ cups

Cook 2 cups fresh or frozen green chickpeas (or
frozen green peas) in a pot of boiling, salted water
for 90 seconds, until just tender. Transfer to an ice
bath to cool quickly. Drain and pat dry. In a small
pan, cook 1 small carrot, diced, and ½ Spanish
onion, diced, together in 1 tablespoon olive oil over
medium-low heat until tender, about 5 minutes.
Set aside to cool. Mix the cooked chickpeas with
the vegetables, ½ cup tahini paste, and the juice of
half a lemon. Thin with 2 to 3 tablespoons of water,
if necessary. Season with salt to taste.

CREMINI MUSHROOMS SHISHLIK WITH HAZELNUTS AND BROCCOLINI

SERVES 6 TO 8 AS A STARTER OR SIDE

Hands-On: 1 hour 50 minutes | Total: 5 hours

Sometimes, the true sign of a great chef, or artist, is showing restraint. This dish is one of those times where perfect execution brings out the best of great ingredients. Grilled over open coals and skewered (shishlik), mushrooms take on just the right texture to balance the tender crunch from Broccolini and sweet hazelnuts. The dukkah is a powderlike topping that combines nuts and spices and really packs a flavor punch. (You can sprinkle it over many other grilled meats, seafoods, and vegetables for a delicious finish.) While cherchi typically refers to a pumpkin salad found in Lebanon or Morocco, Mike puts his own spin, as he often does, on this dish by instead using a base of Broccolini. This is a superb starter or side dish for any occasion.

MUSHROOMS

½ yellow onion, chopped

1 tablespoon ground urfa chile

½ cup plus 1 tablespoon canola oil

2 pounds cremini mushrooms

Kosher salt

2 pounds Broccolini

HAZELNUT CHERCHI

2 cups hazelnuts

1 yellow onion, chopped

2 garlic cloves, chopped

Roughly chopped Broccolini stems (from 2 pounds Broccolini)

2 tablespoons olive oil, plus additional for serving

2 tablespoons white wine vinegar

Lemon juice

Kosher salt

Hazelnut Dukkah (recipe follows)

1 **For the mushrooms:** Puree the onion and urfa in a blender, then slowly stream in the ½ cup canola oil until smooth. Season the mushrooms with salt and toss with the onion marinade to coat. Transfer to a heavy-duty ziplock bag and marinate for at least 1 hour at room temperature, or in the refrigerator for up to 6 hours.

2 Remove the stems of the Broccolini and reserve for the cherchi. Toss the florets with the 1 tablespoon canola oil and season with 2 tablespoons salt.

3 **For the cherchi:** Meanwhile, preheat the oven to 300°F. Spread the hazelnuts in an even layer on a baking sheet. Lightly toast for 7 minutes. Set aside to cool.

4 In a saucepan, cook the onion, garlic, and Broccolini stems together in 2 tablespoons olive oil over low heat for 5 minutes. Add the vinegar and toasted hazelnuts and cover with 2 quarts water. Simmer over low heat until the Broccolini and hazelnuts are tender, about 2 hours. Check periodically and add additional water as needed. Drain and reserve 1 cup of the water.

5 Transfer the cooked vegetables and the 1 cup cooking water to a blender and blend until smooth. Season with the olive oil and lemon juice, and salt to taste. Set the cherchi aside.

6 Open the bottom vent of a charcoal grill completely. Light a charcoal chimney starter filled with charcoal. When the coals are covered with gray ash, pour them onto the bottom grate of the grill.

Adjust the vents as needed to maintain an internal temperature of 300° to 350°F. Coat the top grate with oil; place on the grill. (If using a gas grill, preheat to medium-low [300° to 350°F].)

7 In batches, grill the mushrooms and Broccolini directly over the coals until tender, about 10 minutes.

8 To serve, spread the cherchi across the bottom of a serving plate and top with the grilled Broccolini. Spoon the grilled creminis over the Broccolini, then sprinkle the hazelnut dukkah over the top and serve.

HAZELNUT DUKKAH

Makes ½ cup

Coarsely chop ½ cup toasted hazelnuts and combine with 2 teaspoons toasted sesame seeds, ¾ teaspoon ground coriander, ¾ teaspoon ground cumin, ¾ teaspoon ground urfa chile, ¼ teaspoon Maldon salt, and 1 tablespoon chopped fresh parsley. Use immediately.

DRY-AGED VEAL WITH MUHAMMARA

SERVES 6 TO 8

Hands-On: 45 minutes | Total: 25 hours 45 minutes

"**One part salt,** one part spice, age it for 30 days, and roast it—this veal tastes like the best pork loin of your life," Mike tells me. Admittedly, it seems like a whole lot of effort to find room to age a rack of veal in my fridge for 30 days. But after tasting this cut after it's kissed the grill, along with the spicy red pepper and walnut muhammara sauce, I'm ready to tell my wife that we need another fridge for the sole purpose of re-creating this dish. It's seriously delicious—worth every bit of time and the wait.

1 (6-pound) veal rack

6 tablespoons kosher salt

2 tablespoons Ararat spice (see Note)

Muhammara (recipe follows)

1 Coat the veal rack in salt and Ararat spice and place on a wire rack set inside a rimmed baking sheet. Refrigerate uncovered overnight, or up to 3 weeks (longer is better), rotating and flipping the rack every few days, and draining as necessary.

2 Preheat the oven to 300°F. Roast the veal rack on a clean rack and baking sheet for about 70 minutes, until the internal temperature reaches 130°F.

3 Open the bottom vent of a charcoal grill completely. Light a charcoal chimney starter filled with charcoal. When the coals are covered with gray ash, pour them onto the bottom grate of the grill. Adjust vents as needed to maintain an internal temperature of 300° to 350°F. Coat the top grate with oil; place on the grill. (If using a gas grill, preheat to medium-low [300° to 350°F].)

4 Grill the veal rack for 8 to 10 minutes, until desired degree of doneness (140°F for medium). Lightly tent with foil and let rest for 10 minutes.

5 Slice the veal into individual chops and serve with a few heaping spoonfuls of muhammara on the side.

Note: If you cannot find Ararat spice, make your own: Combine 2 teaspoons ground fenugreek, 2 teaspoons smoked paprika, and 2 teaspoons ground urfa chile.

continued

MUHAMMARA

Makes 1½ cups

1 cup walnuts

2 red bell peppers

1 garlic clove

1 tablespoon
pomegranate molasses

1½ teaspoons smoked
paprika

1½ teaspoons harissa

1½ teaspoons olive oil

2 tablespoons chopped
fresh parsley

2 tablespoons lemon juice

Kosher salt

1 Preheat the oven to 300°F. Spread the walnuts evenly on a baking sheet and lightly toast for 7 minutes. Let cool.

2 Open the bottom vent of a charcoal grill completely. Light a charcoal chimney starter filled with charcoal. When the coals are covered with gray ash, pour them onto the bottom grate of the grill. Adjust vents as needed to maintain an internal temperature of 300° to 350°F. Coat the top grate with oil; place on the grill. (If using a gas grill, preheat to medium-low [300° to 350°F].)

3 Roast the red bell peppers whole on the grill until soft and lightly charred, about 5 minutes. Transfer to a heavy-duty ziplock bag and let cool for 10 minutes. Carefully remove the stem and skin, cut in half, and remove the seeds.

4 Pulse the peppers in a food processor with the walnuts and garlic until it forms a coarse paste. Transfer to a bowl and mix in the pomegranate molasses, paprika, harissa, olive oil, and parsley. Season with lemon juice and salt to taste.

STRAWBERRIES AL HA'ESH WITH FETA-HONEY ICE CREAM

MAKES 4 SERVINGS

Hands-On: 1 hour 15 minutes | Total: 5 hours 30 minutes

Zahav pastry chef Camille Cogswell stands over the open charcoal fire with skewered strawberries, telling me that this dish is something she's been wanting to put on the menu for a long time. *Al ha'esh* is a term used to mean "on the fire"—Isrealis cook so much food in this manner that Michael tells me in city parks there are designated signs to tell overzealous cooks where they can and cannot grill. The house-made ice cream picks up some salty heft from feta cheese that is balanced by honey's sweetness. I'm not a big dessert guy, but you can bet you'll find this simple, tasteful dish being served at dinner parties in my home for years to come.

FETA-HONEY ICE CREAM

2⅔ cups heavy cream

¾ cup whole milk

½ cup honey

11 large egg yolks

½ cup granulated sugar

4 ounces feta cheese, crumbled

2 pounds strawberries, washed and hulled

Rose Syrup (recipe follows)

Extra-virgin olive oil

1 **For the ice cream:** Combine the cream, milk, and honey in a medium saucepan and bring to a simmer, stirring occasionally. Whisk together the egg yolks and sugar in a heatproof bowl. Place a damp kitchen towel under the bowl to hold it in place. Slowly ladle the hot honey cream over the egg yolk mixture while constantly whisking to temper the yolks. Continue until all the liquid has been added to the bowl, one ladleful at a time.

2 Pour the mixture back into the pot, return to the stove, and cook over medium heat, whisking constantly so the eggs don't curdle. Cook over medium-low heat until the mixture reaches 170°F. Remove from the heat and pour into another heatproof container to stop the cooking process. Let cool slightly.

3 Combine the feta cheese and 2 to 3 cups of the warm ice cream base in a blender. Blend together until the mixture is very smooth. Whisk together the contents of the blender and the remaining ice cream base. Strain through a fine mesh strainer into another heatproof container. Chill in the refrigerator until completely cold (at least 4 hours or overnight).

4 Churn the ice cream according to your ice cream machine's instructions. Store in an airtight container in the freezer until ready to serve or up to 1 week.

5 Open the bottom vent of a charcoal grill completely. Light a charcoal chimney starter filled with charcoal. When the coals are covered with gray ash, pour them onto the bottom grate of the grill. Adjust the vents as needed to maintain an internal temperature of 400° to 450°F. (If using a gas grill, preheat to medium-high [400° to 450°F].)

continued

6 Skewer the strawberries through their sides onto metal skewers (or wooden skewers that have been soaked in water), 4 or 5 strawberries per skewer (depending on size). Brush liberally with the cold rose syrup, then place the skewers directly over a bed of white-hot coals, turning as the syrup begins to caramelize, until they have a nice char on all sides and have softened very slightly, about 5 minutes.

7 To serve, place a large scoop of ice cream in the center of a chilled plate and gently press the top with a spoon to create a well for the strawberries and syrup. Lay one skewer over the ice cream. Drizzle with additional rose syrup and good-quality extra-virgin olive oil. Serve immediately.

ROSE SYRUP

Makes ½ cup

Simmer ½ cup sugar, ¼ cup water, and ¼ teaspoon rose water in a small saucepan, stirring to dissolve the sugar, about 5 minutes. Let cool to room temperature and chill until ready to use.

BROOKS REITZ,
owner of Leon's Oyster Shop

Walking into the home that's been converted into an office in Charleston's Upper Peninsula neighborhood, it's hard to find Brooks and team, as they are surrounded by boxes piled from floor to ceiling. "Sorry for the mess," Brooks says.

The reality of being one of Charleston's most successful restaurateurs along with running an equally booming beverage company is that there are a lot of people vying for Brooks's time. A few minutes into our conversation, I can see why—there's a spark to his personality, an undeniable affinity. Put simply, you want to hang out with this guy.

Born and raised in Henderson, Kentucky, Brooks has always had the hospitality business in his blood—his father was a bar owner prior to settling into a life of selling insurance. After high school, Brooks pursued a major in playwriting and screenwriting at Transylvania University in Louisville. Though he was passionate about his studies, it was Pulitzer prize–winning playwright Donald Margulies who counseled Brooks to pursue a different career path. "Donald was able to convey the reality of the business, which pushed me further into hospitality," Brooks recounts.

Brooks had held down jobs at several restaurants throughout his studies, but it was a *New York Times* article he picked up in the college library that would really fan the flames. The Myriad Restaurant Group, known for hot spots such as Nobu and others, was expanding, announcing the opening of Proof on Main in Louisville. Brooks saw it as a great opportunity to get his feet wet locally, while gaining experience with a well-established New York firm. Speaking of New York—during a discovery trip to eat at the city's famed restaurant Balthazar, Brooks got his first taste of a "cinematic restaurant." He realized that becoming a restaurant owner would allow him, in some ways, to remain a playwright—setting a stage, a performance, and an experience for others.

There is an old saying that a jack of all trades is a master of none, but I would argue that Brooks Reitz, owner of Leon's Oyster Shop, is a jack of all trades, master of many. Though Brooks will be the first to admit it, actually cooking in one of his restaurants is not his specialty.

"Let's meet at my office, it's across the street from the restaurant, and it's where I spend most of my time," Brooks told me. He wasn't joking.

Starting as a bartender at Proof on Main, Brooks quickly worked his way up, eventually landing as the general manager at the ripe old age of twenty-four. "Today, I know for a fact that I am a good person to work for—I'm calm, candid, and warm. But I did not start out that way," Brooks says. Youth and wisdom typically do not go hand in hand—nor does life always go as planned.

"I decided to move to Charleston so that I could be closer to my son," Brooks tells me. It was the maturing forces of becoming a father—albeit unplanned—that forged him into the man that he is today.

Stomach growling, I suggest that Brooks and I walk across the street to Leon's—after all, I've got a hankering for the chargrilled oysters. As we make our way, I catch Brooks leaning over, picking up small bits of trash on the sidewalk, arranging the entryway, and chatting to the staff—"It's all about the first impression," he says. A minute later, regular diners are shaking his hand, giving him hugs, and catching up on the local gossip.

Now I know why Brooks suggested that we meet at his office—the distractions and responsibilities of owning a restaurant never seem to cease. But soon we settle at the large bar, he whips me up a signature Jack Rudy Daytripper cocktail, and I dive into the meaty, grilled oysters. They are everything I had imagined—briny, sweet, and made decadent with nutty, melted Parmesan cheese, rendered even more delicious by the smoke of the grill.

Ever the hustler, Brooks first cut his teeth in Charleston by taking over the beverage program at FIG, an establishment known throughout the industry, mainly due to the bright talents of chef Mike Lata. Brooks felt the team could do better, so—playing up FIG's locally sourced mentality—he went to work on creating his own house-made tonic to use at the restaurant. The idea turned out to be a good one—really good. Soon, Brooks found himself selling his tonic to other local restaurants and beyond. He went on to form the Jack Rudy Cocktail Co., named after his serial inventor, daredevil of a great-grandfather. My ears perk when Brooks tells me that Jack once flew his plane illegally under an Ohio River bridge. With a rebel spirit, Brooks continued to grow the side business, while working at FIG, and then another Charleston favorite, The Ordinary.

After a few years, Brooks parlayed the success of Jack Rudy, his newly minted capital, into opening Leon's Oyster Shop—his first foray as an actual owner of a restaurant. It was yet another good idea—this guy is full of 'em. "Leon's was not the norm," Brooks says. "We are just as busy four years later as we were on day one."

After spending a few hours with Brooks, he lets me know that he's got to get back to the office. I tell him to "hit the road, Jack," but I think my humor falls just as flat with Brooks as it does my wife. Anyways, I must admit, I feel guilty taking in the pleasure of food and drink while Brooks heads back to the grind. I ease my mind by rationalizing to myself that a guy with this much luck can only come from Kentucky.

"It's all about the first impression."

As we part ways, I watch Brooks walking back across the street to his office—stopping once again to tidy up, gathering little bits of trash from the street to ensure his guests are welcomed with the best of first impressions.

It becomes clear that Brooks' success is based not on luck or gambling at all. Rather, it's his tireless work ethic—combined with doing all the little things, the right way, that matter the most.

Now, that's something you can bet on.

CHARGRILLED OYSTERS WITH COMPOUND BUTTER

SERVES 4 TO 6 AS AN APPETIZER

Hands-On: 45 minutes | Total: 3 hours 15 minutes

This is one of the most popular dishes served at Leon's, besides their famous fried chicken. Fired by the half dozen, I'd guess at least five hundred or so of these oysters are served during a busy lunch hour. The key to grilling oysters is making sure your grill is super hot, which allows you to cook up batches of oysters quickly and efficiently.

18 oysters, shucked and cleaned

Compound Butter (recipe follows)

¾ cup freshly grated Parmigiano-Reggiano cheese

1 Open the bottom vent of a charcoal grill completely. Light a charcoal chimney starter filled with charcoal. When the coals are covered with gray ash, pour them onto the bottom grate of the grill. Adjust the vents as needed to maintain an internal temperature of 450° to 500°F. Coat the top grate with oil; place on the grill. (If using a gas grill, preheat to high [450° to 500°F].)

2 Top each oyster with 1 teaspoon of compound butter, followed by a generous sprinkle of cheese. Grill the oysters over direct heat for 5 minutes, or until the outer edges just bubble and the cheese is melted.

COMPOUND BUTTER

Makes ¾ cup

Combine ½ cup softened unsalted butter,
¼ cup minced fresh parsley, 1½ tablespoons
Worcestershire sauce, 1½ tablespoons lemon
juice, and 1 teaspoon freshly ground black pepper
until well blended. Transfer the butter onto a sheet
of plastic wrap, shape into a log, and roll up in the
plastic. Refrigerate at least 2 hours to set up and
chill. Freeze any leftover butter for up to 3 months.

SOY-MISO DRESSED GRILLED CORN

SERVES 6 TO 12 AS A SIDE
Hands-On: 35 minutes | Total: 3 hours 15 minutes

Another popular favorite at Leon's, this corn cooks up quickly over the open grill. Poaching the corn first in the soy mixture tenderizes the corn and infuses great flavor—a terrific complement to the char from the heat. But the best part is the dressing—a savory, creamy contrast to the sweet corn that echoes the soy poaching liquid.

If some of these ingredients are new to you, have no fear, most can be readily found at any grocer or specialty store.

POACHING LIQUID AND CORN

6 quarts water

3 cups (24 ounces) soy sauce

6 ears of corn, shucked, cleaned, and cut in half

DRESSING

1 tablespoon soy sauce

¼ cup white miso paste

SPICE BLEND

⅓ cup toasted sesame seeds

1 sheet nori (dried seaweed), crushed (about 1 tablespoon)

½ teaspoon kosher salt

¼ teaspoon togarashi spice blend

Olive oil

Cilantro leaves

1   **To poach the corn:** Bring the water and soy sauce to a boil in a large stockpot over high heat; reduce to a simmer. Add the corn and turn off the heat. Let the corn poach until the liquid comes to room temperature, about 2 hours, then leave in the liquid until ready to use, or up to 24 hours.

2   Open the bottom vent of a charcoal grill completely. Light a charcoal chimney starter filled with charcoal. When the coals are covered with gray ash, pour them onto the bottom grate of the grill. Adjust the vents as needed to maintain an internal temperature of 350° to 400°F. Coat the top grate with oil; place on the grill. (If using a gas grill, preheat to medium [350° to 400°F].)

3   **For the dressing:** Whisk the soy sauce and miso paste in a shallow bowl to combine. Set aside.

4   **For the spice blend:** Combine the sesame seeds, crushed nori, salt, and togarashi spice in a shallow bowl. Set aside.

5   Drain the corn. Brush the ears lightly with olive oil. Place the corn on the hot grill and cook until slightly charred all over, rolling the ears as necessary, about 2 minutes on each side. Remove the corn from the grill with tongs and roll in the dressing to coat. Dredge each ear in the spice blend until coated. Transfer to a serving platter and serve immediately with some sprigs of cilantro.

GRILLED MAHI SANDWICHES

SERVES 4

Hands-On: 40 minutes | Total: 1 hour

Super simple, and super delicious blackened. The fresh mahi fillets, caked in a house-made blackening spice, stand up readily to the hot direct fire on the grill. A bit of love—Duke's mayonnaise (a Southern staple)—and the classic garnish of fresh tomato and lettuce will make you entirely forget that there's no burger on the menu at Leon's.

4 (5-ounce) fillets mahi-mahi

4 tablespoons mayonnaise (preferably Duke's brand), plus additional for serving

Blackening Seasoning (recipe follows)

4 hamburger buns, halved

Crystal hot sauce

4 leaves iceberg lettuce

1 ripe tomato, thinly sliced

1   Open the bottom vent of a charcoal grill completely. Light a charcoal chimney starter filled with charcoal. When the coals are covered with gray ash, pour them onto the bottom grate of the grill. Adjust the vents as needed to maintain an internal temperature of 450° to 500°F. Coat the top grate with oil; place on the grill. (If using a gas grill, preheat to high [450° to 500°F].)

2   Using a pastry brush, paint each fish fillet with 1 tablespoon mayonnaise and generously sprinkle with blackening seasoning. Grill the fillets for 5 minutes on each side, or until the fish is done and flakes easily with a fork. Remove the fish with a spatula and let it rest.

3   Grill the buns, cut-side down, for about 30 seconds or until lightly toasted.

4   Spread an even layer of mayonnaise on the cut side of each half of the bun, and shake on a few dashes of hot sauce as well. Place the fish on the bottom bun, top with lettuce and tomato, and season with a few more shakes of the blackening seasoning. Place the top bun on to assemble the sandwich and enjoy.

BLACKENED SEASONING

Makes ¼ cup

This is also delicious sprinkled on hot buttered corn.

Combine 1½ tablespoons kosher salt, 2 teaspoons freshly ground black pepper, 1 tablespoon paprika, 1½ teaspoons onion powder, ¾ teaspoon dried thyme, and ¼ teaspoon dried oregano. Store in an airtight container in a cool dark place up to 6 months.

THE DAYTRIPPER

SERVES 1

Hands-On: 5 minutes | Total: 5 minutes

I couldn't visit Leon's Oyster Shop without having Brooks whip me up one of his signature cocktails, fortified with some of his own Jack Rudy creations. An homage to one of his favorite Beatles' tunes, this light and refreshing cocktail is perfect for any occasion, best enjoyed during the day. You can find Jack Rudy beverages at fine bottle shops, as well as online.

1½ ounces vodka

¾ ounce lemon juice

½ ounce Jack Rudy sweet tea syrup (see Resources, page 299)

5 drops Jack Rudy lavender bitters (see Resources, page 299)

1   Combine the vodka, lemon juice, and tea syrup in a shaker and shake vigorously until combined. Pour into an ice-filled cocktail glass, garnish with bitters, stir, and serve.

SYLVESTER & MARY HOOVER,
owners of Hoover's Grocery

My first introduction to it came after spending a few days in Greenwood, Mississippi, with fellow author Martha Foose. During those few days that lingered like the Yazoo River, my cup never ran dry, and my plate—and heart—remained full.

Seeking a return to this inimitable piece of earth, I reached out to Martha to ask who has the best grilling game in Greenwood—and that is how I found Sylvester and Mary Hoover.

"I, like those that came before me, was born in the blues. Whatever ill'd 'em, the blues would heal 'em," Sylvester Hoover tells me. His grill lacks any traditional ways to close the vents or damper that are necessary to control temperature. Stuffing the holes with crumpled aluminum foil, and wedging a screwdriver into the hinge, Sylvester smiles, telling me, "I make do."

Inside Hoover's, I meet Sylvester's wife, Mary. Before she greets me with words, I'm flashed a smile that makes me feel as welcome as if she was my own momma. The smile leads to a hug, as is Southern tradition. After exchanging a few pleasantries, we quickly get to work on one of her signatures—peach cake. Like my own momma, I notice nearly nothing is measured—except the love.

Hoover's Grocery is situated in Baptist Town. It received its name due to the baptisms that took place in the 1800s in the small creek that once ran strong, but now only trickles, through the district. After the Emancipation Proclamation, the neighborhood became made up entirely of freed African Americans, but in those days, business owners were largely white, and thereby had even more control to pressure a collective race that had already endured the worst of humanity.

The son of sharecroppers, Sylvester recalls his earliest memories of being dragged on a cotton sack through the rows while his mother picked cotton on the Whittington Plantation. His family was caught in a cyclical existence of debt to the landowners—something Sylvester was able to break by attending school off the plantation.

When I ask about how he met Mary, Sylvester is less than forthcoming. I decide to walk back inside, where Mary is whipping up a batch of coleslaw, and she tells

> "Son, our food doesn't just taste, it feels too."

THE DELTA. There is, perhaps, no place in our country more misunderstood, mythic, and luring. Built primarily on the wrong side of history, most Americans have either shunned the area entirely or, most likely, forgotten its existence altogether. It is isolated. It is complicated. But it is beautiful.

me the story. They were on a basketball trip, and when the two saved seats for each other, Sylvester moved in for the kiss. "I slapped him," Mary tells me. About that time, Sylvester walks back in after lighting up his charcoal fire—he was hip to our conversation. Not skipping a beat, Mary tells him to "Get inside, clean up, and cut up the chicken." When I ask if this is the regular discourse, Sylvester rolls his eyes lovingly, saying, "All the dang time."

Sylvester got his professional start serving as a manager of the Jitney Jungle grocery store chain. When an opportunity came up to purchase Truett Grocery—the famed spot where bluesman Robert Johnson purchased his Prince Albert tobacco—Sylvester became a business owner. He expanded, and downsized, over the years—some planned, others not. Truett burned in 2007. Nowadays, Syl, as he is called by most, is content to have one store, while also leading local tours on civil rights and the history of the blues.

Sylvester might be manning the grill, but he will be the first to admit that the heart and soul of Hoover's, and perhaps Greenwood, is inside. He is speaking of Mary—or Ann, as he calls her. Mary has spent nearly thirty years working in the kitchen—her cooking has been lauded throughout the region, garnering national praise, including from Ms. Oprah Winfrey. But Mary does not shy from sharing about the period in her life when she decided to step away.

"I had buried my father, mother, sister, and brother all within the confines of a few months." Her smile had dimmed, she tells me, and she needed some time to do some soul-searching—outside of the kitchen. After taking some time to travel and visit her own children

and grandkids, Mary took up the responsibility of caring for premature babies—holding them and giving them the same love she fueled into her cooking, to sustain a new generation.

During our conversation, I notice kid after kid walk in from off the street and request everything from a burger and fries to a breakfast sandwich. Mary is patient, she is kind—despite the fact that these kids are anxiously hungry. Minutes later, the kids head back out the door, warm food in hand—but the cash register never rings. "We take care of this community," she tells me.

When the ribs are ready, I devour nearly half a rack, right off the bone, along with a heaping of smoke-laden beans and an extra helping of sweet peach cake. I wash everything down with a cold 40 oz. adult beverage.

After finishing my meal, we peruse our way next door to the Back in the Day Museum, an old home that Sylvester and Mary have converted to show folks how their ancestors lived for generations. It is primitive, to say the least. There is no electricity, but the light cracks through mismatched siding and broken windows. It's almost as though we've lost ourselves in another place and time.

But right on time, Sylvester breaks the silence. "The Delta causes you to rethink all of your senses—the sight of the country, the smell of the water and its low-lying fields, the hums of the blues, and of course, the taste of our food." When I ask about the missing fifth sense, he laughs.

"Son, our food just doesn't just taste, it feels too."

THREE-DOWN RIBS

SERVES 8 TO 10

Hands-On: 1 hour | Total: 2 hours 45 minutes

Sylvester Hoover of Hoover's Grocery tells me that the three-down spareribs cut is the best you can buy. The rack of ribs gets its name from the fact that the ribs, after trimming, weigh less than three pounds—only the very best of the cut is preserved.

Sylvester is adamant about seasoning the meat first with garlic powder, then with a generous sprinkling of seasoned salt. I asked if it really matters that much—he tells me to trust him. After 2 hours on the grill, the meat is bite-off-the bone-rich, and the taste of the salt and garlic is in perfect harmony. I'm a believer. The apples cooked on top of the ribs in the final minutes add just a hint of sweetness. Barbecue sauce can be served on the side—but the real pros know you don't need sauce when the meat tastes this good.

3 (3-pound) racks of three-down spareribs, washed and patted dry

1 tablespoon garlic powder

3 tablespoons seasoned salt, preferably Lawry's brand (see Resources, page 299)

1 red apple, cored and thinly sliced

Barbecue sauce, served warm on the side (optional)

1 Open the bottom vent of a charcoal grill completely. Light a charcoal chimney starter filled with charcoal. When the coals are covered with gray ash, pour them onto the bottom grate of the grill, and then push to one side of the grill. Adjust the vents as needed to maintain an internal temperature of 300° to 350°F. Coat the top grate with oil; place on the grill. (If using a gas grill, preheat to medium [300° to 350°F] on one side.)

2 Prep the ribs by removing the membrane from the bones: Using a small knife and starting at the point of the cut, cut underneath the membrane, but not into the bone. Using a paper towel, grab the loosened membrane and pull it away from the ribs. Continue in this manner until the membrane is removed.

3 Season both sides of the ribs with the garlic powder and then the seasoned salt.

4 Add the ribs to the grill, meat-side down, and cook over direct heat for 30 minutes. Flip the ribs bone-side down and continue to cook over direct heat for 30 minutes. Move the ribs to indirect heat and flip once again onto the meat side; cook for 30 minutes. Finish the ribs by flipping back to bone-side down, topping with the apple slices, and cooking over indirect heat for a final 10 minutes. The ribs should be tender and ¼ inch or so of the bone should show on the sides of the ribs. Remove from the grill, tent with foil, and let rest for 30 minutes.

5 Slice the ribs and serve with sauce on the side, if desired.

SYLVESTER HOOVER'S BARBECUE CHICKEN

SERVES 6 TO 8

Hands-On: 25 minutes | Total: 1 hour 25 minutes

Sylvester prefers to use the thigh and leg cuts from the chicken, both of which stand up nicely to the heat of the grill while the meat stays moist and tender. I caught him using the same seasoning technique, applying the garlic powder first, on the chicken that he used with his ribs—it's his signature. After the skin cooks up to a crispy char, finish the chicken with a coating of your favorite sweet and savory BBQ sauce.

Sylvester tells me that this chicken is almost as good as Mary's fried chicken...which you'll just have to go to Hoover's to try for yourself.

4 pounds chicken thighs and legs, rinsed and patted dry

1 teaspoon garlic powder

1 tablespoon seasoned salt, preferably Lawry's brand (see Resources, page 299)

Barbecue sauce (optional)

1 Open the bottom vent of a charcoal grill completely. Light a charcoal chimney starter filled with charcoal. When the coals are covered with gray ash, pour them onto the bottom grate of the grill, and then push to one side of the grill. Adjust the vents as needed to maintain an internal temperature of 300° to 350°F. Coat the top grate with oil; place on the grill. (If using a gas grill, preheat to medium [300° to 350°F] on one side.)

2 Season all sides of the chicken liberally with the garlic powder and then the seasoned salt.

3 Add the chicken to the grill over direct heat and cook for 15 minutes to sear. Flip the thighs and turn the legs and continue to cook for 10 minutes. Move the chicken to indirect heat, turn again, and cook for an additional 30 minutes, or until the internal temperature reaches 165°F. Finish by slathering the chicken with the sauce. Cover and cook until the sauce has set, about 5 minutes.

MARY'S BAKED BEANS

SERVES 10 TO 12 AS A SIDE

Hands-On: 30 minutes | Total: 2 hours

We fixed up a big vat of these beans and placed them on the grill to pick up plenty of smoke and reduce to a thick, sweet, and spicy combo, then watched as Hoover's patrons came in and asked for the beans throughout the day. It's a good thing I stood around to record the measurements as Mary put them together—otherwise, because she measures with love, I'd likely never get close to the recipe. After a dash of this, and a dash of that—real recipe follows—she pulled out a spoon for tasting. "Darn, that's good," she said. Then it's off to the grill.

2 (28-ounce) cans baked beans, preferably Bush's

⅔ cup frozen seasoning blend vegetables (from 1 [10-ounce] bag PictSweet Farms Recipe Helper)

1 cup barbecue sauce

2 tablespoons ketchup

2 tablespoons yellow mustard

½ teaspoon kosher salt

½ teaspoon garlic powder

1 Open the bottom vent of a charcoal grill completely. Light a charcoal chimney starter filled with charcoal. When the coals are covered with gray ash, pour them onto the bottom grate of the grill, and then push to one side of the grill. Adjust the vents as needed to maintain an internal temperature of 300° to 350°F. (If using a gas grill, preheat to medium [300° to 350°F] on one side.)

2 Combine all the ingredients in a large Dutch oven and mix until incorporated. Cover the pot, place over direct heat, and cook for 30 minutes, rotating every 15 minutes and stirring occasionally. Move to indirect heat and cook for 30 minutes. Remove the lid and cook for a final 30 minutes, until the beans are slightly reduced and bubbly.

SWEET PEACH CAKE

SERVES 8 TO 10

Hands-On: 40 minutes | Total: 1 hour 20 minutes

"Lord, have mercy!"—those were the words that came out of my mouth after taking a deep dive into Ms. Mary's delicious creation. She apologized to me, time and time again, while she was making the cake for using a boxed mix—although she doctors up the mix to her own standards. "I should really be making this from scratch," she said. I eased her concerns by divulging that my Nannie pulled off her famous caramel cake by using a boxed mix too. This recipe is simple and delicious, and a nice change of pace from peach cobbler.

1 teaspoon vegetable oil

2 (15-ounce) cans all-natural sliced peaches, in their juice

1 (15.25-ounce) box white cake mix

2 large eggs, beaten

4 tablespoons butter, melted

½ cup whole milk

1 teaspoon pure vanilla extract

2 tablespoons granulated sugar

1 Open the bottom vent of a charcoal grill completely. Light a charcoal chimney starter filled with charcoal. When the coals are covered with gray ash, pour them onto the bottom grate of the grill, and then push to one side of the grill. Adjust the vents as needed to maintain an internal temperature of 300° to 350°F. (If using a gas grill, preheat to medium [300° to 350°F] on one side.)

2 Coat a large (10- to 12-inch) cast-iron skillet with the vegetable oil. Add the peaches and their juice to the skillet. Using a small knife or kitchen shears, cut the peaches into bite-size pieces.

3 In a mixing bowl, combine the cake mix, eggs, butter, milk, and vanilla and whisk together until smooth and combined. Add the batter to the skillet, pouring evenly on top of the peaches and ensuring that the batter covers the entire top portion of the peaches. Sprinkle the top evenly with the sugar.

4 Place the skillet on the grill over indirect heat. Close the lid and cook, rotating the skillet every 15 minutes, for 35 to 40 minutes, until the cake is golden brown and a wooden pick inserted in the center comes out clean. Remove, allow to cool, and serve.

Part Three

KILLER RECIPES FOR EVERYTHING ON THE GRILL

No matter the course—or the meal—my philosophy is that every-thing can be made better on the grill. After all, that's the code we Serial Grillers live and die by. The following pages round out a slew of my takes on the classics, along with some new ideas that I'm certain will become favorites in your grilling repertoire. Time to get to work.

FIRED STARTERS

GRILLED HALLOUMI CHEESE BITES

SERVES 6

Hands-On: 20 minutes | Total: 4 hours 20 minutes, including 4 hours chilling

If the thought of grilling cheese sounds strange... have no fear. Halloumi is a firm, mild cheese that will stand up well to the heat and the smoke. Rounded out with some of my favorite vegetables that have been marinated then grilled, this starter is sure to please.

½ cup olive oil, plus more for serving

½ cup chopped fresh flat-leaf parsley

2 tablespoons finely chopped garlic (from 4 large cloves)

2 tablespoons white wine vinegar

2 teaspoons grated lemon zest (from 1 lemon)

1 teaspoon kosher salt

¼ teaspoon crushed red pepper

1 (8-ounce) package halloumi cheese, cut into 24 cubes (about 1½ cups)

12 fresh cremini mushrooms (about 8 ounces)

12 cherry tomatoes (about 3½ ounces)

Chopped fresh oregano

1 Whisk together the oil, parsley, garlic, vinegar, lemon zest, salt, and crushed red pepper in a large bowl. Add the cheese, mushrooms, and tomatoes; toss to coat. Transfer the mixture to an 11- x 7-inch baking dish; cover and refrigerate for 4 hours.

2 Open the bottom vent of a charcoal grill completely. Light a charcoal chimney starter filled with charcoal. When the coals are covered with gray ash, pour them onto the bottom grate of the grill, and then push to one side of the grill. Adjust the vents as needed to maintain an internal temperature of 450° to 500°F. Coat the top grate with oil; place on the grill. (If using a gas grill, preheat to high [450° to 500°F] on one side.)

3 Thread two cheese cubes, a mushroom, and a tomato onto each of 12 skewers (starting and ending each skewer with cheese). Discard the marinade mixture in the bowl. Place the skewers on the oiled grates directly over the side with the coals (or the lit side of a gas grill). Grill, covered and turning once, until the cheese is slightly charred and softened and the vegetables are tender, 6 to 8 minutes. Transfer the skewers to a serving platter, drizzle with olive oil, and garnish with oregano.

LOADED QUESO

SERVES 8

Hands-On: 25 minutes | Total: 25 minutes

This ain't your everyday queso. Inspired by the Bob Armstrong Dip from Matt's El Rancho in Austin, Texas, this queso is more meal than appetizer. Sure, you'll recognize the molten white cheese, but as soon as you dig into the spicy sausage, creamy avocado, and savory black bean toppings, you'll be hard pressed to go back to the basic queso.

½ **pound fresh Mexican chorizo**

1 **large avocado (unpeeled), quartered and pitted**

1 **cup drained and rinsed black beans (from 1 [15-ounce] can)**

½ **cup chopped fresh cilantro**

¼ **cup finely chopped white onion**

1 **(4-ounce) can diced green chiles, undrained**

1 **tablespoon fresh lime juice**

1 **teaspoon dried oregano**

½ **teaspoon ground cumin**

½ **teaspoon kosher salt**

1 **pound processed white American cheese, cut into small cubes**

1 **cup whole milk**

Tortilla chips

1   Open the bottom vent of a charcoal grill completely. Light a charcoal chimney starter filled halfway with charcoal. When the coals are covered with gray ash, pour them onto the bottom grate of the grill. Adjust the vents as needed to maintain an internal temperature of 400° to 450°F. Coat the top grate with oil; place on the grill. (If using a gas grill, preheat to medium-high [400° to 450°F].)

2   Place the chorizo on the oiled grates. Grill, uncovered and turning occasionally, until browned and cooked through, 10 to 15 minutes. Transfer to a work surface. Lightly coat the cut sides of the avocado quarters with cooking spray; place, cut-side down, on the grates and grill, uncovered, until slightly charred, 2 to 3 minutes per cut side. Transfer to a work surface. Remove and discard the peel from avocado quarters. Coarsely chop the avocado quarters and the chorizo and keep separate.

3   Stir together the beans, cilantro, onion, chiles, lime juice, oregano, cumin, and ¼ teaspoon of the salt in a bowl. Gently stir in the chopped avocado; set aside.

4   Place the cheese and milk in a 10-inch cast-iron skillet. Place on the grill grates and cook, uncovered and stirring often, until the cheese is melted and smooth, about 10 minutes. Remove from the grill; stir in the chopped chorizo and the remaining ¼ teaspoon salt. Spoon the bean mixture over the top. Serve the queso with tortilla chips.

SKILLET NACHOS

SERVES 6

Hands-On: 7 hours 30 minutes | Total: 16 hours, including 8 hours marinating and 7 hours grilling

This recipe calls for slow roasting a pork butt on the grill to make up a batch of ultimate nachos—but truth be told, you can still use this skillet-on-the-grill technique to whip up any type of nachos: Pick up smoked pork from your favorite pitmaster, or swap in another grilled protein. Be a nacho pro by layering the chips with an even distribution of cheese and toppings for a perfect bite every time.

1 (5-pound) boneless pork shoulder (Boston butt)

2 cups mojo criollo marinade (such as Goya; see Resources, page 299)

1 medium (7-ounce) red onion, thinly sliced (1¼ cups)

1½ teaspoons kosher salt

½ cup fresh lime juice (from about 4 limes)

1 (15-ounce) can black beans, drained and rinsed

1 teaspoon ground cumin

1 teaspoon dried oregano

8 ounces tortilla chips

5 ounces Manchego cheese, shredded

1 large avocado, chopped

¾ cup sour cream

¼ cup chopped fresh cilantro

1 Place the pork and marinade in a 1-gallon ziplock plastic bag. Seal the bag, pressing out excess air. Marinate in the refrigerator for at least 8 hours, or up to 24 hours. Allow the pork to come to room temperature for about 30 minutes before grilling.

2 Stir together the red onion and 1 teaspoon of the salt in a bowl; let stand at room temperature, stirring occasionally, until the onion has slightly softened, about 5 minutes. Stir in the lime juice; let stand, stirring occasionally, until the onion has turned pink, about 30 minutes. Drain and discard the pickling liquid. Cover and chill the pickled onion until ready to use.

3 Open the bottom vent of a charcoal grill completely. Light a charcoal chimney starter filled with charcoal. When the coals are covered with gray ash, pour them onto the bottom grate of the grill, and then push to one side of the grill. Adjust the vents as needed to maintain an internal temperature of 350° to 400°F. Coat the top grill grate with oil; place on the grill. (If using a gas grill, preheat to medium [350° to 400°F] on one side.)

4 Remove the pork from the marinade; discard the marinade. Place the pork on the oiled grates over the side without the coals (or the unlit side of a gas grill). Grill, covered and turning occasionally, until a thermometer inserted in thickest portion of pork registers 200°F, 7 to 8 hours. Transfer the pork to a 12-inch high-sided cast-iron skillet; let stand for 20 minutes. Transfer the pork to a work surface, reserving drippings in skillet. Shred the pork using your hands.

5 Place the skillet with drippings on the grates over the side without the coals. Add the beans, cumin, oregano, and remaining ½ teaspoon salt. Cook, stirring occasionally, until warmed through, about 5 minutes. Remove from the grill; transfer the mixture to a small bowl. Return the skillet to the grates over the side without the coals. Place the tortilla chips in the skillet; spoon the bean mixture evenly over the chips. Top with 2 cups of the shredded pork. (Reserve any remaining pork for another use.) Sprinkle with the cheese. Grill, covered, until the cheese is melted, about 10 minutes. Top with 1 cup of the pickled onions (reserving remaining onions for another use), the avocado, sour cream, and cilantro.

ARTICHOKE BRUSCHETTA

MAKES 6 TOASTS

Hands-On: 20 minutes | Total: 20 minutes

Grilled bread topped with anything is a winner in my book. Quite frankly, you could stop short by just rubbing the charred, warm bread with garlic, but I'm rarely one to stop short of anything (unless we are talking about the famous *Seinfeld* episode). Using jarred marinated artichoke hearts eliminates prep work, while grilling them takes their flavor to a whole new level.

3 (½-inch-thick) rustic Italian bread slices, halved crosswise

8 tablespoons extra-virgin olive oil

1 large garlic clove, halved

1 (12-ounce) jar marinated quartered artichoke hearts, drained

1 tablespoon fresh lemon juice (from 1 lemon)

½ teaspoon kosher salt

¼ teaspoon crushed red pepper

1 Open the bottom vent of a charcoal grill completely. Light a charcoal chimney starter filled with charcoal. When the coals are covered with gray ash, pour them onto the bottom grate of the grill. Adjust the vents as needed to maintain an internal temperature of 450° to 500°F. Coat the top grate with oil; place on the grill. (If using a gas grill, preheat to high [450° to 500°F].)

2 Brush each bread piece on both sides with 1 table-spoon of the oil. Place the bread on the oiled grates. Grill, uncovered, until lightly toasted, 1 to 2 minutes per side. Transfer the toasted bread to a serving platter; rub the tops of each toast with the cut sides of the garlic cloves. Discard garlic cloves.

3 Place the artichoke hearts on the grates. Grill, uncovered and turning occasionally, until slightly charred and tender, 3 to 4 minutes. Transfer to a cutting board and let cool slightly, about 5 minutes. Coarsely chop the artichokes and transfer to a bowl. Add the lemon juice, salt, crushed red pepper, and remaining 2 tablespoons oil; toss to coat. Spread 2 tablespoons artichoke mixture on each toast. Arrange the toasts on a serving platter.

PORK AND BROCCOLI RABE BRUSCHETTA

MAKES 6 TOASTS

Hands-On: 35 minutes | Total: 2 hours

Philly is king when it comes to cheesesteaks, but roast pork topped with crunchy broccoli rabe and smoky provolone is my sandwich of choice when in the City of Brotherly Love—especially when it comes from DiNic's in Reading Terminal Market. This dish is a play on that indulgence, in bite-size form so you can save room for the big plates.

1 small garlic head

5 tablespoons olive oil

3 tablespoons mayonnaise

1¾ teaspoons kosher salt

½ pound pork tenderloin, at room temperature

½ teaspoon freshly ground black pepper

¼ pound fresh broccoli rabe (from 1 bunch), trimmed

1 tablespoon fresh lemon juice (from 1 lemon)

½ teaspoon crushed red pepper

3 (½-inch-thick) rustic sourdough bread slices, halved crosswise

3 ounces shredded mozzarella cheese (about ¾ cup)

3 ounces shredded provolone cheese (about ¾ cup)

1 Open the bottom vent of a charcoal grill completely. Light a charcoal chimney starter filled halfway with charcoal. When the coals are covered with gray ash, pour them onto the bottom grate of the grill. Adjust the vents as needed to maintain an internal temperature of 400° to 450°F. Coat the top grate with oil; place on the grill. (If using a gas grill, preheat to medium-high [400° to 450°F].)

2 Cut and discard the top ½ inch from the garlic head, exposing the garlic cloves. Drizzle with 1 tablespoon of the oil. Wrap in aluminum foil and place on the oiled grates. Grill, covered and turning occasionally, until soft when pierced with a knife, about 1 hour. Let cool for 15 minutes. Remove and discard the foil. Squeeze the roasted garlic from the skins onto a cutting board; discard the skins. Using the broad side of a chef's knife, run the knife back and forth over the roasted garlic until smooth and a paste forms. Stir together the garlic paste, mayonnaise, and ½ teaspoon of the salt in a small bowl until combined; set the garlic mayonnaise aside.

3 Sprinkle the pork with the black pepper and 1 teaspoon of the salt. Place on the grates and grill, uncovered and turning occasionally, until a thermometer inserted in thickest portion of pork registers 145°F, about 15 minutes. Let rest for 10 minutes.

4 Meanwhile, toss together the broccoli rabe and 1 tablespoon of the olive oil in a bowl. Place on the grates and grill, uncovered and turning often, until slightly charred and stems are crisp-tender, about 6 minutes. Transfer to a cutting board and coarsely chop into ½-inch pieces. Transfer to a bowl and add the lemon juice, crushed red pepper, and remaining ¼ teaspoon salt. Toss to coat and set aside.

5 Brush the bread slices on both sides with the remaining 3 tablespoons oil. Place on the grates and grill, uncovered, until lightly toasted, 1 to 2 minutes per side.

6 Thinly slice the pork. Spread 1 tablespoon of the garlic mayonnaise on each toast slice. Spoon 1½ tablespoons broccoli rabe mixture onto each toast; top each with 2 to 3 pork slices. Sprinkle evenly with the cheeses. Arrange the toasts on a small baking sheet. Place the baking sheet on the grates. Grill, covered, until the cheese is melted, about 2 minutes. Transfer the toasts to a serving platter.

GRILLED PEACH AND TALEGGIO BRUSCHETTA

MAKES 6 TOASTS

Hands-On: 25 minutes | Total: 25 minutes

Grilled peaches are a standard at my house no matter the course. The fruit becomes sweeter, more tender, and fragrant after a minute or two over the fire. This is one dish that will make you wish peaches were always in season.

3 medium (5-ounce) peaches, each pitted and cut into 6 wedges

2 tablespoons honey

1 tablespoon sherry vinegar

2 teaspoons fresh thyme leaves

3 tablespoons olive oil

3 (½-inch-thick) rustic sourdough bread slices, halved crosswise

12 ounces Taleggio cheese, thinly sliced

Finely ground sea salt

1 Open the bottom vent of a charcoal grill completely. Light a charcoal chimney starter filled with charcoal. When the coals are covered with gray ash, pour them onto the bottom grate of the grill. Adjust the vents as needed to maintain an internal temperature of 350° to 400°F. Coat the top grate with oil; place on the grill. (If using a gas grill, preheat to medium [350° to 400°F].)

2 Lightly coat the peach wedges with cooking spray; place on the oiled grates. Grill, uncovered, until soft and slightly browned, about 4 minutes per side. Transfer to a bowl. Add the honey, vinegar, and thyme; toss to coat.

3 Brush the oil over each bread slice on both sides; place the bread on the grates. Grill, uncovered, until lightly toasted, 1 to 2 minutes per side. Transfer the toasted bread to a serving platter; immediately top the toasts evenly with cheese slices. Top each toast with 3 peach wedges; garnish with salt.

MEATBALLS WITH SWEET-AND-SOUR SAUCE

MAKES 30 MEATBALLS

Hands-On: 45 minutes | Total: 1 hour

There are never enough meatballs. Just the thought of digging into a few of these guys has my mouth watering. This recipe is a grilled play on Swedish meatballs—a retro savory-sweet appetizer that was a staple of my youth. The little bites of nostalgia are always a party hit. If you can't find lingonberry jam, cranberry sauce works in a pinch.

2 tablespoons salted butter

1 medium (5-ounce) yellow onion, finely chopped (1 cup)

1 large egg, lightly beaten

½ cup heavy cream

⅓ cup dry breadcrumbs

¼ cup chopped fresh flat-leaf parsley

¼ cup chopped fresh dill, plus more for garnish

¼ teaspoon ground allspice

2 teaspoons kosher salt

1 teaspoon freshly ground black pepper

1 pound 85/15 lean ground beef

1 cup lingonberry jam

½ cup white wine vinegar

1 Melt the butter in a small skillet over medium heat. Add the onion and cook, stirring occasionally, until softened, about 5 minutes. Transfer to a small bowl and let cool slightly, about 5 minutes.

2 Stir together the egg, cream, breadcrumbs, parsley, dill, allspice, salt, and pepper in a large bowl. Add the beef and cooled onion and gently mix with your hands until combined. Form the mixture into 30 balls (about 1½ inches in diameter). Thread 3 meatballs onto each of 10 skewers. Arrange the skewers on a baking sheet; cover and refrigerate for 30 minutes.

3 Meanwhile, stir together the jam and vinegar in a small saucepan and bring to a simmer over medium heat. Cook, stirring occasionally, until the jam melts and mixture slightly thickens into a sauce, about 12 minutes. Remove from the heat.

4 Open the bottom vent of a charcoal grill completely. Light a charcoal chimney starter filled halfway with charcoal. When the coals are covered with gray ash, pour them onto the bottom grate of the grill. Adjust the vents as needed to maintain an internal temperature of 350° to 400°F. (If using a gas grill, preheat to medium [350° to 400°F].)

5 Coat a grill-safe wire cooling rack with cooking spray. Place the skewers on the rack; place rack directly on unoiled grates. Grill, covered and turning the skewers occasionally, for 5 minutes. Brush the meatballs with the sauce mixture from the saucepan (about 1 tablespoon per skewer). Cover and continue grilling, turning the skewers occasionally, until the meatballs are browned on all sides and cooked through, about 5 minutes. Transfer the skewers to a serving platter.

6 Return the saucepan with the remaining sauce to the stovetop. Bring to a boil over high heat and cook, stirring often, for 2 minutes. Pour into a small serving bowl. Garnish the skewers with chopped dill, and serve with the sauce.

TWO-STEP BEER BRAT SLIDERS WITH MUSTARD

MAKES 6 SLIDERS

Hands-On: 35 minutes | Total: 1 hour 10 minutes

My wife, Callie, hails from Wisconsin, so I've had my fair share of brats. When we first met, her friends and family had me confused, inviting me over for a barbecue, yet serving me brats. Over the years I've been able to convince her crew that they are in fact grilling out, and not barbecuing.

True Cheeseheads will tell you to first plunge the brats in a mixture of beer and onions, poaching them over the fire until just cooked through—a technique that helps them soak up more delicious flavor while keeping them juicy. After that, it's all about getting that crispy char on the exterior, something you'll easily achieve over direct heat. Serve the sliders with plenty of tangy mustard and a cold beer, of course.

1 large (11-ounce) sweet onion, thinly sliced

3 fresh thyme sprigs

1 (12-ounce) bottle pale lager beer (such as Moosehead)

2 tablespoons coarse-grained mustard, plus more for serving

2 tablespoons apple cider vinegar

1 tablespoon honey

1 teaspoon kosher salt

3 (4-ounce) bratwurst links

6 (2-ounce) mini hoagie rolls (such as King's Hawaiian mini sub rolls), split and lightly grilled

1 Stir together the onion, thyme, beer, mustard, vinegar, honey, and salt in a cast-iron skillet; submerge the bratwurst links in the mixture.

2 Open the bottom vent of a charcoal grill completely. Light a charcoal chimney starter filled with charcoal. When the coals are covered with gray ash, pour them onto the bottom grate of the grill. Adjust the vents as needed to maintain an internal temperature of 350° to 400°F. (If using a gas grill, preheat to medium [350° to 400°F].)

3 Place the skillet with the bratwurst mixture on unoiled grates in the center of the grill. Grill, covered, until the bratwursts are cooked through, about 30 minutes.

4 Remove the bratwursts from the skillet; set aside. Move the skillet to the perimeter of the grill and cook the onion mixture, uncovered and stirring occasionally, until the mixture thickens, about 20 minutes. Remove from the heat; remove and discard the thyme.

5 While the onion mixture cooks, place the bratwursts directly on oiled grates. Grill, uncovered and turning occasionally, until browned and crisp, about 10 minutes. Transfer to a cutting board and let cool slightly, about 5 minutes. Slice each bratwurst in half crosswise at an angle.

6 Spoon 2 tablespoons of the onion mixture into each split roll; top with a bratwurst half and a dollop of mustard. Arrange brats on a serving platter.

BUFFALO SHRIMP-COCKTAIL TOAST

MAKES 24 TOASTS

Hands-On: 25 minutes | Total: 40 minutes

Being the Georgia boy that I am, one of my favorite places to visit is Georgia's beautiful Golden Isles. Life just seems to slow down in the coastal Low Country. On a recent visit, I enjoyed a meal on the water at the famed Jekyll Island Club. A lasting memory from that meal is the local, fresh boiled shrimp served with Buffalo-style sauce, a change of pace from traditional cocktail sauce. I was instantly hooked. This crostini is nice play on that experience.

3 tablespoons unsalted butter, cut into pieces

2 teaspoons finely chopped garlic (from 2 medium cloves)

½ cup Buffalo-style hot sauce

1 tablespoon white vinegar

1 teaspoon kosher salt

4 ounces blue cheese, crumbled (about 1 cup)

4 ounces cream cheese, softened

3 tablespoons finely chopped fresh chives, plus more for garnish

1 tablespoon fresh lemon juice

½ teaspoon freshly ground black pepper

24 extra-large raw shrimp (about 1 pound), peeled and deveined

2 tablespoons olive oil

24 (¼-inch-thick) baguette slices, lightly grilled

1. Heat the butter and garlic in a small saucepan over low heat. Cook, stirring often, until the butter melts and is foamy, about 2 minutes. Remove from the heat and whisk in the hot sauce, vinegar, and ¼ teaspoon of the salt until combined. Set the Buffalo sauce aside.

2. Stir together the blue cheese, cream cheese, chives, lemon juice, pepper, and ¼ teaspoon of the salt in a bowl until combined. Toss together the shrimp, oil, and remaining ½ teaspoon salt in a separate bowl.

3. Open the bottom vent of a charcoal grill completely. Light a charcoal chimney starter filled halfway with charcoal. When the coals are covered with gray ash, pour them onto the bottom grate of the grill. Adjust the vents as needed to maintain an internal temperature of 450° to 500°F. Coat the top grate with oil; place on the grill. (If using a gas grill, preheat to high [450° to 500°F].)

4. Place the shrimp on the oiled grates. Grill, uncovered, until pink and opaque, 2 to 3 minutes per side. Transfer to a large bowl, add one-quarter of the reserved Buffalo sauce, and toss to coat. Pour the remaining sauce into a small serving bowl.

5. Spread 1 tablespoon blue cheese mixture evenly onto each baguette slice; top each with one shrimp. Transfer to a serving platter and garnish with chopped chives. Serve immediately with the Buffalo sauce in the serving bowl.

GRILL-ROASTED CLAMS WITH CHILE OIL

SERVES 4

Hands-On: 40 minutes | Total: 40 minutes

The sweet, delicate flavor of meaty clams takes on just a wisp of smoke flavor with a quick roast on the grill. Silky, spicy chile oil makes these finger-licking delicious. This is a quick and easy appetizer that can make a weeknight feel like a special occasion, especially when paired with a crisp Chardonnay. For a heartier version, serve the clams alongside some fresh buttered pasta with plenty of freshly cracked pepper.

Buy the freshest clams possible. They should close tightly when you tap the shell, otherwise move on to the next ones until you have a couple dozen prime clams for cooking up this delicious starter.

½ cup olive oil

¼ cup finely chopped drained Calabrian chiles (from 1 [6-ounce] jar chiles in oil)

2 tablespoons finely chopped garlic (from 6 medium cloves)

¾ teaspoon kosher salt

1 tablespoon grated lemon zest (from 2 lemons)

24 littleneck clams, scrubbed

2 tablespoons chopped fresh mint

Lemon wedges

1 Combine the olive oil, chiles, garlic, and salt in a small saucepan and bring to a gentle simmer over low heat. Cook, stirring occasionally, until fragrant, about 4 minutes. Let cool for 10 minutes. Stir in the lemon zest and set the chile oil aside.

2 Open the bottom vent of a charcoal grill completely. Light a charcoal chimney starter filled halfway with charcoal. When the coals are covered with gray ash, pour them onto the bottom grate of the grill. Adjust the vents as needed to maintain an internal temperature of 450° to 500°F. Coat the top grate with oil; place on the grill. (If using a gas grill, preheat to high [450° to 500°F].)

3 Place the clams on the oiled grates. Grill, uncovered, until the clams pop open, 8 to 10 minutes. Discard any clams that do not open. Transfer the clams to a serving platter, being careful not to spill clam juices. Spoon ½ teaspoon or more, if desired, of the chile oil over each clam; sprinkle evenly with the mint. Serve with lemon wedges.

BLUE CRABS WITH TABASCO DRAWN BUTTER

MAKES 6 CRABS

Hands-On: 35 minutes | Total: 35 minutes

Soft-shell crab season lasts a hot minute, which means you need to eat as many as you can while you've got the chance. My favorite part of this recipe is the Tabasco-laden drawn butter. It adds the perfect dose of richness, spice, and acidity for sweet, tender crab.

6 live soft-shell blue crabs

1 cup (8 ounces) salted butter, cubed

2 tablespoons Tabasco pepper sauce

1 tablespoon fresh lemon juice (from 1 lemon)

1 teaspoon kosher salt

1 bay leaf

Chopped fresh flat-leaf parsley

Lemon wedges

1 Place the crabs, underside facing up, on a work surface. Working with one crab at a time, plunge the tip of a small paring knife into the crab head (about 1 inch below the mouth). Pull off and discard the triangular shell on the underside of the crab. Using your fingers, clean out the gills, lungs, and center of the crab. Rinse the crab under cold running water and return to the work surface; pat dry.

2 Cut the cleaned crabs in half lengthwise. Arrange on a baking sheet and refrigerate, uncovered, until ready to use, or up to 12 hours.

3 Melt the butter in a small saucepan over medium-low heat until it begins to foam and the milk solids sink to the bottom, skimming and discarding foam as needed, 6 to 7 minutes. Carefully pour the butter through a fine-mesh strainer into a small saucepan. Stir in the Tabasco, lemon juice, salt, and bay leaf.

4 While the butter melts, open the bottom vent of a charcoal grill completely. Light a charcoal chimney starter filled with charcoal. When the coals are covered with gray ash, pour them onto the bottom grate of the grill, and then push to one side of the grill. Adjust the vents as needed to maintain an internal temperature of 450° to 500°F. (If using a gas grill, preheat to high [450° to 500°F] on one side.)

5 Pour one-third of the Tabasco butter into a small bowl and set aside for serving. Pour an additional one-third of the Tabasco butter into a large bowl and set aside.

6 Brush the crabs with remaining one-third of the Tabasco butter. Place the crabs, shell-side down, on unoiled grates directly over the side with the coals (or the lit side of a gas grill). Grill, uncovered and turning occasionally, until grill marks appear, 4 to 5 minutes. Transfer the crabs to the grates over the side without the coals (or the unlit side of a gas grill). Grill, uncovered and turning occasionally, until the crabs are red and cooked through, 8 to 10 minutes.

7 Transfer the crabs to the Tabasco butter in the large bowl and gently toss to coat. Arrange the crabs on a serving platter and garnish with parsley. Serve with the Tabasco butter in the small serving bowl and the lemon wedges.

SMOKIN' SALADS

GRILLED HEIRLOOM CAPRESE SALAD 175

GRILLED BEET, CHARRED ONION, AND GOAT CHEESE SALAD 177

GRILLED CAESAR SALAD WITH SANS-EGG DRESSING 178

NEW-SCHOOL NIÇOISE SALAD WITH ANCHOVY VINAIGRETTE 180

GRILLED BRUSSELS SPROUT–FETA SALAD WITH SMOKED OLIVE OIL VINAIGRETTE 183

GRILLED POTATO SALAD 184 | GRILLED CHICKEN SALAD 187

GRILLED PANZANELLA SALAD 188

GRILLED HEIRLOOM CAPRESE SALAD

SERVES 6

Hands-On: 20 minutes | Total: 20 minutes

It's hard to beat the classic caprese, but as with most ingredients, something magical happens to vine-ripe tomatoes grilled over fire. Be sure to cut the tomatoes thick and keep the grill uncovered so they don't get too soft. The old saying that great meals start with great ingredients is key here. As much as I am all about serial grilling—including grilling every season—this recipe should be reserved solely for summertime. Whether you grow 'em yourself or patronize your farmers' market, use only the best vine-ripe tomatoes you can find.

1¾ pounds large heirloom tomatoes

1 pint heirloom cherry tomatoes, halved

8 ounces fresh mozzarella cheese, torn into small pieces

1 teaspoon kosher salt

½ teaspoon freshly ground black pepper

½ cup extra-virgin olive oil

2 tablespoons balsamic vinegar

½ cup packed medium-size fresh basil leaves

1 Open the bottom vent of a charcoal grill completely. Light a charcoal chimney starter filled with charcoal. When the coals are covered with gray ash, pour them onto the bottom grate of the grill. Adjust the vents as needed to maintain an internal temperature of 450° to 500°F. Coat the top grate with oil; place on the grill. (If using a gas grill, preheat to high [450° to 500°F].)

2 Cut the large tomatoes crosswise into 1-inch-thick slices and pat dry. Place on the oiled grates. Grill, uncovered, until lightly charred, 1 to 2 minutes per side.

3 Arrange the tomato slices on a serving platter; sprinkle with the cherry tomatoes, cheese, salt, and pepper. Drizzle with the oil and vinegar. Sprinkle with the basil leaves.

GRILLED BEET, CHARRED ONION, AND GOAT CHEESE SALAD

SERVES 4

Hands-On: 30 minutes | Total: 1 hour 30 minutes

All aboard! This salad will have you riding the beet train whether you've been a fan of this earthy root or not. When exposed to high heat from the grill, the sugars in the beets caramelize and the result is delectable. Tossed with arugula, charred onion, creamy goat cheese, and nutty sunflower seeds in a tangy vinaigrette, the beets create a super satisfying salad that is a healthy winner in my book.

3 medium-size red beets (about 1 pound), peeled and trimmed

5 tablespoons olive oil

1 teaspoon kosher salt

1 small (4-ounce) white onion, halved crosswise

2 tablespoons apple cider vinegar

1 teaspoon honey

½ teaspoon freshly ground black pepper

4 ounces baby arugula (about 4 cups)

2 ounces goat cheese, crumbled (about ½ cup)

¼ cup chopped scallions (about 2 scallions)

3 tablespoons salted sunflower seed kernels

1 Open the bottom vent of a charcoal grill completely. Light a charcoal chimney starter filled with charcoal. When the coals are covered with gray ash, pour them onto the bottom grate of the grill, and then push to one side of the grill. Adjust vents as needed to maintain an internal temperature of 400° to 450°F. (If using a gas grill, preheat to medium-high [400° to 450°F] on one side.)

2 Place the beets on a large sheet of aluminum foil. Drizzle with 2 tablespoons of the oil and sprinkle with ½ teaspoon of the salt. Wrap the foil securely around the beets. Place the beets, foil-seam-side up, on unoiled grates over the side without the coals (or the unlit side of a gas grill). Grill, covered, until the beets are tender when pierced with a fork, 1 hour to 1 hour and 15 minutes. Remove and discard the foil.

3 Place the beets and the halved onion on oiled grates over the side with the coals (or the lit side of a gas grill). Grill, uncovered and turning occasionally, until lightly charred, 10 to 12 minutes. Remove from the grill and let stand for 10 minutes. Cut each beet into 6 wedges. Coarsely chop the onion.

4 Whisk together the remaining 3 tablespoons oil with the vinegar, honey, pepper, and remaining ½ teaspoon salt in a large bowl. Add the chopped onion and toss to coat. Add the arugula and toss gently to combine. Arrange the mixture evenly on a serving platter and top with the beet wedges. Sprinkle with the goat cheese, scallions, and sunflower kernels.

GRILLED CAESAR SALAD WITH SANS-EGG DRESSING

SERVES 4

Hands-On: 30 minutes | Total: 30 minutes

Over the years I've had to adapt my traditional Caesar dressing to meet the needs of friends, and my wife, when they were expecting because raw eggs are too risky. I began to experiment with avocados and a touch of mayo to mimic the standard raw egg and oil emulsion. Though different in texture than the classic dressing, the flavor of this remake is delicious. Charring the romaine lettuce picks up some nice, smoky flavor and provides a warm contrast to the cool, creamy dressing.

½ cup mayonnaise

½ cup water

3 tablespoons grated Parmesan cheese

3 tablespoons fresh lemon juice (from 1 lemon)

1 tablespoon Worcestershire sauce

½ medium avocado, pitted and peeled

4 anchovies (from 1 [4-ounce] jar)

1 medium garlic clove, smashed

3 romaine lettuce hearts (about 8 ounces total), halved lengthwise

3 (¾-inch-thick) rustic bread slices (about 3 ounces total)

1 teaspoon kosher salt

1 teaspoon freshly ground black pepper

2 ounces Parmesan cheese, shaved (about 1 cup)

3 tablespoons extra-virgin olive oil

1 Open the bottom vent of a charcoal grill completely. Light a charcoal chimney starter filled with charcoal. When the coals are covered with gray ash, pour them onto the bottom grate of the grill. Adjust the vents as needed to maintain an internal temperature of 400° to 450°F. Coat the top grate with oil; place on the grill. (If using a gas grill, preheat to medium-high [400° to 450°F].)

2 Combine the mayonnaise, water, grated Parmesan, lemon juice, Worcestershire sauce, avocado half, anchovies, and garlic in a blender. Process until smooth, 30 seconds to 1 minute, stopping to scrape down the sides as needed. Set the dressing aside.

3 Coat the lettuce and bread with cooking spray and sprinkle evenly with the salt and pepper. Place the lettuce, cut-side down, on the oiled grates. Grill, uncovered without turning, until charred, 2 to 3 minutes. Remove from the grill. Place the bread on the grates and grill, uncovered, until grill marks appear, 3 to 4 minutes per side. Remove from the grill and allow to cool 1 minute.

4 Cut the bread into ¾-inch cubes. Coarsely chop the lettuce and arrange on a serving platter. Sprinkle with bread cubes and shaved Parmesan. Drizzle with the dressing and the olive oil.

NEW-SCHOOL NIÇOISE SALAD WITH ANCHOVY VINAIGRETTE

SERVES 4

Hands-On: 1 hour | Total: 1 hour 20 minutes

I've been fortunate to spend quite a bit of time traveling and working on the French Riviera. Or as I like to say, working hard, or hardly working? Either way, one of my favorite meals there is a classic Niçoise salad. Like gumbo in the South, each Riviera café or chef puts his or her own unique spin on their iconic dish. The one thing that stays pretty consistent in France is that the tuna is almost always from a can. When I take the reins, a thick tuna steak grilled rare is the centerpiece, but I also like to grill the potatoes and green beans. A traditional anchovy vinaigrette keeps the classic flavors in the mix. Though we might not be enjoying this meal in the South of France, my grilled spin on Niçoise rivals any you'll find there.

4 large eggs

3 tablespoons red wine vinegar

2 tablespoons finely chopped shallot (from 1 small [2-ounce] shallot)

½ teaspoon grated garlic (from 1 medium clove)

½ teaspoon freshly ground black pepper

5 anchovies (from 1 [5-ounce] can), finely chopped

9 tablespoons extra-virgin olive oil

12 ounces baby Yukon Gold potatoes (about 1½ inches in diameter), unpeeled

3 (6-ounce) skinless sushi-grade yellowfin tuna fillets (about 1½ inches thick)

¾ teaspoon kosher salt

8 ounces fresh haricots verts (French green beans), trimmed

1½ cups heirloom grape tomatoes, halved

¼ cup pitted Niçoise olives, halved

1. Bring a small pot of water to a boil on a stovetop over high heat. Add the eggs and boil, uncovered, for 10 minutes. Remove from water, plunge into a bowl filled with ice water, and cool for about 10 minutes. Set aside.

2. Whisk together the vinegar, shallot, garlic, pepper, anchovies, and 6 tablespoons of the oil in a bowl until combined. Set aside.

3. Open the bottom vent of a charcoal grill completely. Light a charcoal chimney starter filled with charcoal. When the coals are covered with gray ash, pour them onto the bottom grate of the grill. Adjust the vents as needed to maintain an internal temperature of 400° to 450°F. Coat the top grate with oil; place on the grill. (If using a gas grill, preheat to medium-high [400° to 450°F].)

4. Prick the potatoes with a fork. Place in a microwavable bowl and microwave on HIGH until tender-firm when pierced with a fork, about 5 minutes.

5. Pat the tuna fillets dry and rub with 1 tablespoon of the oil. Sprinkle evenly with salt. Place on the oiled grates. Grill, uncovered, until grill marks appear on each side, about 2½ minutes per side for rare, or to desired degree of doneness. Remove from the grill. Toss the potatoes in 1 tablespoon of the oil and place on the grates. Grill, uncovered and turning occasionally, until grill marks appear, 4 to 5 minutes. Remove from the grill. Toss the haricots verts in the remaining 1 tablespoon oil and place on the grates. Grill, uncovered and turning occasionally, until charred, 4 to 5 minutes. Remove from the grill.

6. Cut the tuna into ⅓-inch-thick slices. Cut the potatoes and haricots verts in half. Arrange the tuna, potatoes, haricots verts, tomatoes, and olives on a serving platter. Peel the eggs (discarding the shells), and cut in half lengthwise. Top the salad with the eggs and drizzle with the vinaigrette.

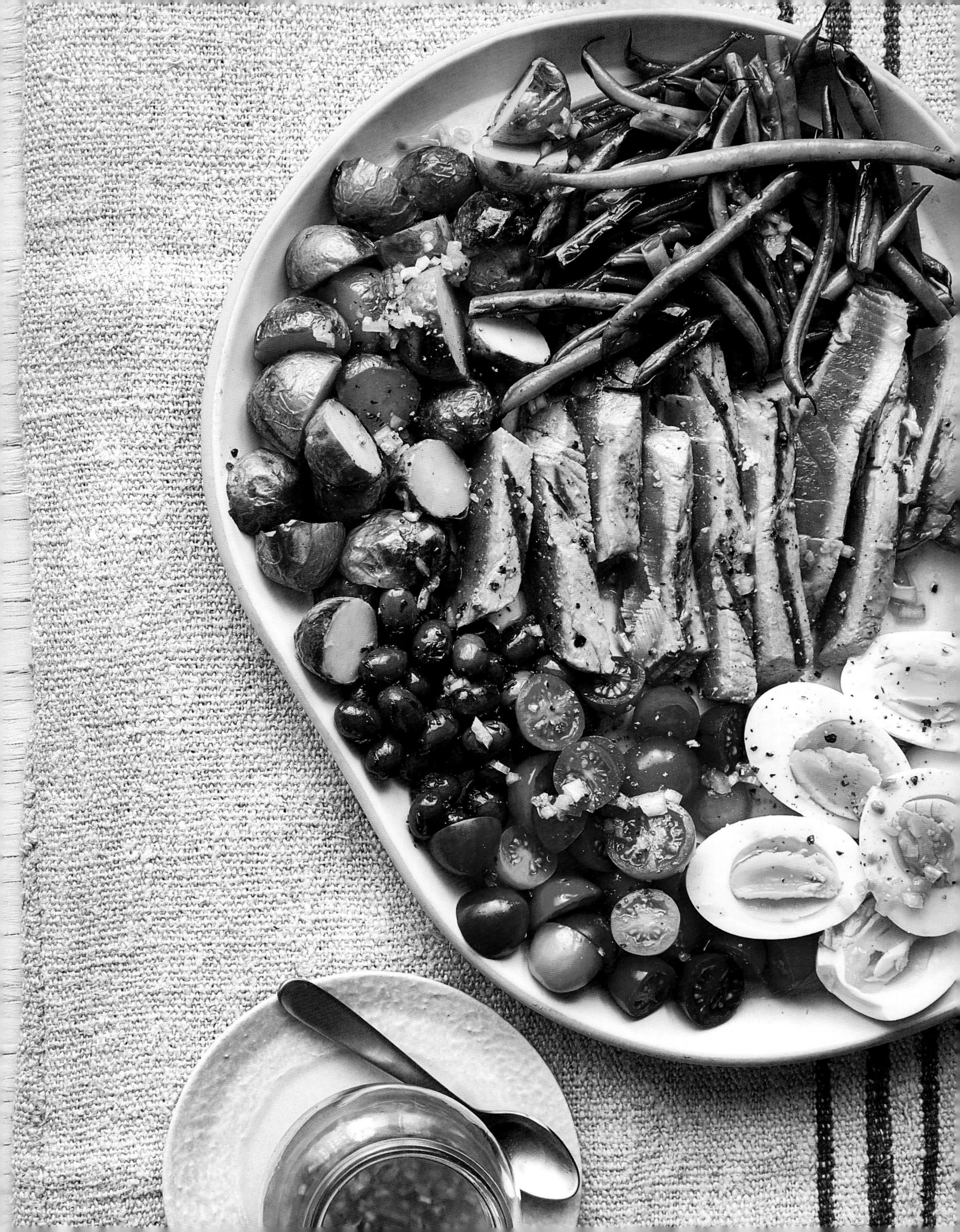

GRILLED BRUSSELS SPROUT–FETA SALAD WITH SMOKED OLIVE OIL VINAIGRETTE

SERVES 4

Hands-On: 35 minutes | Total: 3 hours 50 minutes, including 3 hours smoking

Okay, okay, I'm finally going to "give up the goods" on this recipe. For years it has been one of the recipes served in my home that my friends request the most. Smoking the olive oil takes the salad over the top, so don't skip the step. You'll have leftover oil for a future use as a finishing oil or in other dressings, so it's worth the effort. Buy the best quality brine-packed feta for this recipe too. My secret is out.

½ cup cherrywood chips

2 cups olive oil

¼ cup fresh lemon juice (from 2 lemons)

4 teaspoons honey

2 teaspoons Dijon mustard

2 teaspoons kosher salt

1 teaspoon freshly ground black pepper

1 pound fresh Brussels sprouts, halved lengthwise

16 large lacinato kale leaves (from 1 bunch)

1 large lemon, cut crosswise into 10 rounds and seeded

1 cup diagonally sliced celery (from 2 stalks)

3 ounces feta cheese, crumbled (about ¾ cup)

1 Soak the wood chips in water for 20 minutes; drain. Light a charcoal chimney starter filled one-quarter full with charcoal. When the coals are covered with gray ash, pour them on the bottom grate of the grill. Scatter soaked wood chips over the hot coals. Adjust the vents as needed to maintain an internal temperature of about 200°F. (If using a gas grill, place soaked wood chips in an aluminum foil packet; poke several holes in the packet. Place the packet directly on burners; preheat to very low [about 200°F].)

2 Pour the oil into a disposable aluminum pan and place on the unoiled grates. Smoke the oil, covered, until it has a smoky flavor, about 3 hours. Remove from the grill. (If using a gas grill, discard the packet with the wood chips.)

3 Whisk together 3 tablespoons of the smoked oil, the lemon juice, honey, mustard, 1 teaspoon of the salt, and ½ teaspoon of the pepper in a bowl until combined. (Reserve remaining smoked oil for another use.) Set the dressing aside.

4 Refill the charcoal chimney starter with briquettes, and light. When the briquettes are covered with gray ash, pour them on the bottom grate of the grill. Adjust the vents as needed to maintain an internal temperature of 400° to 450°F. Coat the top grate with oil; place on the grill. (If using a gas grill, preheat to medium-high [400° to 450°F].)

5 Place the Brussels sprouts on the oiled grates. Grill, covered and turning occasionally, until tender, 8 to 10 minutes. Remove from the grill. Place the kale leaves on the grates; grill, uncovered, until charred on one side, 1 to 2 minutes. Remove from the grill. Carefully place the lemon slices on the grates; grill, uncovered, until charred on one side, about 2 minutes. Remove from the grill.

6 Remove and discard the stems from the kale leaves and coarsely chop the leaves. Toss together the chopped kale leaves, Brussels sprouts, celery, and remaining 1 teaspoon salt and ½ teaspoon pepper in a large bowl. Add the smoked oil dressing and toss to coat. Arrange the mixture on a serving platter, top with the lemon slices, and sprinkle with the feta.

GRILLED POTATO SALAD

SERVES 6

Hands-On: 1 hour | Total: 1 hour 30 minutes

This hefty salad is lightened a bit by cutting the mayonnaise with thick Greek-style yogurt. The salad shines as a tangy, rich, and satisfying side, especially when paired with a grilled pork tenderloin or juicy burgers.

10 large new potatoes (about 3½ pounds), unpeeled

8 tablespoons olive oil

1¼ teaspoons kosher salt

¼ cup plain whole-milk Greek yogurt

¼ cup mayonnaise

2 tablespoons fresh lemon juice (from 1 lemon)

¾ teaspoon freshly ground black pepper

3 tablespoons chopped fresh dill

1 Open the bottom vent of a charcoal grill completely. Light a charcoal chimney starter filled with charcoal. When the coals are covered with gray ash, pour them onto the bottom grate of the grill. Adjust the vents as needed to maintain an internal temperature of 350° to 400°F. (If using a gas grill, preheat to medium [350° to 400°F].)

2 Place the potatoes on a large sheet of aluminum foil. Rub with 1 tablespoon of the oil and sprinkle with ½ teaspoon of the salt. Wrap the foil securely around the potatoes. Place the potatoes, foil-seam-side up, on the unoiled grates. Grill, covered and turning occasionally, until the potatoes are firm-tender when pierced with a fork, about 45 minutes. Unwrap and let cool 10 minutes. Cut into 1-inch pieces.

3 Whisk together 5 tablespoons of the oil, the yogurt, mayonnaise, lemon juice, pepper, and remaining ¾ teaspoon salt in a large bowl until smooth.

4 Place a large cast-iron skillet on the grates and heat until very hot. Add 1 tablespoon of the oil to the skillet. Add half of the potato pieces and cook, uncovered, until browned, 5 to 6 minutes, stirring once halfway through cook time. Remove the potatoes from the skillet. Wipe the skillet clean and repeat the process with the remaining 1 tablespoon oil and potato pieces. Allow the potatoes to cool completely, about 20 minutes.

5 Add the cooled potatoes and dill to the dressing in the bowl; toss to coat.

GRILLED CHICKEN SALAD

SERVES 6

Hands-On: 40 minutes | Total: 40 minutes

My mama's chicken salad is a staple in my home, especially during the summer months when I love to put together a cold supper of chicken salad and boiled eggs with some sliced tomatoes and pickles. We also are constantly entertaining at our house, which means we often have a lot of leftovers. One day, I used leftover grilled chicken in chicken salad instead of the traditional poached chicken we grew up using. Dang...was it ever good! I can't always wait for leftovers, so now I fire up the grill when we're craving Mama's chicken salad.

6 (8-ounce) bone-in, skinless chicken breasts

1½ teaspoons kosher salt

1½ teaspoons freshly ground black pepper

1 cup mayonnaise

½ cup extra-virgin olive oil

6 tablespoons fresh lemon juice (from 2 lemons)

1 cup finely chopped celery (from 2 stalks)

1 cup finely chopped red onion (from 1 medium onion)

¼ teaspoon cayenne pepper

1 Open the bottom vent of a charcoal grill completely. Light a charcoal chimney starter filled with charcoal. When the coals are covered with gray ash, pour them onto the bottom grate of the grill. Adjust the vents as needed to maintain an internal temperature of 400° to 450°F. Coat the top grate with oil; place on the grill. (If using a gas grill, preheat to medium-high [400° to 450°F].)

2 Sprinkle the chicken with 1 teaspoon of the salt and ½ teaspoon of the black pepper. Place the chicken on the oiled grates. Grill, covered and turning occasionally, until a thermometer inserted in the thickest portion of the chicken registers 165°F, 15 to 20 minutes. Remove from the grill and let stand for 10 minutes. Shred the chicken into large pieces; discard the bones.

3 Whisk together the mayonnaise, oil, and lemon juice in a large bowl until smooth. Stir in the celery, onion, cayenne pepper, and remaining ½ teaspoon salt and 1 teaspoon black pepper until combined. Add the shredded chicken and toss to coat.

GRILLED PANZANELLA SALAD

SERVES 6

Hands-On: 20 minutes | Total: 20 minutes

The ideal way to get the crispy, crunchy croutons that are the best part of any classic Italian bread salad is on the grill. The other genius part of the recipe is using the natural juices from the tomatoes as the base of a dressing that infuses the bread, arugula, and basil with that delicious and distinctive tomato essence.

5 ounces French bread (from 1 [12-ounce] loaf)

1¾ pounds large heirloom tomatoes, halved crosswise

¼ cup olive oil

2 tablespoons balsamic vinegar

2 teaspoons finely chopped garlic (from 2 medium cloves)

1 teaspoon kosher salt

¾ teaspoon freshly ground black pepper

2 cups packed baby arugula

1 cup torn fresh basil leaves

1   Open the bottom vent of a charcoal grill completely. Light a charcoal chimney starter filled with charcoal. When the coals are covered with gray ash, pour them onto the bottom grate of the grill. Adjust the vents as needed to maintain an internal temperature of 400° to 450°F. (If using a gas grill, preheat to medium-high [400° to 450°F].)

2   Cut the bread crosswise into 1-inch-thick slices. Coat the slices with cooking spray and place on the unoiled grates. Grill, uncovered, until grill marks appear, 3 to 4 minutes per side. Remove from the grill and allow to cool 1 minute. Tear into 1-inch pieces.

3   Gently squeeze the seeds and juice from the tomato halves into a large bowl; chop the squeezed tomato halves. Add the oil, vinegar, garlic, salt, and pepper to the tomato liquid and whisk to combine. Add the torn bread, chopped tomatoes, arugula, and basil; toss to combine.

SIZZLIN' SIDES

GRILLED BACON-WRAPPED ASPARAGUS BUNDLES 193

CAULIFLOWER STEAKS 194 | GRILLED CORN WITH DILL BUTTAH AND FETA 197

SKEWERED OKRA 199 | CHARRED BROCCOLI RABE 200

GRILLED TRUMPET MUSHROOMS 203 | GRILLED BAKED BEANS 205

SMOKY SUMMER SQUASH 206

GRILLED ARTICHOKES WITH SOUR CREAM DIPPING SAUCE 209

REDNECK POTATOES 211 | GRILLED CHEESE FRIES 212

GRILLED BACON-WRAPPED ASPARAGUS BUNDLES

SERVES 4
Hands-On: 15 minutes | Total: 15 minutes

Grilled asparagus is made even better with bacon. Seriously, what isn't made better with bacon? Because the two items have varied cooking times, it's important to slightly cook the bacon prior to wrapping up and grilling the asparagus bundles. Use the best, thick-cut bacon you can find. My go-to is Benton's bacon from my neck of the woods in Tennessee. I like to pair the bundles with grilled steaks or chops.

2 thick-cut bacon slices (3 ounces)

1 bunch (about 14 ounces) fresh asparagus, trimmed

1 tablespoon olive oil

½ teaspoon kosher salt

½ teaspoon freshly ground black pepper

1 tablespoon extra-virgin olive oil

2 teaspoons balsamic glaze

1 tablespoon chopped fresh chives

1 Open the bottom vent of a charcoal grill completely. Light a charcoal chimney starter filled with charcoal. When the coals are covered with gray ash, pour them onto the bottom grate of the grill. Adjust the vents as needed to maintain an internal temperature of 400° to 450°F. Coat the top grate with oil; place on the grill. (If using a gas grill, preheat to medium-high [400° to 450°F].)

2 Place the bacon on a microwavable plate between two paper towels. Microwave on HIGH until cooked through but still pliable, about 1½ minutes. Set aside at room temperature until cool enough to handle, about 5 minutes.

3 Toss together the asparagus, olive oil, salt, and pepper in a bowl; divide evenly into four portions with the asparagus tips pointing in the same direction. Cut the bacon slices in half crosswise. Wrap one bacon piece around each asparagus bundle, leaving tips exposed, and secure bundle with kitchen twine.

4 Place the bundles on the oiled grates. Grill, covered and turning often, until the bacon is crispy and the asparagus is lightly charred, 8 to 10 minutes. Transfer to a serving platter. Drizzle with extra-virgin olive oil and balsamic glaze and sprinkle with the chives.

CAULIFLOWER STEAKS

SERVES 6

Hands-On: 30 minutes | Total: 30 minutes

These days, cauliflower is all the rage and used for everything, from spins on rice, to pizza crusts, to a buffalo'd snack. And for good reason...this meaty vegetable satisfies, pure and simple. My preferred method is to cut the heads into thick "steaks" and season them simply before tossing them on the grill. The steaks are a great side, but can also be a lighter vegetarian main dish.

1 large (2-pound) cauliflower head

½ cup extra-virgin olive oil

1 tablespoon smoked paprika

1½ teaspoons kosher salt

1 teaspoon freshly ground black pepper

1 tablespoon truffle oil or fruity extra-virgin olive oil

¼ cup chopped fresh flat-leaf parsley

1 Open the bottom vent of a charcoal grill completely. Light a charcoal chimney starter filled with charcoal. When the coals are covered with gray ash, pour them onto the bottom grate of the grill. Adjust the vents as needed to maintain an internal temperature of 400° to 450°F. Coat the top grate with oil; place on the grill. (If using a gas grill, preheat to medium-high [400° to 450°F].)

2 Cut the cauliflower head lengthwise into six (1-inch-thick) slices, leaving the stem intact to hold the florets together. Brush all sides of the cauliflower steaks with ¼ cup of the olive oil; sprinkle evenly with the paprika, salt, and pepper. Place on the oiled grates. Grill, uncovered, until starting to char and soften, 6 to 8 minutes. Brush the tops and sides of the steaks with the remaining ¼ cup olive oil and flip. Grill until charred and softened, 6 to 8 minutes. Transfer to a serving platter, drizzle with the truffle oil, and sprinkle with the parsley.

GRILLED CORN WITH DILL BUTTAH AND FETA

SERVES 8

Hands-On: 30 minutes | Total: 30 minutes

Part of the fun of cooking this recipe is just saying *buttah*. It should roll off your tongue slowly, like a Deep South drawl, emulating the rich smoothness that melting butter adds to deliciously sweet and smoky corn. Gild the lily by finishing the ears with some salty, tangy feta.

½ cup (4 ounces) unsalted butter, softened

2 tablespoons chopped fresh dill, plus more for garnish

1 teaspoon grated lemon zest plus ½ tablespoon fresh juice (from 1 lemon)

1 teaspoon kosher salt

1 teaspoon freshly ground black pepper

8 ears fresh yellow corn, shucked

1 ounce feta cheese, crumbled (about ¼ cup)

1 Open the bottom vent of a charcoal grill completely. Light a charcoal chimney starter filled with charcoal. When the coals are covered with gray ash, pour them onto the bottom grate of the grill. Adjust the vents as needed to maintain an internal temperature of 450° to 500°F. Coat the top grate with oil; place on the grill. (If using a gas grill, preheat to high [450° to 500°F].)

2 Stir together the butter, dill, lemon zest and juice, salt, and pepper in a bowl until well combined. (If making ahead, store in the refrigerator, covered, for up to 5 days; let come to room temperature 5 minutes before using.)

3 Place the corn on the oiled grates. Grill, uncovered and turning often, until charred on all sides, about 8 minutes. Transfer to a serving platter. Brush each corn ear with 1½ tablespoons of the dill butter and sprinkle with ½ tablespoon of the feta. Garnish with additional dill.

SKEWERED OKRA

SERVES 4

Hands-On: 15 minutes | Total: 30 minutes

Okra, a classic Southern ingredient that's often fried—or found hidden in gumbos or pots of purple hull peas—is one of my favorite vegetables. I often make it the star of the show, instead of serving as a backup singer. Be sure to source fresh, young okra: The pods should be tender and not woody.

1 pound fresh okra

3 tablespoons soy sauce

2 tablespoons honey

2 tablespoons olive oil

1 teaspoon garlic powder

1 tablespoon toasted sesame seeds

¼ teaspoon flaky sea salt

1 Open the bottom vent of a charcoal grill completely. Light a charcoal chimney starter filled with charcoal. When the coals are covered with gray ash, pour them onto the bottom grate of the grill. Adjust the vents as needed to maintain an internal temperature of 450° to 500°F. Coat the top grate with oil; place on the grill. (If using a gas grill, preheat to high [450° to 500°F].)

2 Toss together the okra, soy sauce, honey, oil, and garlic powder in a bowl. Let stand at room temperature for 10 minutes. Remove the okra from the marinade; reserve 3 tablespoons of the marinade and discard the rest.

3 Thread five okra pods onto two parallel skewers so that each skewer pierces the pods ½ inch from each end. Repeat with the remaining okra, skewering about five okra onto every two parallel skewers. Place on the oiled grates. Grill, uncovered, until slightly charred, 4 to 6 minutes, flipping the skewers once halfway through cook time. Transfer to a serving platter. Drizzle with the reserved marinade and sprinkle with the sesame seeds and salt.

CHARRED BROCCOLI RABE

SERVES 4

Hands-On: 15 minutes | Total: 15 minutes

Looks can be deceiving. Though it looks like a cross between broccoli and asparagus, broccoli rabe—also called rapini—is a leafy cruciferous vegetable that is closely related to the turnip. It's slightly bitter, with nutty flavors coming from the charred florets. It's an Italian favorite so Italian flavors like EVOO, Parmesan, and red pepper flakes are delicious accents. A squeeze of smoky lemon adds brightness.

1 pound fresh broccoli rabe, trimmed

4 tablespoons extra-virgin olive oil

½ teaspoon kosher salt

½ teaspoon freshly ground black pepper

2 medium lemons, halved crosswise

⅛ teaspoon crushed red pepper

½ ounce Parmesan cheese, shaved

1 Open the bottom vent of a charcoal grill completely. Light a charcoal chimney starter filled with charcoal. When the coals are covered with gray ash, pour them onto the bottom grate of the grill. Adjust the vents as needed to maintain an internal temperature of 400° to 450°F. Coat the top grate with oil; place on the grill. (If using a gas grill, preheat to medium-high [400° to 450°F].)

2 Brush the broccoli rabe with 2 tablespoons of the oil and sprinkle with the salt and black pepper. Place the broccoli rabe and lemon halves, cut-side down, on the oiled grates. Grill, uncovered, until the broccoli rabe and lemon halves are charred, about 6 minutes, turning the broccoli rabe halfway through cook time. Transfer the broccoli rabe to a serving platter. Squeeze the juice (you should have about 3 tablespoons) from the lemon halves into a small bowl (discard the seeds). Stir the crushed red pepper and remaining 2 tablespoons oil into the lemon juice. Drizzle the mixture over the broccoli rabe and sprinkle with the Parmesan shavings. Discard the squeezed lemon halves.

GRILLED TRUMPET MUSHROOMS

SERVES 4

Hands-On: 10 minutes | Total: 20 minutes

This side is mandatory when serving a thick, juicy grilled steak. Meaty, tender trumpet mushrooms are a great choice for the grill, but you could sub portobellos or button mushrooms. Rosemary is the ideal herb to bridge all the savory, earthy flavors, so stick to the recipe there.

8 fresh trumpet mushrooms (10 ounces), quartered lengthwise

¼ cup extra-virgin olive oil

2 medium garlic cloves, grated on a Microplane (1 teaspoon)

1 teaspoon chopped fresh rosemary

¾ teaspoon kosher salt

¼ teaspoon freshly ground black pepper

⅛ teaspoon crushed red pepper

1 Open the bottom vent of a charcoal grill completely. Light a charcoal chimney starter filled with charcoal. When the coals are covered with gray ash, pour them onto the bottom grate of the grill. Adjust the vents as needed to maintain an internal temperature of 400° to 450°F. Coat the top grate with oil; place on the grill. (If using a gas grill, preheat to medium-high [400° to 450°F].)

2 Place the mushrooms on a plate. Stir together the oil, garlic, rosemary, salt, black pepper, and crushed red pepper in a small bowl. Measure and reserve 1 tablespoon of the oil mixture in a separate small bowl. Brush the mushrooms with the remaining mixture; let stand at room temperature 10 minutes.

3 Place the mushrooms on the oiled grates. Grill, uncovered and turning occasionally, until tender and slightly charred on all cut sides, 6 to 9 minutes. Transfer to a serving platter and drizzle with the reserved oil mixture.

GRILLED BAKED BEANS

SERVES 8

Hands-On: 40 minutes | Total: 1 hour 40 minutes

Baked beans are a hefty, affordable side dish fit for a crowd. I like to up the flavor ante of the cookout classic by grilling the base ingredients—a mixture of peppers and onions. After that, it's all about adding the remaining tried-and-true ingredients and letting the heat from the grill work its magic. Serve from the Dutch oven right off the grill to retain heat and keep the beans deliciously warm for when you go back for seconds.

1 large (10-ounce) yellow onion, cut into ½-inch-thick slices

2 medium poblano chiles (about 5 ounces)

2 medium Hungarian wax peppers (about 5 ounces)

2 medium jalapeño chiles (about 3 ounces)

1 tablespoon olive oil

4 thick-cut bacon slices (about 3½ ounces), chopped

2 (14½-ounce) cans pinto beans, drained and rinsed

2 (14½-ounce) cans Great Northern beans, drained and rinsed

1 cup water

½ cup ketchup

¼ cup packed light brown sugar

2 tablespoons molasses

1 tablespoon yellow mustard

2 teaspoons chili powder

1 teaspoon kosher salt

½ teaspoon freshly ground black pepper

3 tablespoons apple cider vinegar

1 Open the bottom vent of a charcoal grill completely. Light a charcoal chimney starter filled with charcoal. When the coals are covered with gray ash, pour them onto the bottom grate of the grill, and then push to one side of the grill. Adjust the vents as needed to maintain an internal temperature of 450° to 500°F. Coat the top grate with oil; place on the grill. (If using a gas grill, preheat to high [450° to 500°F] on one side.)

2 Toss together the onion, poblanos, wax peppers, jalapeños, and oil in a large bowl. Place the vegetables on the oiled grates directly over the side with the coals (or the lit side of a gas grill). Grill, uncovered, until charred on all sides, about 12 minutes, turning halfway through cook time. Transfer the onion to a cutting board. Return the poblanos, wax peppers, and jalapeños to the large bowl; cover with plastic wrap and let stand until cool enough to handle, about 10 minutes.

3 Roughly chop the onion. Remove and discard the skin, stems, and seeds from the poblanos, wax peppers, and jalapeños and roughly chop. Set the chopped vegetables aside.

4 Place a Dutch oven on the grates directly over the side with the coals (or the lit side of a gas grill). Add the bacon to the pot and cook, stirring often, until crispy, about 5 minutes. Transfer the bacon with a slotted spoon to a plate lined with paper towels, reserving the drippings in the pot. Add the chopped vegetables to the pot, along with the pinto beans, Great Northern beans, water, ketchup, sugar, molasses, mustard, chili powder, salt, and pepper. Move the Dutch oven to the grates over the side without the coals (or the unlit side of a gas grill). Cover the Dutch oven and close the grill. Cook until the beans are tender and the sauce has thickened, about 1 hour. Stir in the vinegar and sprinkle with the bacon.

SMOKY SUMMER SQUASH

SERVES 4

Hands-On: 15 minutes | Total: 25 minutes

Tender, yellow squash is a Southern summertime favorite. The best part is that the vegetable takes on other flavors so well. While I enjoy the fresh taste of squash when it is baked or steamed, the flavor imparted by grilling makes it my preferred approach. Fresh basil provides a nice color contrast and lots of complementary summer flavor.

1 pound yellow squash, cut into ½-inch-thick slices

3 tablespoons extra-virgin olive oil

2 teaspoons smoked paprika

2 teaspoons garlic powder

1 teaspoon kosher salt

½ teaspoon freshly ground black pepper

1 tablespoon fresh lemon juice (from 1 lemon)

¼ cup torn fresh basil

1 Open the bottom vent of a charcoal grill completely. Light a charcoal chimney starter filled with charcoal. When the coals are covered with gray ash, pour them onto the bottom grate of the grill. Adjust the vents as needed to maintain an internal temperature of 450° to 500°F. Coat the top grate with oil; place on the grill. (If using a gas grill, preheat to high [450° to 500°F].)

2 Brush the squash slices with 2 tablespoons of the oil and sprinkle evenly with the paprika, garlic powder, salt, and pepper. Let stand at room temperature for 10 minutes.

3 Place the squash on the oiled grates. Grill, uncovered, until charred on both sides, 3 to 5 minutes per side. Transfer to a serving platter. Drizzle with the lemon juice and remaining 1 tablespoon oil and sprinkle with the basil.

GRILLED ARTICHOKES WITH SOUR CREAM DIPPING SAUCE

SERVES 4

Hands-On: 45 minutes | Total: 1 hour

This is a foolproof way to make delicious artichokes on the grill. Grilling the trimmed artichokes in foil packets traps moisture, steaming them until they are perfectly tender. Once they're cooked, a quick char over the direct heat of the grill enhances their meaty flavor. The creamy sour cream dipping sauce is a nice change of pace from artichokes' usual lemon-butter dunk.

4 (13-ounce) globe artichokes

2 medium lemons, halved crosswise

2 tablespoons olive oil

1½ teaspoons kosher salt

1 teaspoon freshly ground black pepper

6 tablespoons water

½ cup sour cream

1 medium garlic clove, grated on a Microplane (½ teaspoon)

1 tablespoon finely chopped fresh chives, plus more for garnish

2 teaspoons fresh lemon juice (from 1 lemon)

1. Open the bottom vent of a charcoal grill completely. Light a charcoal chimney starter filled with charcoal. When the coals are covered with gray ash, pour them onto the bottom grate of the grill, and then push to one side of the grill. Adjust the vents as needed to maintain an internal temperature of 450° to 500°F. Coat the top grate with oil; place on the grill. (If using a gas grill, preheat to high [450° to 500°F] on one side.)

2. Trim and discard the brown ends from the artichoke stems. Trim and discard the top third of each artichoke. Fill a medium bowl with water and squeeze juice from the halved lemons into the water (discarding the seeds). Add the squeezed lemon halves and artichokes to the lemon water. Working with one artichoke at a time, cut into quarters and peel off the thick outer leaves (leaving only tender light-green leaves). Scoop out and discard the fuzzy thistle. Return to the lemon water until ready to use, preferably within a few hours.

3. Drain the artichokes and transfer to a large bowl. Add the oil, 1 teaspoon of the salt, and ¾ teaspoon of the pepper; toss to coat. Place half the artichokes on an aluminum foil sheet; add 3 tablespoons water and wrap the foil around the artichokes. Repeat the process with the remaining artichokes and 3 tablespoons water.

4. Place the artichoke packets on the oiled grates over the side without the coals (or the unlit side of a gas grill). Grill, covered, until the artichokes are tender when pierced with a knife, 18 to 20 minutes. Carefully remove the artichokes from the foil packets; discard the foil. Place the artichokes on the oiled grates directly over the side with the coals (or the lit side of a gas grill); grill, uncovered and turning occasionally, until charred on all sides, about 6 minutes.

5. Meanwhile, stir together the sour cream, garlic, chives, lemon juice, and remaining ½ teaspoon salt and ¼ teaspoon pepper in a serving bowl. Transfer the artichokes to a serving platter; garnish with additional chives and serve with the sour cream sauce.

REDNECK POTATOES

SERVES 8

Hands-On: 35 minutes | Total: 1 hour 20 minutes

Odds are, you have enjoyed some version of this dish at some point. It's an easy, satisfying casserole that is also referred to as party potatoes or funeral potatoes because it's an ideal covered dish to take anywhere. By now you know that I'm going to tell you that you don't know what you're missing until you've tried the grilled version. I prefer using indirect heat for most dishes grilled in a skillet, which leaves room to grill some sort of protein directly over the coals while the casserole comes together. Once the potatoes are tender, move the skillet over direct heat to develop a flavorful crust on the bottom and to amplify the bubbling cheesy goodness on top. Garnish with crispy bacon and chives and get ready to soak up praise from friends and family.

4 thick-cut bacon slices (about 3½ ounces)

1 large (9½-ounce) sweet onion, chopped (2 cups)

4 tablespoons unsalted butter

1 (32-ounce) package frozen diced hash browns (such as Ore-Ida)

1 (10½-ounce) can cream of chicken soup (such as Campbell's)

8 ounces sour cream

8 ounces white Cheddar cheese, shredded (about 2 cups)

1½ teaspoons kosher salt

1 teaspoon freshly ground black pepper

3 tablespoons chopped fresh chives

1   Open the bottom vent of a charcoal grill completely. Light a charcoal chimney starter filled with charcoal. When the coals are covered with gray ash, pour them onto the bottom grate of the grill, and then push to one side of the grill. Adjust the vents as needed to maintain an internal temperature of 350° to 400°F. (If using a gas grill, preheat to medium [350° to 400°F] on one side.)

2   Place a large cast-iron skillet on unoiled grates over the side without the coals (or the unlit side of a gas grill). Add the bacon to the skillet and cook until crispy, 8 to 10 minutes, turning once halfway through cook time. Transfer the bacon to a cutting board, reserving the drippings in the skillet. Let the bacon cool 5 minutes, then roughly chop.

3   Add the onion and butter to the skillet and cook, stirring occasionally, until the onion is slightly caramelized, about 10 minutes. Add the potatoes and stir to coat. Add the soup, sour cream, cheese, salt, and pepper and stir until combined. Cover and cook, undisturbed, until the potatoes are tender, about 40 minutes. Move the skillet to the side with the coals (or the lit side of a gas grill). Cook, covered, until the cheese is bubbly and the potatoes on the bottom of the skillet begin to brown, about 8 minutes.

4   Remove the skillet from the grill and sprinkle with the reserved chopped bacon and the chives.

GRILLED CHEESE FRIES

SERVES 6

Hands-On: 20 minutes | Total: 35 minutes

Say hello to your new addiction. I'm obsessed with Mexican-style corn and so this recipe was inspired by the flavors of that popular street food. Unlike the usual soggy cheese fries soaked in molten orange "cheese" sauce, these grilled potatoes remain sturdy and crisp even after the drizzle of crema and crumbled queso fresco. So dig in now, *and* dig in later. You'll be sad when they're gone.

2 large (8-ounce) russet potatoes

3 tablespoons olive oil

1 teaspoon grated lime zest plus 1 tablespoon fresh juice (from 1 lime)

2 teaspoons smoked paprika

1 teaspoon garlic powder

1 teaspoon onion powder

1 teaspoon kosher salt

½ teaspoon freshly ground black pepper

¼ cup crema

1 ounce queso fresco, crumbled (about ¼ cup)

¼ cup chopped fresh cilantro

Lime wedges

1 Open the bottom vent of a charcoal grill completely. Light a charcoal chimney starter filled with charcoal. When the coals are covered with gray ash, pour them onto the bottom grate of the grill. Adjust the vents as needed to maintain an internal temperature of 450° to 500°F. Coat the top grate with oil; place on the grill. (If using a gas grill, preheat to high [450° to 500°F].)

2 Prick the potatoes all over with a fork. Place on a microwavable plate and microwave on HIGH until just tender, 7 to 8 minutes. Let cool to room temperature, 10 to 15 minutes. Cut into long wedges, about ¾ inch thick.

3 Toss together the potato wedges, oil, lime zest and juice, paprika, garlic powder, onion powder, salt, and pepper in a large bowl. Place on the oiled grates. Grill, uncovered, until the wedges are charred on the cut sides, 2 to 3 minutes per cut side. Transfer to a serving platter, drizzle with the crema, and sprinkle with the queso fresco and cilantro. Serve with lime wedges.

HOT HANDHELDS

ZA'ATAR-SPICED WINGS

SERVES 6 (4 OR 5 WINGS PER PERSON)

Hands-On: 30 minutes | Total: 1 hour 30 minutes, including 1 hour marinating

Chicken wings hot off the grill are heavenly. I like recipes that deviate from the usual barbecue or buffalo spice. Za'atar is a Middle Eastern seasoning—generally a blend of tangy sumac, thyme, oregano, marjoram, sesame seeds, and salt. It's an aromatic blend that amps up the flavors of grilled meats and melds beautifully with charcoal's smoke so that the end result is familiarly addictive yet deliciously new.

¼ cup canola oil

¼ cup fresh lemon juice (from 2 lemons)

3 tablespoons za'atar

3 tablespoons honey

1 teaspoon ground sumac

2 teaspoons kosher salt

3 pounds chicken wings (about 13 wings), wing flats, drumettes, and tips separated, and tips discarded

3 tablespoons chopped fresh cilantro

1 teaspoon toasted sesame seeds

1 Whisk together the oil, lemon juice, za'atar, honey, sumac, and 1 teaspoon of the salt in a large bowl. Add the wing pieces; toss to coat. Cover and refrigerate for 1 to 2 hours.

2 Open the bottom vent of a charcoal grill completely. Light a charcoal chimney starter filled with charcoal. When the coals are covered with gray ash, pour them onto the bottom grate of the grill, and then push to one side of the grill. Adjust the vents as needed to maintain an internal temperature of 400° to 450°F. Coat the top grate with oil; place on the grill. (If using a gas grill, preheat to medium-high [400° to 450°F] on one side.)

3 Remove the wings from the marinade; discard the marinade. Place the wings on the oiled grates directly over the side with the coals (or the lit side of a gas grill). Grill, covered, until charred, 8 to 10 minutes, turning once halfway through cook time. Move the wings to the side without the coals (or the unlit side of a gas grill). Grill, covered, until a thermometer inserted in thickest portion of the wings registers 160°F, about 10 minutes. Transfer the wings to a serving platter; sprinkle with cilantro, sesame seeds, and remaining 1 teaspoon salt.

CAJUN WINGS

SERVES 6 (4 OR 5 WINGS PER PERSON)

Hands-On: 30 minutes | Total: 30 minutes

This is my preferred spin on Buffalo wings, just made a bit better with some Cajun love. Start with a dry rub of traditional Cajun and Creole ingredients (in a pinch you can use your favorite Cajun seasoning blend). The grilling technique that I use with all my wing recipes is key here. You want to start the wings over direct heat to get the skin golden and crispy, and then finish over indirect heat. I like to toss these guys in Crystal hot sauce mixed with melted butter. The dry rub and sauce are a one-two punch that makes these wings winners.

2 teaspoons kosher salt

1½ teaspoons paprika

¾ teaspoon onion powder

¾ teaspoon garlic powder

½ teaspoon dried oregano

½ teaspoon freshly ground black pepper

¼ teaspoon cayenne pepper

3 pounds chicken wings (about 13 wings), wing flats, drumettes, and tips separated, and tips discarded

1 (6-ounce) bottle Crystal hot sauce

½ cup (4 ounces) unsalted butter, cubed

1 Stir together the salt, paprika, onion powder, garlic powder, oregano, black pepper, and cayenne pepper in a large bowl. Add the wing pieces and toss to coat.

2 Open the bottom vent of a charcoal grill completely. Light a charcoal chimney starter filled with charcoal. When the coals are covered with gray ash, pour them onto the bottom grate of the grill, and then push to one side of the grill. Adjust the vents as needed to maintain an internal temperature of 400° to 450°F. Coat the top grate with oil; place on the grill. (If using a gas grill, preheat to medium-high [400° to 450°F] on one side.)

3 Place the hot sauce and butter in a saucepan and place on the oiled grates directly over the side with the coals (or the lit side of a gas grill). Cook, whisking often, until the butter melts and the mixture is smooth, 4 to 5 minutes. Remove from the heat.

4 Place the wings on the oiled grates directly over the side with the coals. Grill, covered, until charred, about 8 minutes, turning once halfway through cook time. Move the wings to the side without the coals (or the unlit side of a gas grill). Grill, covered, until a thermometer inserted in thickest portion of the wings registers 160°F, about 10 minutes. Transfer the wings to a large bowl; add the buttered hot sauce and toss to coat. Arrange on a serving platter.

SPICY GOCHUJANG WINGS

SERVES 6

Hands-On: 30 minutes | Total: 30 minutes

This spicy-sweet approach to wings relies on one of my favorite Korean condiments—gochujang. Have no fear, even mainstream grocery stores often stock this fermented red pepper paste, as well as the red pepper flakes (gochugaru) used in the rub, in the international aisle. If not, hit the Asian market or buy it online; it's worth keeping a tub in the fridge. The wings are less spicy than you might think. The savory and sweet sauce tempers the heat just enough that you can't stop eating them. Don't blame this guy if you eat the whole bunch!

½ cup gochujang

¼ cup rice vinegar

3 tablespoons granulated sugar

2 tablespoons toasted sesame oil

1½ tablespoons soy sauce

2 teaspoons gochugaru (Korean red pepper flakes)

2 teaspoons kosher salt

1 teaspoon freshly ground black pepper

3 pounds chicken wings (about 13 wings), wing flats, drumettes, and tips separated, and tips discarded

1 Whisk together the gochujang, vinegar, sugar, sesame oil, and soy sauce in a large bowl until smooth.

2 Open the bottom vent of a charcoal grill completely. Light a charcoal chimney starter filled with charcoal. When the coals are covered with gray ash, pour them onto the bottom grate of the grill, and then push to one side of the grill. Adjust the vents as needed to maintain an internal temperature of 400° to 450°F. Coat the top grate with oil; place on the grill. (If using a gas grill, preheat to medium-high [400° to 450°F] on one side.)

3 Stir together the gochugaru, salt, and black pepper in a small bowl. Sprinkle the mixture over the wing pieces. Place the wings on the oiled grates directly over the side with the coals (or the lit side of a gas grill). Grill, covered, until charred, 8 to 10 minutes, turning once halfway through cook time. Move the wings to the side without the coals (or the unlit side of a gas grill). Grill, covered, until a thermometer inserted in thickest portion of the wings registers 160°F, about 10 minutes. Transfer the wings to the sauce in the bowl and toss to coat. Arrange on a serving platter.

TACOS AL PASTOR

SERVES 8

Hands-On: 25 minutes | Total: 1 hour 25 minutes, including 1 hour marinating

This prized dish of Central Mexico came about because of the migration of Lebanese Christians who wanted to re-create the foods of their homeland. Called *tacos árabes* by Puebla, Mexico, locals, they are a delicious amalgamation of cultures through food. The marinade includes allspice, a spice typical to Lebanese and Middle Eastern cuisine. Local taco shops skewer and roast the meats on large spits much like shawarma, then slice it to order and fold in a tortilla-reminiscent of the soft pitas of the Middle East. Using skirt steak here provides a similar experience but scaled for a smaller crowd.

STEAK

¼ cup olive oil

¼ cup fresh lime juice (from 2 limes)

¼ cup chopped fresh cilantro

2 teaspoons chili powder

1 teaspoon ground allspice

8 medium garlic cloves, minced (3 tablespoons)

1 (1½-pound) skirt steak (½ inch thick), cut in half crosswise

1½ teaspoons kosher salt

1 teaspoon freshly ground black pepper

SALSA

5 guajillo chiles, seeded

4 cups boiling water

3 tablespoons fresh lime juice (from 2 limes)

1 teaspoon kosher salt

½ teaspoon light brown sugar

FOR SERVING

16 (5-inch) corn tortillas

1 small (5-ounce) white onion, chopped (about ¾ cup)

Cilantro sprigs

Lime wedges

1 Marinate the steak: Whisk together the oil, lime juice, cilantro, chili powder, allspice, and garlic in a bowl. Add the steak and toss to coat. Cover and refrigerate for 1 to 2 hours.

2 Meanwhile, prepare the salsa: Place the chiles in a heatproof bowl and pour the boiling water over them. Let stand for 30 minutes. Drain the chiles, reserving ¼ cup of the soaking liquid. Combine the chiles and reserved soaking liquid with the lime juice, salt, and sugar in a blender. Process until smooth, about 1 minute, stopping to scrape down the sides as needed.

3 Open the bottom vent of a charcoal grill completely. Light a charcoal chimney starter filled with charcoal. When the coals are covered with gray ash, pour them onto the bottom grate of the grill. Adjust vents as needed to maintain an internal temperature of 400° to 450°F. Coat the top grate with oil; place on the grill. (If using a gas grill, preheat to medium-high [400° to 450°F].)

4 Remove the steak from the marinade, discarding marinade, and sprinkle with the salt and pepper. Place on the oiled grates. Grill, uncovered, until charred on both sides, 3 to 4 minutes per side. Transfer to a cutting board and let rest for 8 minutes. Slice against the grain crosswise.

5 Working in batches, place the tortillas on the oiled grates; grill until lightly charred, 20 to 30 seconds per side.

6 Fill the tortillas evenly with steak, onion, and cilantro sprigs. Top evenly with the salsa and serve with the lime wedges.

PORK GYROS

SERVES 6

Hands-On: 20 minutes | Total: 1 hour 40 minutes, including 1 hour marinating

Most Americans think of beef or lamb when it comes to gyros, but an authentic Greek gyro is traditionally filled with pork. I ate my fill of these during my travels in Greece, usually holding one in my hand, tzatziki dripping down my arm, while navigating the local narrow streets on a motorcycle. To re-create the Greek classic, I like to use pork tenderloin to ensure the meat is super tender. You can also use this marinade for chicken, beef, or lamb, if that's more your speed.

PORK

½ cup plain whole-milk Greek yogurt

¼ cup red wine vinegar

1½ tablespoons dried oregano

1 tablespoon garlic powder

1 tablespoon paprika

2 teaspoons kosher salt

1 teaspoon freshly ground black pepper

1½ pounds pork tenderloin, cut into ½-inch cubes

TZATZIKI

¾ cup plain whole-milk Greek yogurt

¼ cup finely chopped seeded cucumber (from 1 small [7-ounce] cucumber)

2 tablespoons red wine vinegar

2 tablespoons chopped fresh dill

1 teaspoon kosher salt

1 teaspoon freshly ground black pepper

1 teaspoon granulated sugar

FOR SERVING

6 (8-inch) pita rounds, halved crosswise

3 cups shredded iceberg lettuce (from 1 [8-ounce] package)

2 cups chopped seeded tomato (from 2 medium [6-ounce] tomatoes)

1 Marinate the pork: Whisk together the yogurt, vinegar, oregano, garlic powder, paprika, salt, and pepper in a large bowl. Add the pork and toss to coat. Cover and refrigerate for 1 to 2 hours.

2 Meanwhile, prepare the tzatziki: Stir together all the ingredients in a bowl. Cover and refrigerate until ready to use, or up to a few days.

3 Open the bottom vent of a charcoal grill completely. Light a charcoal chimney starter filled with charcoal. When the coals are covered with gray ash, pour them onto the bottom grate of the grill. Adjust the vents as needed to maintain an internal temperature of 400° to 450°F. Coat the top grate with oil; place on the grill. (If using a gas grill, preheat to medium-high [400° to 450°F].)

4 Remove the pork from marinade; discard the marinade. Thread the pork evenly onto 12 (6-inch) skewers. Place the skewers on the oiled grates. Grill, covered and turning occasionally, until the pork is charred and a thermometer inserted in thickest portion of the pork registers 145°F, 6 to 8 minutes. Remove from the heat.

5 Wrap the pita halves in damp paper towels. Microwave on HIGH until softened, 30 to 45 seconds. Fill the pita halves evenly with the pork, lettuce, and tomatoes. Drizzle with the tzatziki.

CHILI CHEESE DOGS

SERVES 8

Hands-On: 20 minutes | Total: 20 minutes

A good chili dog is hard to beat. It's a savory handheld that really hits the spot. I like to make both the dogs and the chili on the grill for undeniable smoky flavor, plus it keeps the kitchen clean. It's hard for me to eat a chili dog and not think of football. I often make a big ole pot of chili on game day and serve it alongside a platter of grilled dogs next to all the toppings for a perfect tailgate meal right at home.

1½ cups Chili on the Grill (page 266)

8 hot dog buns, split

8 beef hot dogs

4 ounces sharp Cheddar cheese, shredded (about 1 cup)

1 cup thinly sliced scallions (from 10 scallions)

6 tablespoons yellow mustard

½ cup pickled jalapeño chiles (optional)

1 Open the bottom vent of a charcoal grill completely. Light a charcoal chimney starter filled with charcoal. When the coals are covered with gray ash, pour them onto the bottom grate of the grill. Adjust the vents as needed to maintain an internal temperature of 400° to 450°F. Coat the top grate with oil; place on the grill. (If using a gas grill, preheat to medium-high [400° to 450°F].)

2 Bring the chili to a simmer in a small saucepan on a stovetop over medium-high heat, stirring occasionally. Remove from the heat and cover to keep warm.

3 Coat the cut sides of the buns with cooking spray and place, cut-side down, on the oiled grates. Grill, uncovered, until toasted and golden brown, 2 to 3 minutes. Transfer to a plate. Place the hot dogs on the oiled grates. Grill, uncovered and turning often, until slightly charred on all sides, 6 to 7 minutes.

4 Place one hot dog in each bun. Top evenly with chili, cheese, scallions, mustard, and jalapeños (if desired).

TRIPLE CHEESEBURGERS

SERVES 6

Hands-On: 35 minutes | Total: 1 hour 35 minutes

In the '90s, every McDonald's was dominated by the Monopoly game, but when I was a kid it was their triple cheeseburger that caught my interest. That indulgent burger debuted around the time of the remake of the *Dick Tracy* movie with Warren Beatty; why such memories persist in my mind is anyone's guess, but the idea of three patties and two slices of cheese still excites me. Instead of a thick patty, I like how three smaller patties provide more surface area so you get more crispy char on the meat. Nowadays, I prefer a high-quality spin on the Triple C, hand-forming the patties and making homemade pickles. But I'm not willing to give up the American cheese: You can't have a worthy re-creation of this burger without it. Give these a try at your next cookout and you'll agree that three patties are better than one.

1 cup water

1 cup apple cider vinegar

½ cup granulated sugar

¼ cup pickling spice

¼ cup plus 2 teaspoons kosher salt

1 medium English cucumber (unpeeled), cut into 3-inch pieces

2 pounds 90/10 lean ground beef sirloin

1½ tablespoons Worcestershire sauce

1½ teaspoons freshly ground black pepper

6 sesame seed hamburger buns, split

¾ cup mayonnaise

12 (½-ounce) slices American cheese

1. Stir together the water, vinegar, sugar, pickling spice, and the ¼ cup salt in a saucepan and bring to a boil over high heat. Thinly slice the cucumber pieces into ¼-inch planks and place in a heatproof bowl. Pour the boiling liquid over the cucumber. Cover and refrigerate for 1 hour.

2. Open the bottom vent of a charcoal grill completely. Light a charcoal chimney starter filled with charcoal. When the coals are covered with gray ash, pour them onto the bottom grate of the grill. Adjust the vents as needed to maintain an internal temperature of 400° to 450°F. Coat the top grate with oil; place on the grill. (If using a gas grill, preheat to medium-high [400° to 450°F].)

3. Place the beef, Worcestershire sauce, pepper, and remaining 2 teaspoons salt in a bowl; mix gently using your hands. Form into 18 (¼-inch-thick) patties. Place on the oiled grill grates. Grill, uncovered, until a thermometer inserted in thickest portion of the patties registers 160°F, 2 to 3 minutes per side. Coat the cut sides of the buns with cooking spray. Place on the oiled grates, cut-side down, and grill until toasted, about 30 seconds.

4. Spread 1 tablespoon mayonnaise on each bun half. Place a patty on each bottom bun half. Layer each with a cheese slice, a patty, a cheese slice, and another patty. Top with the refrigerated pickles, then the bun tops. (Store leftover pickles in pickling liquid, covered, in refrigerator up to 10 days.)

DEBRIS PO'BOY

SERVES 6

Hands-On: 25 minutes | Total: 3 hours 15 minutes

Chuck roast seems to always be on sale at my local grocery—especially on Sundays. Though I'm all for a low-and-slow roast in the oven or slow cooker on the weekend, I prefer throwing this bad boy on the grill until the exterior is crusty and caramelized. Once it's got a good exterior char, I finish cooking the roast in a Dutch oven until it is fall-apart moist and tender, "debris" style. Of course, you can serve the beef as a traditional roast with all the fixings, but I like it shredded and piled in a classic po'boy, dressed with the trimmings and reserved drippings. Keep a bowl of that savory drippings nectar close for dunking.

1 (3-pound) boneless chuck roast

2 teaspoons kosher salt

1½ teaspoons freshly ground black pepper

3 cups unsalted beef stock

¾ cup (6 ounces) salted butter, softened

6 (8-inch-long) portions Italian bread, split

6 tablespoons mayonnaise

12 (¾-ounce) slices provolone cheese

3 cups shredded iceberg lettuce (from 1 head)

12 thin tomato slices (from 1 large [12-ounce] tomato)

24 dill pickle chips

Crystal hot sauce (optional)

1 Open the bottom vent of a charcoal grill completely. Light a charcoal chimney starter filled with charcoal. When the coals are covered with gray ash, pour them onto the bottom grate of the grill. Adjust vents as needed to maintain an internal temperature of 300° to 350°F. Coat the top grate with oil; place on the grill. (If using a gas grill, preheat to medium-low [300° to 350°F].)

2 Season the beef with the salt and pepper. Place on the oiled grates. Grill, covered and turning occasionally, until browned on all sides, 15 to 20 minutes. Transfer to a large Dutch oven. Pour the stock over the beef and place the Dutch oven on the grates. Grill, covered, until the beef is fork-tender and a thermometer inserted in thickest portion registers 145°F, about 2½ hours. Remove the pot from the heat. Transfer the beef to a cutting board (reserving drippings in the pot); let rest for 15 minutes.

3 Spread the butter evenly on the cut sides of the bread. Place the bread, cut-side down, on the oiled grates and grill until just golden brown, about 45 seconds. Remove from the grill.

4 Shred the beef with a fork. Spread the mayonnaise evenly on the bread tops. Place two cheese slices on each bread bottom. Top evenly with the shredded beef, lettuce, tomato, pickles, and hot sauce (if desired). Pour the reserved beef drippings into a serving bowl; serve alongside the sandwiches.

BIG PLATES

EGGPLANT MEDITERRANEAN 233 | CHICKEN THIGHS WITH HERB SALSA 234

EAST NASHVILLE HOT CHICKEN 237 | GRILLED TURKEY BREAST 239

SPATCHCOCKED WHOLE CHICKEN 240 | GRILLED VEGGIE PIZZA 243

BAYOU PIZZA 244 | CAROLINA WHITE CLAM PIZZA 246

GRILLED WHOLE POMPANO 249 | REDFISH ON THE HALF SHELL 250

GRILLED SALMON WITH CREAMY CUCUMBER RELISH 253 | SMOKED GREEK RIBS 254

COUNTRY-STYLE RIBS WITH PEACH SALSA 257

GRILLED PORK BELLY WITH PEACH VINEGAR SAUCE 259

SORGHUM-GLAZED PORK CHOPS WITH COUSCOUS 261 | PORCHETTA 262

COUNTRY SAUSAGE BOLOGNESE 265 | CHILI ON THE GRILL 266

BEEF KAFTA WITH QUICK LABNEH 269 | BBQ MEATLOAF 271

BEEF FILLET STROGANOFF 272

EGGPLANT MEDITERRANEAN

SERVES 6

Hands-On: 35 minutes | **Total:** 1 hour 35 minutes, including 1 hour marinating

Now and then, you need a break from the heavy stuff, and that's where this recipe comes in. The meaty texture of eggplant is light when it needs to be and yet can be stick-to-your-ribs satisfying just the same. I love serving this as a main dish to carnivore friends and seeing how they are totally satisfied after the meal, rarely asking, "Where's the beef?"

4 cups chicken stock

6 medium garlic cloves, smashed

2 large sprigs fresh oregano, plus chopped leaves for garnish

1 tablespoon plus 1 teaspoon kosher salt

1 tablespoon black peppercorns

3 cups ice

2 medium eggplants (about 3½ pounds)

½ teaspoon freshly ground black pepper

¾ cup diced plum tomatoes (from 2 medium tomatoes)

½ cup diced English cucumber (from 1 medium cucumber)

¼ cup diced red onion (from 1 medium onion)

2 tablespoons red wine vinegar

1 tablespoon extra-virgin olive oil

2 ounces feta cheese, crumbled (about ½ cup)

1 Bring the stock, garlic, oregano sprigs, 1 tablespoon of the salt, and the peppercorns to a boil in a medium saucepan over high heat. Remove from the heat, cover, and let stand for 10 minutes. Add the ice to the saucepan and stir until melted.

2 Partially peel the eggplants by peeling in alternating stripes. Cut the eggplants lengthwise into 1-inch-thick slabs. Place in an 11- x 7-inch baking dish and pour over the stock mixture. Let marinate at room temperature for 1 hour. Remove the eggplant from the marinade; discard the marinade. Pat the eggplant dry.

3 Open the bottom vent of a charcoal grill completely. Light a charcoal chimney starter filled with charcoal. When the coals are covered with gray ash, pour them onto the bottom grate of the grill. Adjust the vents as needed to maintain an internal temperature of 450° to 500°F. Coat the top grate with oil; place on the grill. (If using a gas grill, preheat to high [450° to 500°F].)

4 Coat the eggplant slabs with cooking spray and sprinkle with the ground black pepper and ¾ teaspoon of the salt. Place on the oiled grates and grill, covered, until the eggplant is tender and grill marks appear, 5 to 6 minutes per side. Transfer the eggplant to a cutting board and let cool for 5 minutes. Roughly chop the eggplant into 1- to 2-inch pieces and arrange on a serving platter.

5 Toss together the tomatoes, cucumber, onion, vinegar, oil, and remaining ¼ teaspoon salt in a medium bowl. Sprinkle the mixture evenly over the eggplant and sprinkle with the feta and chopped oregano.

CHICKEN THIGHS WITH HERB SALSA

SERVES 4

Hands-On: 30 minutes | Total: 30 minutes

All you novice grillers out there: This recipe is going to be your go-to. Chicken thighs are one of the most forgivable cuts of meat to grill. Inattentive cooks are often surprised to find that they are still moist and juicy inside even if over-charred outside. I don't recommend that, but it's nice to know. To add even more depth and moisture, I love to serve meaty grilled thighs with a fresh herb salsa, typically just using a mix of whatever fresh herbs I have on hand. The secret of the salsa is the anchovy. Don't skip this ingredient! It provides the savory umami flavor that brings all the other flavors together.

8 boneless, skinless chicken thighs (about 2 pounds)

1 teaspoon kosher salt

½ teaspoon freshly ground black pepper

¼ cup chopped shallot (about 1 medium shallot)

2 tablespoons capers, drained

2 tablespoons chopped fresh flat-leaf parsley

2 tablespoons chopped fresh mint

2 tablespoons chopped fresh basil

1 teaspoon fresh thyme leaves

3 medium garlic cloves, chopped (about 1 tablespoon)

4 anchovy fillets

¼ cup olive oil

2 cups hot cooked white rice

1 Open the bottom vent of a charcoal grill completely. Light a charcoal chimney starter filled with charcoal. When the coals are covered with gray ash, pour them onto the bottom grate of the grill. Adjust vents as needed to maintain an internal temperature of 400° to 450°F. Coat the top grate with oil; place on the grill. (If using a gas grill, preheat to medium-high [400° to 450°F].)

2 Sprinkle the chicken evenly with the salt and pepper. Place on the oiled grates. Grill, covered, until charred on both sides and a thermometer inserted in thickest portion of the chicken registers 170°F, about 5 minutes per side.

3 Meanwhile, place the shallot, capers, parsley, mint, basil, thyme, garlic, and anchovy fillets on a cutting board. Chop the mixture until the consistency resembles a rough paste; drizzle with the oil.

4 Remove the chicken from the grill and place directly on the shallot mixture on the cutting board. Let rest for 5 minutes. Slice the chicken against the grain into ½-inch-thick slices and toss gently with the shallot mixture. Serve directly off the cutting board, family style, alongside hot rice.

EAST NASHVILLE HOT CHICKEN

SERVES 4

Hands-On: 35 minutes | Total: 8 hours 35 minutes, including 8 hours marinating

Being a longtime resident of East Nashville, I'm hesitant to even include this recipe. I still have not come to terms with Nashville's rapid ascent as a city, or the fact that hot chicken has become our food of export. Most folks incorrectly liken hot chicken to buffalo-style chicken. Classic hot chicken includes a paste—almost a batter—of molten butter or oil, sugar, and spice that's a deep heat that hits you more in the gut than tongue. The classic hot chicken is fried, but this grilled spin is awesome. Serve the usual way, with soft white bread and tart dill pickles, and it's a taste of home, no matter where you're from.

4 bone-in, skin-on chicken breasts (about 1 pound)

2 cups dill pickle juice

1 cup water

1 tablespoon plus 2 teaspoons kosher salt

1 cup canola oil

2 tablespoons light brown sugar

2 tablespoons cayenne pepper

1 tablespoon paprika

1 tablespoon freshly ground black pepper

8 (1-ounce) white sandwich bread slices

20 dill pickle chips

1 Place the chicken, pickle juice, water, and 1 tablespoon of the salt in a large ziplock plastic bag. Seal the bag and marinate in the refrigerator for 8 to 12 hours. Remove the chicken from the bag; discard the marinade. Set the chicken aside at room temperature.

2 Open the bottom vent of a charcoal grill completely. Light a charcoal chimney starter filled with charcoal. When the coals are covered with gray ash, pour them onto the bottom grate of the grill. Adjust the vents as needed to maintain an internal temperature of 400° to 450°F. (If using a gas grill, preheat to medium-high [400° to 450°F].)

3 Combine the oil, sugar, cayenne, paprika, and black pepper in a small grill-safe saucepan; place on unoiled grates. Cook, uncovered and stirring often, until tiny bubbles form and the sugar melts, 3 to 4 minutes. Remove from the heat. Pour the mixture into a heatproof bowl and allow to cool slightly, about 10 minutes.

4 Sprinkle the chicken with the remaining 2 teaspoons salt. Coat the top grate with oil; place the chicken on the oiled grates. Grill, covered, until a thermometer inserted in thickest portion of the chicken registers 160°F, 10 to 12 minutes per side. Remove from the heat and let cool for 5 minutes.

5 Dip the chicken, one breast at a time, in the oil-sugar mixture. Place two bread slices on each of four serving plates; top one slice on each plate with a chicken breast and five pickle chips.

GRILLED TURKEY BREAST

SERVES 8

Hands-On: 20 minutes | Total: 2 hours 30 minutes, including 1 hour standing

It's easy to overlook turkey, relegating it to the Thanksgiving table and forgetting about the tasty bird the rest of the year. Here is a recipe you can give thanks for whenever the mood strikes, no matter the season. A turkey breast can serve a whole family or just a few and yield plenty of leftovers. Some are intimidated by turkey—perhaps after one too many dry birds or because it reminds us of uncomfortable holidays we'd rather forget. Fear not. Follow this recipe and rest assured you'll have a flavorful and juicy end result that will become an anytime favorite.

1 (5- to 6-pound) bone-in, skin-on turkey breast

½ cup (4 ounces) unsalted butter, softened

1½ tablespoons chopped fresh thyme

1½ tablespoons chopped fresh rosemary

1½ tablespoons chopped garlic (from 3 medium cloves)

1 tablespoon grated lemon zest (from 2 lemons)

1 tablespoon kosher salt

1 teaspoon freshly ground black pepper

1 Let the turkey stand at room temperature for 1 hour. Stir together the butter, thyme, rosemary, garlic, lemon zest, salt, and pepper in a bowl; set aside.

2 Open the bottom vent of a charcoal grill completely. Light a charcoal chimney starter filled with charcoal. When the coals are covered with gray ash, pour them onto the bottom grate of the grill, and then push to one side of the grill. Adjust the vents as needed to maintain an internal temperature of about 350°F. Coat the top grate with oil; place on the grill. (If using a gas grill, preheat to medium-low [about 350°F] on one side.)

3 Loosen the skin from the turkey breast by inserting your fingers, gently pushing between skin and meat. Rub the butter mixture under the loosened skin. Place the turkey, skin-side up, on the oiled grates over the side without the coals (or the unlit side of a gas grill). Grill, covered, until a thermometer inserted in thickest portion of the turkey registers 150°F, 1 hour to 1 hour and 20 minutes, rotating the turkey 45 degrees occasionally.

4 Move the turkey, skin-side down, to the oiled grates directly over the side with the coals (or the lit side of a gas grill). Grill, covered, until the skin is golden brown and a thermometer inserted in thickest portion of the breast registers 155°F, 6 to 8 minutes, rotating occasionally. Transfer to a cutting board. Loosely cover the turkey with aluminum foil and let rest for 15 minutes (internal temperature will rise to 165°F). Slice and serve.

SPATCHCOCKED WHOLE CHICKEN

SERVES 4

Hands-On: 30 minutes | Total: 1 hour 30 minutes

A properly grilled whole chicken should be a part of any grillmaster's repertoire. The problem is, it ain't easy. Cooking the dark meat to perfection while keeping the white meat from becoming jerky, all while simultaneously attempting to master perfectly crispy skin, has left cooks baffled since the invention of the grill. There is a better way, my friends! By removing the backbone, you are able to open the chicken like a book, flattening it at the breastbone to create more surface area and allowing the chicken to grill more evenly. Start skin-side down over direct heat to get that perfect char on the skin and then flip the bird and move it over to indirect heat to grill the meat evenly to temperature.

1 (3- to 4-pound) whole chicken, giblets removed and discarded

½ cup (4 ounces) unsalted butter, softened

1 tablespoon chopped fresh sage

1 teaspoon chopped fresh rosemary

1 teaspoon chopped fresh thyme

3 medium garlic cloves, grated on a Microplane (2 teaspoons)

2½ teaspoons kosher salt

1 teaspoon freshly ground black pepper

¼ cup chopped fresh flat-leaf parsley

1 Open the bottom vent of a charcoal grill completely. Light a charcoal chimney starter filled with charcoal. When the coals are covered with gray ash, pour them onto the bottom grate of the grill, and then push to one side of the grill. Adjust the vents as needed to maintain an internal temperature of 400° to 450°F. Coat the top grate with oil; place on the grill. (If using a gas grill, preheat to medium-high [400° to 450°F] on one side.)

2 Place the chicken, breast-side down, on a cutting board. Using poultry shears, cut along both sides of the backbone and remove the backbone. (Discard or reserve for stock.) Turn the chicken breast-side up and open the underside of the chicken like a book. Using the heel of your hand, press firmly against the breastbone until it cracks.

3 Stir together the butter, sage, rosemary, thyme, garlic, 1½ teaspoons of the salt, and ½ teaspoon of the pepper in a bowl. Rub the butter mixture under the chicken skin and all over the chicken. Sprinkle the chicken all over with the remaining 1 teaspoon salt and ½ teaspoon pepper. Tuck the wing tips under the breasts.

4 Place the chicken, skin-side down, on the oiled grill grates directly over the side with the coals (or the lit side of a gas grill). Grill, covered, until browned, 5 to 10 minutes. Flip the chicken and move to the oiled grates on the side without the coals (or the unlit side of a gas grill). Grill, covered, until a thermometer inserted in thickest portion of the chicken registers 165°F, about 50 minutes. Transfer the chicken to a cutting board and let rest for 15 minutes. Carve and sprinkle with the parsley.

GRILLED VEGGIE PIZZA

SERVES 6 (TWO 10-INCH PIZZAS)

Hands-On: 55 minutes | Total: 6 hours, including 5 hours making and rising the dough

Unless you are fortunate enough to own a wood-fired pizza oven, about the only way to emulate your favorite pizzeria creation is to throw that baby on a red-hot grill. And grilled vegetables are right at home atop a smoky, savory pizza. One bite into this delicious loaded combo with a nice contrast of textures and flavors and I bet you won't even notice it is sans meat. The combo of fontina, a creamy Italian cow's milk cheese, and tangy and salty ricotta salata is something you'll crave on every pizza you eat from now on. Serve the pizzas alongside a grilled salad (pages 172 to 189), and a glass or two of pinot noir.

1 medium (8-ounce) red onion, cut into ½-inch pieces

1 medium (7-ounce) yellow bell pepper, cut into ½-inch pieces

4 ounces fresh cremini mushrooms, sliced

1 medium (4-ounce) tomato, cut into 1-inch pieces

1 teaspoon kosher salt

4 tablespoons olive oil

Coarse cornmeal, for the peel

2 (12-ounce) dough portions from Master Pizza Dough (page 247), stretched into two 11-inch rounds

12 ounces fontina cheese, shredded (about 3 cups)

½ cup jarred marinated quartered artichoke hearts, drained

4 tablespoons sliced black olives

Crumbled ricotta salata cheese

Fresh basil leaves

1   Open the bottom vent of a charcoal grill completely. Light a charcoal chimney starter filled with charcoal. When the coals are covered with gray ash, pour them onto the bottom grate of the grill, and then push to one side of the grill. Adjust the vents as needed to maintain an internal temperature of around 500°F. Coat the top grate with oil; place on the grill. (If using a gas grill, preheat to very high [500°F and up].)

2   Toss together the onion, bell pepper, mushrooms, tomato, salt, and 2 tablespoons of the oil in a bowl. Transfer the vegetables to a grilling basket coated with oil and arrange in a single layer. Place the grilling basket on the oiled grates directly over the side with the coals (or the lit side of a gas grill). Grill, covered and stirring occasionally, until the vegetables are tender and lightly charred, about 8 minutes. Remove from the grill; let cool for 5 minutes.

3   Sprinkle a pizza peel with cornmeal; place 1 stretched dough round on the peel and brush with 1 tablespoon of the oil. Sprinkle with 1½ cups of the fontina, half of the grilled vegetables, ¼ cup of the artichoke hearts, and 2 tablespoons of the olives. Slide the pizza onto the oiled grates directly over the side with the coals (or the lit side of a gas grill). Grill, covered, until the bottom of the crust is golden brown and charred in spots, 1 to 2 minutes. Move the pizza to the oiled grates over the side without the coals (or the unlit side of a gas grill). Grill, covered, until the top of the pizza is bubbly, 6 to 8 minutes. Remove from the grill. Repeat with the remaining pizza dough, oil, fontina, grilled vegetables, artichoke hearts, and olives.

4   Garnish the pizzas with the ricotta salata and basil leaves.

BAYOU PIZZA

SERVES 6 (TWO 10-INCH PIZZAS)

Hands-On: 55 minutes | Total: 6 hours, including 5 hours making and rising the dough

The unique flavors and rich history of southern Louisiana cooking is appreciated throughout the world. It's a mash-up of flavors based on a blend of cultures, including Acadian, French, Spanish, Native American, West African, Haitian, and Western European, and built upon the readily available ingredients of Bayou Country. One of the ways to best enjoy all the flavors of Louisiana cuisine is in one bite, so I put them all on a pizza. I can hear a sigh from all the Italians out there, but hear me out...and taste this first. The pizza sauce here is inspired by remoulade—this one is a mix of the Creole and Cajun-style sauces. The unique sauce anchors the toppings to the crisp, grilled crust. Topped with spicy Cajun andouille, smoked Gouda, corn, peppers, and onions and hot sauce, I promise this recipe is a worthy pizza combo that you'll serve proudly to friends and family.

⅔ cup mayonnaise

1 scallion, sliced (2 tablespoons), plus more for garnish

1½ tablespoons Creole mustard

2 teaspoons hot sauce (such as Crystal)

1 teaspoon fresh lime juice (from 1 lime)

½ teaspoon kosher salt

¼ teaspoon freshly ground black pepper

8 ounces andouille sausage

1 medium (8-ounce) red bell pepper, cut into 2-inch strips

1 medium (6-ounce) ear fresh corn, shucked

Coarse cornmeal, for the peel

2 (12-ounce) dough portions from Master Pizza Dough (page 247), stretched into two 11-inch rounds

12 ounces smoked Gouda cheese, shredded (about 3 cups)

½ cup thinly sliced red onion (from 1 medium onion)

1 Open the bottom vent of a charcoal grill completely. Light a charcoal chimney starter filled with charcoal. When the coals are covered with gray ash, pour them onto the bottom grate of the grill, and then push to one side of the grill. Adjust the vents as needed to maintain an internal temperature of about 500°F. Coat the top grate with oil; place on the grill. (If using a gas grill, preheat to very high [500°F and up] on one side.)

2 Stir together the mayonnaise, scallion, mustard, hot sauce, lime juice, salt, and black pepper in a bowl; set the sauce aside.

3 Place the sausage, bell pepper, and corn on the oiled grates directly over the side with the coals (or the lit side of a gas grill). Grill, uncovered, until the sausage is heated through and the vegetables are charred and tender, about 3 minutes per side. Transfer to a cutting board and let cool slightly, about 10 minutes. Slice the sausage into ½-inch-thick half-moons. Cut the bell pepper into ½-inch pieces. Cut the corn from the cob, discarding the cob.

4 Sprinkle a pizza peel with cornmeal and place one stretched dough round on the peel. Spread half of the sauce on the surface of the dough. Sprinkle with 1½ cups of the cheese. Top with ¼ cup of the red onion and half of the sausage, bell pepper, and corn. Slide the pizza onto the oiled grates directly over the side with the coals (or the lit side of a gas grill). Grill, covered, until golden brown and lightly charred on the bottom, 1 to 2 minutes. Move the pizza to the oiled grates over the side without the coals (or the unlit side of a gas grill). Grill, covered, until the top of the pizza is bubbly, 6 to 8 minutes. Remove from the grill. Repeat with the remaining pizza dough, sauce, cheese, red onion, sausage, bell pepper, and corn. Garnish the pizzas with sliced scallions.

CAROLINA WHITE CLAM PIZZA

SERVES 6 (TWO 10-INCH PIZZAS)

Hands-On: 55 minutes | Total: 6 hours, including 5 hours making and rising the dough

While New Haven, Connecticut, may be the birthplace of the white clam pie, I prefer to source my seafood as close to home as possible, so briny sweet clams from the Carolinas are often my go-tos. If you can't get littlenecks, buy the freshest type of clams you can find and chop them into bite-size pieces.

Coarse cornmeal, for the work surface

2 (12-ounce) dough portions from Master Pizza Dough (recipe follows), stretched into two 11-inch rounds

4 tablespoons olive oil

5 ounces pecorino Romano cheese, finely grated (about 2 cups)

36 littleneck clams (about 3 pounds), shucked

3 teaspoons finely chopped garlic (from 4 medium cloves)

1 teaspoon chopped fresh oregano

1　Open the bottom vent of a charcoal grill completely. Light a charcoal chimney starter filled with charcoal. When the coals are covered with gray ash, pour them evenly onto the bottom grate of the grill, and then push to one side of the grill. Adjust the vents as needed to maintain an internal temperature of around 500°F. Coat the top grate with oil; place on the grill. (If using a gas grill, preheat to very high [500°F and up] on one side.)

2　Sprinkle a pizza peel with cornmeal; place one stretched dough round on the peel. Brush with 1 tablespoon of the oil. Sprinkle with 1 cup of the cheese, 18 clams, 1½ teaspoons of the garlic, and ½ teaspoon of the oregano. Drizzle with 1 tablespoon of the oil. Slide the pizza onto the oiled grates directly over the side with the coals (or the lit side of a gas grill). Grill, uncovered, until the bottom of the crust is golden brown and charred in spots, 1 to 2 minutes. Move the pizza to the oiled grates over the side without the coals (or the unlit side of a gas grill). Grill, covered, until the dough is crispy on the bottom and the cheese is melted, 8 to 10 minutes. Remove from the grill. Repeat with the remaining pizza dough, oil, cheese, clams, garlic, and oregano.

MASTER PIZZA DOUGH

Makes 2 (12-ounce) portions pizza dough

1 cup warm (100° to 110°F) water

2 tablespoons light rye flour

1 teaspoon honey

Up to 3¼ cups (about 13⅞ ounces) bread flour, plus more for the work surface

1½ teaspoons active dry yeast (from 1 envelope)

1½ teaspoons kosher salt

1 Combine the water, rye flour, honey, 1 cup of the bread flour, and 1 teaspoon of the yeast in the bowl of a heavy-duty electric mixer fitted with a dough hook; stir together until smooth with a wooden spoon. Cover and let stand at room temperature until the surface is bubbly, about 3 hours.

2 With the mixer running on low speed, gradually add the salt, 1¼ cups of the bread flour, and the remaining ½ teaspoon yeast. Increase to medium-low speed and continue mixing until the dough pulls away from sides of the bowl, about 6 minutes, adding up to 1 cup additional bread flour, as needed, until the dough is no longer wet but still slightly tacky. Transfer the dough to a lightly greased bowl. Cover and let stand at room temperature until doubled in volume, about 1 hour.

3 Transfer the dough to a work surface lightly dusted with bread flour. Divide the dough into two pieces (about 12 ounces each) and shape each into a ball. Cover with a towel and let rise until puffy, about 45 minutes.

4 Using a floured rolling pin on a floured surface, flatten and stretch the dough into a 10-inch round, about ¼ inch thick. Use immediately.

GRILLED WHOLE POMPANO

SERVES 4

Hands-On: 30 minutes | **Total:** 30 minutes

Antoine's is a storied New Orleans French Quarter establishment known throughout the world, and it was there that I first experienced this fish. Pompano, a firm, thick, pan-size white fish averaging about 2 pounds, is readily found in Atlantic and Gulf waters, as well as in Louisiana's Lake Pontchartrain. At Antoine's it is served *en papillote*, or in a parchment envelope where it steams with shrimp, crabmeat, wine, and butter. This grilled pompano is simpler yet more boldly flavored. While fennel seed is most closely associated with sausage in this country, it is delicious with grilled fish and you'll find it in seafood dishes throughout the Mediterranean. The slightly sweet, licorice flavor of the fennel seeds marries well with the tender, distinctive flavor of the smoke-kissed pompano.

2 (2-pound) whole skin-on pompano, cleaned and scaled

2 tablespoons olive oil

1 teaspoon ground fennel seeds

2 teaspoons kosher salt

1 teaspoon freshly ground black pepper

½ teaspoon crushed red pepper

6 sprigs fresh mint

1 small lemon, thinly sliced

1 garlic head, halved horizontally

1 Open the bottom vent of a charcoal grill completely. Light a charcoal chimney starter halfway filled with charcoal. When the coals are covered with gray ash, pour them onto the bottom grate of the grill. Adjust the vents as needed to maintain an internal temperature of 400° to 450°F. Coat the top grate with oil; place on the grill. (If using a gas grill, preheat to medium-high [400° to 450°F].)

2 Place the fish on a large rimmed baking sheet. Score both sides of each fish with a sharp knife, making four or five parallel cuts per side. Rub the fish evenly with the oil. Stir together the fennel, salt, black pepper, and crushed red pepper in a small bowl. Sprinkle the mixture on the surface and in the cavity of each fish. Stuff the cavities evenly with the mint, lemon slices, and garlic.

3 Transfer the fish to the oiled grates. Grill, covered, until a thermometer inserted in the thickest portion of the fish registers 140°F, 5 to 6 minutes per side. Transfer to a serving platter and serve.

REDFISH ON THE HALF SHELL

SERVES 4

Hands-On: 25 minutes | Total: 25 minutes

There is perhaps no better-tasting game fish than redfish, aka red drum. Found in Gulf waters, this fighting fish is a sportsman's favorite that was long considered a trash fish. But then, in the 1980s, Chef Paul Prudhomme's famous blackened redfish recipe spread like wildfire across the country. Soon after, the species was almost extinct. Fortunately the redfish population is bountiful again, so catch them if you can, and keep inside the limits! Redfish have dense skin with large scales, so they are good for cooking skin-on to more easily remove the flesh from the skin after cooking. Or serve it "on the half shell" in its cradle of crisped-up skin. Basting the fish in seasoned butter adds loads of flavor. A squeeze of concentrated juices from grilled lemons and a splattering of chopped parsley are all that's needed to serve.

½ cup (4 ounces) unsalted butter, melted

3 tablespoons chopped fresh flat-leaf parsley, plus more for garnish

2 tablespoons Cajun seasoning (such as Slap Ya Mama; see Resources, page 299)

1 tablespoon chopped garlic (from 3 medium cloves)

1 tablespoon fresh lemon juice (from 1 lemon)

1½ teaspoons kosher salt

1 teaspoon freshly ground black pepper

4 (10-ounce) skin-on redfish fillets, scales left on

2 lemons, halved crosswise

1 Open the bottom vent of a charcoal grill completely. Light a charcoal chimney starter filled with charcoal. When the coals are covered with gray ash, pour them evenly onto the bottom grate of the grill. Adjust the vents as needed to maintain an internal temperature of 350° to 400°F. Coat the top grate with oil; place on the grill. (If using a gas grill, preheat to medium [350° to 400°F].)

2 Stir together the butter, parsley, Cajun seasoning, garlic, lemon juice, salt, and pepper in a bowl. Place the redfish, skin-side down, on the oiled grates; brush with half of the butter mixture. Grill, covered and basting occasionally with the remaining butter mixture, until the fish is cooked through, 12 to 15 minutes.

3 While the redfish cooks, place the lemon halves, cut-side down, on the oiled grates. Grill until the lemons are lightly charred and start to release their juices, 4 to 5 minutes. Garnish the redfish with the chopped parsley and serve with the grilled lemon halves.

GRILLED SALMON WITH CREAMY CUCUMBER RELISH

SERVES 4

Hands-On: 25 minutes | Total: 35 minutes

Its richness and meaty texture make salmon one of the easier varieties of fish to grill. The trick is to simply let the fillets be after placing them on the grates. Allow time and temperature to do the work for you and you won't need to worry about the fish sticking. Instead you'll have uniform crispy skin and moist and tender fish. A cool, creamy, crunchy cucumber relish flavored with dill is a natural with grilled salmon.

4 (6-ounce) skin-on salmon fillets

1 tablespoon olive oil

1 teaspoon freshly ground black pepper

2 teaspoons kosher salt

½ cup plain whole-milk Greek yogurt

¼ cup whole buttermilk

¼ cup finely chopped fresh dill

1 small garlic clove, grated (½ teaspoon)

2 teaspoons grated lemon zest plus 1 tablespoon fresh juice (from 1 lemon)

1 cup chopped seeded peeled cucumber (from 1 [8-ounce] cucumber)

¼ cup finely chopped red onion (from 1 [3-ounce] onion)

Extra-virgin olive oil

1. Brush the salmon with the olive oil and sprinkle evenly with the pepper and 1 teaspoon of the salt. Let stand at room temperature for 20 minutes.

2. Meanwhile, stir together the yogurt, buttermilk, dill, garlic, lemon zest and lemon juice, and remaining 1 teaspoon salt in a bowl. Refrigerate until ready to use.

3. Open the bottom vent of a charcoal grill completely. Light a charcoal chimney starter halfway filled with charcoal. When the coals are covered with gray ash, pour them onto the bottom grate of the grill, and then push to one side of the grill. Adjust the vents as needed to maintain an internal temperature of 400° to 450°F. Coat the top grate with oil; place on the grill. (If using a gas grill, preheat to medium-high [400° to 450°F] on one side.)

4. Place the salmon, skin-side down, on the oiled grates directly over the side with the coals (or the lit side of a gas grill). Grill, covered, until grill marks appear, about 4 minutes. Carefully turn each fillet over with a fish spatula and move to the oiled grates over the side without the coals (or the unlit side of a gas grill). Grill, covered, until just cooked through, about 3 minutes. Transfer to a plate lined with paper towels and let rest for 5 minutes.

5. While the fish rests, add the cucumber and onion to the yogurt-dill mixture and stir to combine. Place a salmon fillet on each of four plates and spoon ½ cup cucumber relish on top of each. Drizzle with extra-virgin olive oil.

SMOKED GREEK RIBS

SERVES 6

Hands-On: 30 minutes | Total: 2 hours 30 minutes

Alabama is famous for having some of the best 'cue in the BBQ belt. In addition to the state's creamy white sauce for barbecue chicken, Greek immigrants to Alabama are credited with cooking up some of the best ribs around. Cooked over hardwood charcoal or wood fires, the heavily dry-rubbed ribs are fall-off-the-bone tender, tangy, and divine. The rules for basting the ribs with the vinegar and honey mixture are loose, but if you want my rule, I say to baste when you pop off the top of each fresh cold beer.

5 teaspoons kosher salt

4 teaspoons grated lemon zest (from 2 lemons)

4 teaspoons dried oregano

4 teaspoons garlic powder

2 teaspoons crushed red pepper

2 (3-pound) slabs St. Louis–style pork spareribs

½ cup red wine vinegar

2 tablespoons honey

1 teaspoon freshly ground black pepper

1   Stir together the salt, lemon zest, oregano, garlic powder, and crushed red pepper in a bowl. Rub the mixture evenly over the ribs. Whisk together the vinegar, honey, and black pepper in a separate bowl.

2   Open the bottom vent of a charcoal grill completely. Light a charcoal chimney starter filled halfway with charcoal. When the coals are covered with gray ash, pour them onto the bottom grate of the grill, and then push to one side of the grill. Adjust the vents as needed to maintain an internal temperature of 350° to 400°F. Coat the top grate with oil; place on the grill. (If using a gas grill, preheat to medium [350° to 400°F] on one side.)

3   Place the ribs, meaty-side down, on the oiled grates directly over the side with the coals (or the lit side of a gas grill). Grill, covered, until lightly browned and charred, about 15 minutes, turning once halfway through cook time. Move the ribs to the oiled grates over the side without the coals (or the unlit side of a gas grill). Grill, covered and brushing occasionally with the vinegar mixture, until a thermometer inserted in thickest portion of the ribs registers 195°F, 1 hour and 30 minutes to 1 hour and 45 minutes. Transfer the ribs to a cutting board and let rest for 10 to 15 minutes. Cut into individual ribs.

COUNTRY-STYLE RIBS WITH PEACH SALSA

SERVES 6

Hands-On: 30 minutes | **Total:** 1 hour 45 minutes

It's a bit of a misnomer to call these *ribs* since they are actually cut from the blade end of the loin. But like pork butt (shoulder), sometimes having a strange name is a good thing, especially when it conjures up delicious food. The smoky, tender grilled pork is mouthwatering on its own, but it's out of sight with a refreshing, spicy-sweet salsa served on the side.

3 pounds bone-in country-style pork ribs

2 teaspoons paprika

2¼ teaspoons kosher salt

1½ teaspoons freshly ground black pepper

2 cups chopped peeled peaches (about 3 medium peaches)

1 cup chopped seeded cucumber (about 1 medium cucumber)

½ cup diced red onion (1 small onion)

¼ cup fresh lime juice (from 2 large limes)

¼ cup extra-virgin olive oil

3 tablespoons chopped fresh cilantro

3 tablespoons thinly sliced fresh mint

2 teaspoons finely chopped unseeded jalapeño chile (from 1 medium jalapeño)

1 Open the bottom vent of a charcoal grill completely. Light a charcoal chimney starter filled halfway with charcoal. When the coals are covered with gray ash, pour them onto the bottom grate of the grill, and then push to one side of the grill. Adjust vents as needed to maintain an internal temperature of 350° to 400°F. Coat the top grate with oil; place on the grill. (If using a gas grill, preheat to medium [350° to 400°F] on one side.)

2 Sprinkle the ribs evenly with the paprika, 1½ teaspoons of the salt, and 1 teaspoon of the black pepper. Place the ribs on the oiled grates directly over the side with the coals (or the lit side of a gas grill). Grill, covered, until slightly browned and charred, about 15 minutes, turning once halfway through cook time. Move the ribs to the oiled grates over the side without the coals (or the unlit side of a gas grill). Grill, covered, until a thermometer inserted in thickest portion of the ribs registers 195°F, 1 hour to 1 hour and 15 minutes. Transfer the ribs to a cutting board and let rest for 10 minutes. Cut into individual ribs.

3 Toss together the peaches, cucumber, onion, lime juice, oil, cilantro, mint, jalapeño, and remaining ¾ teaspoon salt and ½ teaspoon pepper in a bowl. Serve the salsa alongside the ribs.

GRILLED PORK BELLY WITH PEACH VINEGAR SAUCE

SERVES 6

Hands-On: 35 minutes | Total: 4 hours

Pork belly is one of the foods of the gods. Pork belly becomes bacon when it is cured and smoked, and of course, it is difficult to overstate the popularity of bacon. But not to be overlooked, the fatty, tender uncured belly is rendered heavenly over the fire and flames of the grill. The fat melts with the sweet spices and creates a caramelized crust, or *bark*, that is irresistible. A sweet-tart stovetop peach vinegar sauce adds a bright note that cuts through the richness of the meat and creates a symphony of porky deliciousness.

2 medium white onions (about 1 pound), quartered

4 celery stalks, cut into 2-inch pieces

3 medium carrots, cut into 2-inch pieces

1 tablespoon paprika

1 tablespoon freshly ground black pepper

2 teaspoons onion powder

1½ tablespoons plus ¼ teaspoon kosher salt

1 (4-pound) pork belly

1 cup packed light brown sugar

⅓ cup water

1 cup apple cider vinegar

1 cup finely chopped peaches (from 2 [6-ounce] unpeeled peaches)

1 Open the bottom vent of a charcoal grill completely. Light a charcoal chimney starter filled with charcoal. When the coals are covered with gray ash, pour them onto the bottom grate of the grill. Adjust the vents as needed to maintain an internal temperature of 450° to 500°F. (If using a gas grill, preheat to high [450° to 500°F].)

2 Place the onions, celery, and carrots in a high-sided roasting pan (just large enough to fit the pork belly). Stir together the paprika, pepper, onion powder, and the 1½ tablespoons salt in a small bowl. Score the skin side of the pork with a sharp knife, making ¾-inch-deep slits down the length of the pork, leaving about ¾ inch between each slit. Rub the paprika mixture over the surface and into the slits of the pork. Place the pork, skin-side up, on top of the vegetables in the roasting pan. Place on the unoiled grill grates. Cook, covered, for 20 minutes. Adjust vents as needed to reduce grill internal temperature to 300° to 350°F. (If using a gas grill, reduce temperature to medium-low [300° to 350°F].) Cook, covered, until the pork is very tender and the fat is dark brown and crispy, about 3 hours. Transfer the pork to a cutting board; discard the vegetables.

3 Meanwhile, combine the sugar and water in a saucepan on a stovetop over medium-high heat. Cook, stirring occasionally, until the sugar dissolves, about 5 minutes. Continue cooking, undisturbed, until the mixture turns a dark caramel brown, about 5 minutes. Add the vinegar all at once; use caution as the mixture will splatter. Bring to a boil over medium-high heat. Add the peaches and cook, uncovered and stirring occasionally, until the sauce is reduced and slightly thickened, about 5 minutes. Strain the sauce through a fine-mesh strainer into a heatproof bowl; discard the solids. Stir in the remaining ¼ teaspoon salt. Cut the pork into 1-inch chunks and drizzle with the peach sauce.

SORGHUM-GLAZED PORK CHOPS WITH COUSCOUS

SERVES 4

Hands-On: 35 minutes | Total: 3 hours 30 minutes, including 2 hours brining

When it comes to deliciously tender, juicy pork chops, a brine is a game-changer. If time is of the essence, you can skip the brine, but be sure your grilling game is on point or you risk drying out the meat. A sweet and spicy sorghum glaze guarantees these chops will be top-notch. Fruity, nutty couscous provides an ideal backdrop to absorb all the juicy drippings from the chops.

4 cups water

1 cup granulated sugar

1¼ cups apple cider vinegar

½ cup plus 3½ teaspoons kosher salt

4 double-cut, bone-in pork loin chops (1¼ pounds), frenched

4 tablespoons olive oil

2½ teaspoons freshly ground black pepper

1 cup sorghum syrup

1 medium leek, chopped (about 1 cup)

1¼ cups low-sodium chicken stock

1 cup uncooked couscous

1 cup orange segments (from 1 large orange)

½ cup pomegranate arils

½ cup slivered almonds, toasted

⅓ cup chopped fresh flat-leaf parsley

1 Whisk together the water, sugar, 1 cup of the vinegar, and ½ cup of the salt in a bowl until dissolved. Place the pork in a large ziplock plastic freezer bag or brining bag; add the brining mixture and seal the bag. Refrigerate for 2 to 3 hours.

2 Remove the pork from the brine and discard the brine. Pat the pork dry with paper towels. Rub the pork with 2 tablespoons of the oil and sprinkle with 2 teaspoons of the salt and 1 teaspoon of the pepper. Let stand at room temperature for 30 minutes.

3 Meanwhile, whisk together the sorghum syrup, 1 teaspoon of the pepper, and the remaining ¼ cup vinegar in a bowl. Measure and transfer ½ cup sorghum mixture to a small bowl and set aside for serving. Reserve the remaining sorghum mixture for brushing the pork.

4 Open the bottom vent of a charcoal grill completely. Light a charcoal chimney starter filled with charcoal. When the coals are covered with gray ash, pour them onto the bottom grate of the grill, and then push to one side of the grill. Adjust the vents as needed to maintain an internal temperature of 350° to 400°F. Coat the top grate with oil; place on the grill. (If using a gas grill, preheat to medium [350° to 400°F] on one side.)

5 Place the pork on the oiled grates directly over the side with the coals (or the lit side of a gas grill). Grill, covered, until a thermometer inserted in thickest portion of the pork registers 125°F, about 12 minutes per side. (If the pork starts to burn, move to the side of the grill without the coals [or the unlit side of a gas grill].) Brush the pork with the sorghum mixture reserved for brushing; continue grilling, turning occasionally, until the pork is glazed and a thermometer inserted in thickest portion of the pork registers 135°F for medium, 6 to 8 minutes. Transfer to a serving platter and brush with ½ cup of the sorghum mixture reserved for serving. Tent loosely with foil and let rest for 15 minutes. (Internal temperature will increase to 145°F while resting.)

6 While the pork rests, heat the remaining 2 tablespoons oil in a small saucepan on a stovetop over medium-high heat. Add the leek and cook, stirring occasionally, until softened, about 5 minutes. Add the stock and bring to a boil over high. Stir in the couscous and remaining 1½ teaspoons salt and ½ teaspoon pepper; cover and remove from the heat. Let stand for 5 minutes. Fluff the couscous with a fork and stir in the orange segments, pomegranate arils, almonds, and parsley. Serve the couscous alongside the pork chops.

PORCHETTA

SERVES 16

Hands-On: 35 minutes | Total: 11 hours 35 minutes, including 8 hours chilling

Be forewarned: If you serve this at your next dinner party, odds are you will also be hosting the next dinner party, and the next…and so on. This showstopper is a host's best-kept secret because you do most of the prep the day before, and then enjoy your guests while the grill works its magic. It's impressive to set this grilled beauty on the table—then slice, serve, and watch your guests swoon.

2 tablespoons fennel seeds

1½ tablespoons cumin seeds

1 tablespoon coriander seeds

¼ cup country-style Dijon mustard

¼ cup olive oil

10 medium garlic cloves, grated on a Microplane (2 tablespoons)

3 tablespoons chopped fresh rosemary

3 tablespoons chopped fresh thyme

2 tablespoons kosher salt

1½ tablespoons freshly ground black pepper

2 teaspoons crushed red pepper

1 (2- to 3-pound) boneless center-cut pork loin roast, trimmed

1 (5- to 6-pound) skin-on pork belly

1 Toast the fennel, cumin, and coriander in a small skillet over medium heat, stirring occasionally, until fragrant, 1 to 2 minutes. Grind the spices using a mortar and pestle, or place in a small ziplock plastic bag and crush with the bottom of a heavy skillet. Transfer the mixture to a small bowl and stir in the mustard, oil, garlic, rosemary, thyme, salt, black pepper, and crushed red pepper. Set aside.

2 Using a long, sharp knife, slice the pork loin horizontally in half (lengthwise) without cutting through the other side, leaving ½ inch on the uncut side. Open the loin to lay flat (like an opened book). Place the loin between two plastic wrap sheets. Using the flat side of a meat mallet or the back of a small, heavy skillet, pound the loin to a ½-inch thickness that is about 10 inches square. Spread half of the mustard mixture evenly over the loin, leaving a ½-inch border at the edges. Tightly roll up the loin.

3 Place the pork belly, skin-side up, on a cutting board. Pierce the skin all over with the tip of a paring knife or skewer. Flip the belly and score the flesh, ⅓ inch deep, in a checkerboard pattern. Rub the remaining mustard mixture over the flesh side of the belly. Place the rolled loin lengthwise down the middle of the belly. Roll the belly up around the loin and tie with kitchen twine at 2-inch intervals. Place the porchetta on a wire rack set over a rimmed baking sheet. Chill, uncovered, for 8 hours or overnight.

4 Let the porchetta stand at room temperature for 1 hour before grilling. Meanwhile, open the bottom vent of a charcoal grill completely. Light a charcoal chimney starter filled with charcoal. When the coals are covered with gray ash, pour them onto the bottom grate of the grill, and then push to one side of the grill. Adjust the vents as needed to maintain an internal temperature of 300° to 350°F. Coat the top grate with oil; place on the grill. (If using a gas grill, preheat to medium-low [300° to 350°F] on one side.)

5 Place the porchetta on the oiled grates over the side without the coals (or the unlit side of a gas grill). Grill, covered and rotating occasionally, until a thermometer inserted in thickest portion of the pork registers 125°F, 2 to 2½ hours. Transfer the porchetta to the oiled grates directly over the side with the coals (or the lit side of a gas grill). Grill, covered and turning occasionally, until the skin is golden brown and crispy and a thermometer inserted in thickest portion of the pork registers 140°F, about 15 minutes. Transfer to a cutting board and loosely cover with aluminum foil. Let rest for 20 minutes. (Internal temperature will increase to 145°F while resting.) Remove and discard the twine. Slice the pork into 1-inch slices.

COUNTRY SAUSAGE BOLOGNESE

SERVES 4

Hands-On: 1 hour | Total: 2 hours 30 minutes

The key to this dish is allowing the flavors of the wine, consommé, and tomato paste to cook down and concentrate, uncovered on the grill, to get a saucy, smoky sauce that cloaks the pappardelle pasta. Using a country-style breakfast sausage infuses the sauce with just the right balance of seasoning—the traditional sage, thyme, and fennel—to make this a comfort classic.

1 pound ground breakfast sausage

1 cup finely chopped sweet onion (from 1 [10-ounce] onion)

1 cup finely chopped carrots (from 3 medium carrots)

3 large garlic cloves, smashed

1 (6-ounce) can tomato paste

3 bay leaves

1 teaspoon kosher salt

1 teaspoon freshly ground black pepper

½ teaspoon ground cinnamon

1 (750-ml) bottle dry red wine

2 cups water

1 (10½-ounce) can beef consommé or beef stock

16 ounces uncooked pappardelle pasta

3 ounces pecorino Romano cheese, grated (about ¾ cup)

2 tablespoons finely chopped fresh flat-leaf parsley

1 Open the bottom vent of a charcoal grill completely. Light a charcoal chimney starter filled with charcoal. When the coals are covered with gray ash, pour them onto the bottom grate of the grill. Adjust the vents as needed to maintain an internal temperature of 400° to 450°F. (If using a gas grill, preheat to medium-high [400° to 450°F].)

2 Place a large Dutch oven on the unoiled grates. Place the sausage in the Dutch oven and cook, stirring occasionally, until cooked through and crispy bits have formed on the bottom, about 8 minutes. Move the sausage to the side of the pot and add the onion, carrots, and garlic. Cook, stirring occasionally, until tender, 5 to 6 minutes. Add the tomato paste, bay leaves, salt, pepper, and cinnamon; cook, stirring often, for 1 minute. Add the wine and let the mixture come to a boil. Cook, stirring occasionally, until the liquid evaporates by half, about 20 minutes. Stir in the water and consommé. Adjust the vents as needed to reduce grill internal temperature to 300° to 350°F. (If using a gas grill, reduce temperature to medium-low [300° to 350°F].) Cook, uncovered, until the mixture has thickened and becomes saucy, about 1½ hours. Remove from the heat, discard the bay leaves, and cover to keep warm.

3 Prepare the pasta according to package directions. Add the cooked pasta to the sausage mixture in the Dutch oven and toss to coat. Sprinkle with the cheese and parsley.

CHILI ON THE GRILL

SERVES 6

Hands-On: 1 hour 20 minutes | Total: 1 hour 20 minutes

There is chili, and then there is chili from the grill. Cooking the ingredients in an open searing-hot Dutch oven in a covered grill allows the ingredients to get both a flavorful browning without losing any natural juices to the flames and plenty of smoky flavor. The result is a complex, delicious chili. It is formidable on its own in a bowl with your preferred garnishes, or as the key component of the Chili Cheese Dogs on page 225.

2 tablespoons olive oil

1 medium (8-ounce) yellow onion, chopped (1 cup)

1½ tablespoons minced garlic (from 4 medium cloves)

2 pounds 80/20 lean ground beef

2½ tablespoons chili powder

2 teaspoons kosher salt

1½ teaspoons ground cumin

1½ teaspoons ground cinnamon

½ teaspoon unsweetened cocoa

¼ teaspoon ground allspice

¼ teaspoon cayenne pepper

1 (15-ounce) can tomato sauce

1 cup water

1 tablespoon red wine vinegar

1 Open the bottom vent of a charcoal grill completely. Light a charcoal chimney starter filled with charcoal. When the coals are covered with gray ash, pour them onto the bottom grate of the grill. Adjust the vents as needed to maintain an internal temperature of 400° to 450°F. (If using a gas grill, preheat to medium-high [400° to 450°F].)

2 Place a cast-iron Dutch oven on the unoiled grates. Add the oil and heat until shimmering. Add the onion and cook, stirring occasionally, until softened, about 5 minutes. Add the garlic and cook, stirring constantly, until fragrant, about 1 minute. Add the ground beef and cook, breaking up chunks with a wooden spoon, until browned, 8 to 10 minutes. Stir in the chili powder, salt, cumin, cinnamon, cocoa, allspice, and cayenne. Cook, stirring constantly, until fragrant, about 1 minute. Stir in the tomato sauce, water, and vinegar and allow the mixture to come to a simmer.

3 Adjust the vents as needed to reduce grill internal temperature to 250° to 300°F. (If using a gas grill, reduce temperature to low [250° to 300°F].) Cook, covered and stirring occasionally, until the meat is tender and the sauce has thickened, about 1 hour.

BEEF KAFTA WITH QUICK LABNEH

SERVES 4

Hands-On: 20 minutes | Total: 50 minutes

My mama's side of the family hails from Beirut, immigrating several generations ago to south Georgia and beyond. We might have settled in the South and learned to make perfect fried chicken, but we also brought plenty of recipe standards from the old country. The combo of onion, parsley, garlic, and allspice mixed into beef is an amalgam of flavors that transports me to my childhood. The recent accessibility of quality, thick Greek yogurt makes the process of churning out *labneh*—a tangy Middle Eastern cream cheese—achievable. A shmear of labneh on warm, crusty grilled flatbread topped with the savory kafta is unbelievably delicious. Sub ground lamb or even venison for the beef depending on your tastes and the season.

1 cup plain whole-milk Greek yogurt

2 tablespoons fresh lemon juice (from 1 lemon)

1 teaspoon kosher salt

1 pound 80/20 lean ground beef

¼ cup finely chopped onion (from 1 small onion)

2 tablespoons chopped fresh flat-leaf parsley, plus more for garnish

3 medium garlic cloves, grated on a Microplane (2 teaspoons)

½ teaspoon ground allspice

½ teaspoon freshly ground black pepper

4 (6-inch-round) flatbreads (such as Toufayan)

2 tablespoons olive oil

1 Place the yogurt in a fine-mesh strainer set over a bowl and drain in the refrigerator for 30 minutes. Discard the liquid in the bowl. Transfer the drained yogurt to a small bowl and stir in the lemon juice and ¼ teaspoon of the salt. Cover and refrigerate until ready to use, or up to 1 week.

2 Open the bottom vent of a charcoal grill completely. Light a charcoal chimney starter filled with charcoal. When the coals are covered with gray ash, pour them onto the bottom grate of the grill. Adjust the vents as needed to maintain an internal temperature of 350° to 400°F. Coat the top grate with oil; place on the grill. (If using a gas grill, preheat to medium [350° to 400°F].)

3 Stir together the ground chuck, onion, parsley, garlic, allspice, pepper, and remaining ¾ teaspoon salt in a bowl. Divide into four equal portions. Shape each portion into a 5-inch-long log around one (8- to 12-inch) skewer.

4 Place the skewers on the oiled grates. Grill, uncovered and turning every 5 minutes, until charred on all sides and a thermometer inserted in thickest portion of the meat registers 160°F, 15 to 20 minutes. Transfer the skewers to a serving platter.

5 Brush both sides of the flatbreads evenly with the oil. Place on the oiled grates and grill, uncovered, until lightly charred, 1 to 2 minutes per side. Serve alongside the skewers and yogurt sauce and garnish with parsley.

BBQ MEATLOAF

SERVES 6

Hands-On: 25 minutes | Total: 3 hours

Meatloaf is so comforting and homey. My wife, Callie, makes it whenever the temp drops and evenings become long. This recipe involves a two-step process of cooking the loaf to temperature, and then searing thick slices to develop grill marks and a flavorful char on the exterior while maintaining tender deliciousness inside. Meatloaf really shines the next day too. I love it cold, sandwiched between slices of white bread with a slice or two of American cheese. Oh, and don't forget the potato chips.

2 large eggs

1¼ cups fresh breadcrumbs (about 3 ounces)

¾ cup finely chopped white onion (from 1 large onion)

¼ cup whole milk

1 tablespoon Worcestershire sauce

1½ teaspoons kosher salt

1 teaspoon freshly ground black pepper

¾ cup Memphis-style barbecue sauce

1 pound 80/20 lean ground beef

8 ounces ground pork

1 Stir together the eggs, breadcrumbs, onion, milk, Worcestershire sauce, salt, pepper, and ¼ cup of the barbecue sauce in a large bowl. Let stand until the breadcrumbs soften, about 5 minutes. Add the beef and pork, stirring gently to combine. Shape the mixture into a 4- x 8-inch loaf and place on an ungreased sheet of aluminum foil.

2 Open the bottom vent of a charcoal grill completely. Light a charcoal chimney starter filled with charcoal. When the coals are covered with gray ash, pour them onto the bottom grate of the grill, and then push to one side of the grill. Adjust the vents as needed to maintain an internal temperature of 350° to 400°F. (If using a gas grill, preheat to medium [350° to 400°F] on one side.)

3 Place the foil with the meatloaf on the unoiled grates over the side without the coals (or the unlit side of a gas grill). Grill, covered, until a thermometer inserted in thickest portion of the meatloaf registers 155°F, 1½ to 2 hours. Remove from the grill and let stand for 45 minutes.

4 Refill the charcoal chimney and light. When the briquettes are covered with gray ash, pour them onto the bottom grate of the grill. Adjust the vents as needed to maintain an internal temperature of 450° to 500°F. Coat the top rack with oil; place on the grill. (If using a gas grill, preheat to high [450° to 500°F].)

5 Cut the meatloaf crosswise into six even slices. Place the slices on the oiled grates and grill, uncovered, until grill marks appear, about 3 minutes per side. Brush the slices evenly on top with the remaining ½ cup barbecue sauce and grill for 1 minute per side.

BEEF FILLET STROGANOFF

SERVES 4

Hands-On: 45 minutes | Total: 45 minutes

I spent much of my 1980's childhood hanging with my best pal, R.C., playing our favorite game, 1942, on the Nintendo. When dinner rolled around, R.C.'s mom, Jamie, would often serve up a heaping bowl of one of my favorites—beef stroganoff. It was likely the boxed "helper" version, but I always stuck around for that creamy, sour cream–soaked pasta laced with tender beef. This is a grown-up version that's got that comforting, classic taste, only elevated by top-notch ingredients. Every bite of this is yummy nostalgia for me.

4 (5-ounce) beef tenderloin filets mignons (1½ inches thick)

1¼ teaspoons kosher salt

¾ teaspoon freshly ground black pepper

2 tablespoons salted butter

8 ounces sliced fresh button mushrooms

¾ cup (6 ounces) dry red wine

1 tablespoon plus 2 teaspoons all-purpose flour

2½ cups beef stock

2 teaspoons Dijon mustard

⅓ cup sour cream

16 ounces uncooked campanelle pasta

2 teaspoons chopped fresh dill

1. Open the bottom vent of a charcoal grill completely. Light a charcoal chimney starter filled with charcoal. When the coals are covered with gray ash, pour them onto the bottom grate of the grill. Adjust the vents as needed to maintain an internal temperature of 400° to 450°F. Coat the top grate with oil; place on the grill. (If using a gas grill, preheat to medium-high [400° to 450°F].)

2. Sprinkle the filets with 1 teaspoon of the salt and ½ teaspoon of the pepper. Place the beef on the oiled grates and grill, covered, until a thermometer inserted in thickest portion of the beef registers 140°F, 4 to 5 minutes per side. Transfer to a cutting board and let rest for 15 minutes. Thinly slice against the grain.

3. While the beef rests, place a large grill-safe skillet on the oiled grates. Add the butter and cook until melted. Add the mushrooms and cook, stirring occasionally, until well browned, 6 to 8 minutes. Add the wine and cook, stirring occasionally, until almost evaporated, about 5 minutes. Add the flour and cook, stirring often, for 1 minute. Stir in the stock, mustard, and remaining ¼ teaspoon each salt and pepper and let the mixture come to a boil. Boil, stirring occasionally, until slightly thickened, 2 to 3 minutes. Remove from the heat and let stand for 5 minutes. Stir in the sour cream and cover to keep warm.

4. Prepare the pasta according to package directions. Add the pasta to the sauce in the skillet and toss to coat. Divide the pasta evenly among four bowls. Top evenly with the sliced beef and sprinkle with the dill.

DESSERTS

GRILLED WATERMELON 277

GRILLED STRAWBERRIES WITH CHOCOLATE-AMARETTO SAUCE 278

GRILLED FIGS WITH WHIPPED MASCARPONE 280

GRILLED PEAR-GORGONZOLA TOASTS 283

GRILLED-DOUGHNUT ICE CREAM SANDWICHES 285

GRILLED SALTED CARAMEL-PECAN BREAD PUDDING 286

GRILLED CHOCOLATE LAVA CAKES 289 | GRILLED CHOCOLATE POUND CAKE 290

GRILLED BANANAS À LA MODE WITH CHOCOLATE DRIZZLE AND PEANUTS 293

GRILLED S'MORES 294 | GRILLED PEACH COBBLER 296

GRILLED WATERMELON

SERVES 8

Hands-On: 10 minutes | Total: 10 minutes

The concentrated sweetness and hint of smoke that juicy melon gets from a brief rest on a hot grill adds surprising pizzazz to a refreshing dessert that is big on flavor and short on hassle. Sweeten things up, in a healthy way, by adding a rich, creamy dollop of vanilla Greek yogurt. The best desserts are all about sensory balance—here, hot meets cold, and creamy and juicy counter crunchy and chewy.

8 (1-inch-thick) seedless watermelon wedges with rinds

½ cup vanilla whole-milk Greek yogurt

¼ cup roasted salted pistachios, roughly chopped

2 teaspoons crystallized ginger, finely chopped

½ teaspoon grated orange zest (from 1 orange)

Freshly ground black pepper

1 Open the bottom and top vents of a charcoal grill completely. Light a charcoal chimney starter filled halfway with charcoal. When the coals are covered with gray ash, pour them onto the bottom grate of the grill. Adjust the vents as needed to maintain an internal temperature of 450° to 500°F. Coat the top grate with oil; place on the grill. (If using a gas grill, preheat to high [450° to 500°F].)

2 Place the watermelon wedges on the oiled grates; grill, uncovered, until grill marks appear, 1 to 2 minutes per side.

3 Place a grilled watermelon wedge on each of eight serving plates. Top the wedges evenly with the yogurt, pistachios, ginger, and orange zest. Garnish with pepper.

GRILLED STRAWBERRIES WITH CHOCOLATE-AMARETTO SAUCE

SERVES 4

Hands-On: 15 minutes | Total: 15 minutes

Grilled sweet, slightly tart strawberries combined with a decadent amaretto-spiked chocolate sauce is one of the best ways to experience the delicious harmony of the classic pairing. Enjoy with a flute of Champagne, rosé, or prosecco for a sparkling finish.

16 medium-size fresh strawberries (about 13 ounces), hulled

1 tablespoon honey

4 ounces bittersweet chocolate, roughly chopped

¼ cup heavy cream

1 tablespoon light corn syrup

1 tablespoon amaretto (almond liqueur)

¼ teaspoon kosher salt

2 tablespoons chopped almonds, toasted

1 Open the bottom and top vents of a charcoal grill completely. Light a charcoal chimney starter filled halfway with charcoal. When the coals are covered with gray ash, pour them onto the bottom grate of the grill. Adjust the vents as needed to maintain an internal temperature of 450° to 500°F. Coat the top grate with oil; place on the grill. (If using a gas grill, preheat to high [450° to 500°F].)

2 Thread four strawberries, lengthwise through the hulled stems, on each of four (8-inch-long) skewers. Brush the strawberries evenly with the honey. Place the skewers on the oiled grates and grill, uncovered and turning occasionally, until grill marks appear, 1 to 2 minutes total. Arrange the skewers on a serving platter.

3 Stir together the chocolate, cream, corn syrup, amaretto, and salt in a medium microwavable bowl. Microwave on HIGH until melted and smooth, about 1 minute, stirring after 30 seconds. Drizzle 1 tablespoon chocolate sauce over each skewer; sprinkle evenly with the almonds. Pour the remaining chocolate sauce into a small bowl and serve with the skewers for dipping.

GRILLED FIGS WITH WHIPPED MASCARPONE

SERVES 6

Hands-On: 10 minutes | Total: 10 minutes

Sweet and jammy ripe figs are even more delicious when they're flame kissed. Any fruit grilled, in my opinion, is always a safe bet for dessert, but I especially enjoy the flavor of figs combined with creamy whipped mascarpone.

12 medium-size fresh figs (about 13 ounces), halved lengthwise

8 ounces mascarpone cheese

¼ cup heavy cream

1½ tablespoons honey

2 teaspoons molasses

¼ cup pomegranate arils

¼ teaspoon flaky sea salt

Fresh mint leaves

1   Open the bottom and top vents of a charcoal grill completely. Light a charcoal chimney starter filled halfway with charcoal. When the coals are covered with gray ash, pour them onto the bottom grate of the grill. Adjust the vents as needed to maintain an internal temperature of 400° to 450°F. Coat the top grate with oil; place on the grill. (If using a gas grill, preheat to medium-high [400° to 450°F].)

2   Place the figs, cut-side down, on the oiled grates. Grill, uncovered, until softened and lightly charred, about 3 minutes, flipping halfway through cook time. Remove from the grill.

3   Whisk together the mascarpone, cream, and honey in a medium bowl until soft peaks form, 1 to 2 minutes. Spoon ⅓ cup mixture onto each of six plates; top each with four fig halves. Drizzle the plates evenly with the molasses and sprinkle evenly with the pomegranate arils and salt. Garnish with mint.

GRILLED PEAR– GORGONZOLA TOASTS

SERVES 12

Hands-On: 22 minutes | Total: 22 minutes

Equally fitting for dessert or offered as an elegant appetizer for a group, these sweet-and-savory crostini are delicious served with an after-dinner glass of moscato.

3 firm ripe Bartlett pears, cut into ¼-inch-thick wedges

4 ounces cream cheese, softened

4 ounces Gorgonzola cheese, crumbled

4 tablespoons unsalted butter, softened

2 tablespoons dry sherry

36 French bread baguette slices, toasted

½ cup finely chopped candied pecans

2 tablespoons finely chopped fresh rosemary

¼ cup honey

1 Open the bottom and top vents of a charcoal grill completely. Light a charcoal chimney starter filled halfway with charcoal. When the coals are covered with gray ash, pour them onto the bottom grate of the grill. Adjust the vents as needed to maintain an internal temperature of 350° to 400°F. Coat the top grate with oil; place on the grill. (If using a gas grill, preheat to medium [350° to 400°F].)

2 Place the pear wedges on the oiled grates and grill, covered, until golden, 1 to 2 minutes on each side. Remove from the grill.

3 Stir together the cream cheese, Gorgonzola, butter, and sherry. Spread about ½ tablespoon of the cheese mixture on each baguette slice and top with some grilled pear. Sprinkle with the pecans and rosemary and drizzle with the honey.

GRILLED-DOUGHNUT ICE CREAM SANDWICHES

SERVES 4

Hands-On: 10 minutes | Total: 10 minutes

The stars here—leftover glazed doughnuts—get revived on the grill, warming up the glaze, softening the centers, and toasting the edges. One bite and you'll be as happy as a kid in an ice cream shop. The trick to these treats is to buy a pint-size container of ice cream, remove the carton, and literally slice the frozen cylinder into disks for four perfectly sized sandwich fillings.

4 glazed doughnuts, cut in half horizontally

1 pint ice cream of choice

Garnishes: choice of candy sprinkles, chopped toasted nuts, toasted shredded coconut, miniature chocolate chips

1 Open the bottom and top vents of a charcoal grill completely. Light a charcoal chimney starter filled halfway with charcoal. When the coals are covered with gray ash, pour them onto the bottom grate of the grill. Adjust the vents as needed to maintain an internal temperature of 300° to 350°F. Coat the top grate with oil. (If using a gas grill, preheat to medium-low [300° to 350°F].)

2 Place the doughnuts, cut-side down, on the oiled grates. Grill, uncovered, until toasted and light grill marks appear, about 2 minutes. Flip and grill until the tops begin to brown, about 30 seconds. Remove from the grill.

3 Cut the packaging away from the ice cream, exposing one large cylinder. Slice the cylinder crosswise into four even rounds. Place an ice cream slice on each bottom doughnut half; cover each with a top doughnut half. Place desired garnishes on separate small plates and roll the ice cream sandwich edges in the garnishes. Serve immediately.

GRILLED SALTED CARAMEL–PECAN BREAD PUDDING

SERVES 6

Hands-On: 45 minutes | Total: 1 hour 45 minutes

My wife gets upset with me when I throw stale bread in the yard to feed the birds. At first, I thought she'd seen one too many Hitchcock movies and was afraid of birds. But I soon realized that she was hoping I'd put that bread to use in this delicious recipe. Bread pudding is a homey comfort in heavy rotation at our house during cooler months. Truth be told, like grilling, it should be enjoyed every season of the year.

8 cups cubed (1-inch pieces) day-old brioche bread (about 10 ounces)

2 large eggs

2 large egg yolks

1½ cups half-and-half

¼ cup granulated sugar

¼ cup packed dark brown sugar

1½ teaspoons vanilla extract

½ teaspoon ground cinnamon

½ teaspoon kosher salt

1½ cups toasted pecan halves, roughly chopped

½ cup salted caramel sauce (such as Stonewall Kitchen)

1 Preheat the oven to 350°F. Arrange the bread cubes in an even layer on a large rimmed baking sheet. Bake in the preheated oven until lightly toasted, about 10 minutes. Set aside.

2 Open the bottom and top vents of a charcoal grill completely. Light a charcoal chimney starter filled with charcoal. When the coals are covered with gray ash, pour them onto the bottom grate of the grill, and then push to one side of the grill. Adjust the vents as needed to maintain an internal temperature of 350° to 400°F. (If using a gas grill, preheat to medium [350° to 400°F] on one side.)

3 Spray six (6-ounce) ramekins with cooking spray, place on a rimmed baking sheet, and set aside. Whisk together the eggs, egg yolks, half-and-half, granulated sugar, brown sugar, vanilla, cinnamon, and salt in a large bowl until smooth. Add the toasted bread cubes and toss to coat. Let the mixture stand at room temperature for 20 minutes, stirring occasionally. Stir in the pecans. Spoon the mixture evenly into the prepared ramekins.

4 Place the baking sheet with ramekins on the grates over the side without the coals (or on the unlit side of a gas grill). Grill, covered, until the bread pudding is set, about 35 minutes, rotating the baking sheet once halfway through cook time. Transfer the ramekins to a wire rack and let cool for 30 minutes. Drizzle evenly with the salted caramel sauce.

GRILLED CHOCOLATE LAVA CAKES

SERVES 6

Hands-On: 40 minutes | Total: 2 hours, including 1 hour chilling

I've yet to meet anyone who doesn't like this dessert. You get the same great *aha!* experience of the liquefied, molten chocolate as you do with an oven-cooked lava cake, but with the grill you get the smoky flavors that give the chocolate a divine complexity. I like topping mine off with a scoop or two of ice cream or even lightly sweetened whipped cream to create irresistible contrasts.

¼ cup heavy cream

8 ounces bittersweet chocolate, chopped

½ cup (4 ounces) unsalted butter

2 large eggs

2 large egg yolks

¼ cup granulated sugar

1 teaspoon vanilla extract

½ teaspoon kosher salt

3 tablespoons all-purpose flour

Vanilla ice cream

1 Combine the cream and 2 ounces of the chocolate in a small microwavable bowl. Microwave on HIGH until smooth and melted, about 45 seconds, stirring after 20 seconds. Chill the filling, uncovered, until firm, about 1 hour.

2 Open the bottom and top vents of a charcoal grill completely. Light a charcoal chimney starter filled with charcoal. When the coals are covered with gray ash, pour them onto the bottom grate of the grill, and then push to one side of the grill. Adjust the vents as needed to maintain an internal temperature of 350° to 400°F. (If using a gas grill, preheat to medium [350° to 400°F] on one side.)

3 Spray six (6-ounce) ramekins with cooking spray; place on a rimmed baking sheet and set aside. Place the butter and remaining 6 ounces chocolate in a medium microwavable bowl. Microwave on HIGH until the mixture is smooth and melted, about 1½ minutes, stirring every 30 seconds. Cool for 10 minutes.

4 Combine the eggs, egg yolks, sugar, vanilla, and salt in a medium bowl. Whisk vigorously until pale and thickened, 2 to 3 minutes. Whisk in the cooled butter-chocolate mixture. Gently fold in the flour. Spoon half of the batter evenly into the prepared ramekins. Place about 1 tablespoon of the chilled cream-chocolate filling in the center of each partially filled ramekin. Top each evenly with the remaining batter.

5 Place the baking sheet with ramekins on the grates over the side without the coals (or on the unlit side of a gas grill). Grill, covered, until the tops of cakes are set but still have a slight jiggle, about 18 minutes, rotating the sheet once halfway through cook time. Let the cakes cool slightly in the ramekins, about 5 minutes. Top with ice cream.

GRILLED CHOCOLATE POUND CAKE

SERVES 6

Hands-On: 25 minutes | Total: 3 hours, including 2½ hours baking and cooling

Let me tell you, friends, there's pound cake and then there's chocolate pound cake. It's hard to beat the ease of this recipe when the craving for dessert hits. Grilling slices of pound cake toasts the edges and adds tenderness to the center as it warms. A big ole dollop of cream and raspberries pushes this sweet ending into overdrive.

1½ cups all-purpose flour, plus more for the pan

½ cup unsweetened cocoa powder

½ teaspoon kosher salt

¼ teaspoon baking soda

1¼ cups (10 ounces) unsalted butter, softened

1½ cups granulated sugar

3 large eggs, at room temperature

1½ teaspoons vanilla extract

½ cup sour cream

¾ cup heavy cream

3 tablespoons powdered sugar, plus more for garnish

2 cups fresh raspberries

1 Preheat the oven to 325°F. Grease and flour a 9- x 5-inch loaf pan. Whisk together the flour, cocoa powder, salt, and baking soda in a medium bowl. Set aside.

2 Beat ¾ cup of the butter in the bowl of a heavy-duty stand mixer fitted with a paddle attachment on medium-high speed until smooth, 1 to 2 minutes. Gradually add the granulated sugar, beating until light and fluffy, about 3 minutes. Add the eggs, one at a time, beating until just incorporated after each addition. Stir in the vanilla. Add the flour mixture in three additions, alternating with the sour cream, beginning and ending with the flour mixture, and beating on low speed after each addition. Pour the batter into the prepared loaf pan.

3 Bake in the preheated oven until a wooden toothpick inserted in the center of the cake comes out clean, about 1 hour and 15 minutes. Cool the cake in the pan on a wire rack for 10 minutes. Remove from the loaf pan and cool completely on a wire rack, about 1 hour.

4 Open the bottom and top vents of a charcoal grill completely. Light a charcoal chimney starter filled with charcoal. When the coals are covered with gray ash, pour them onto the bottom grate of the grill. Adjust the vents as needed to maintain an internal temperature of 350° to 400°F. Coat the top grill grate with oil; place on the grill. (If using a gas grill, preheat to medium [350° to 400°F].)

5 Cut the cooled cake into twelve (½-inch-thick) slices. Spread the remaining ½ cup butter evenly on both sides of the slices. Place the slices on the oiled grates. Grill, uncovered, until grill marks appear, about 2 minutes per side. Remove from the grill.

6 Whisk together the cream and powdered sugar in a bowl until soft peaks form, about 2 minutes. Place two cake slices on each of six serving plates. Top evenly with the whipped cream and the raspberries. Garnish with powdered sugar.

GRILLED BANANAS À LA MODE WITH CHOCOLATE DRIZZLE AND PEANUTS

SERVES 8

Hands-On: 20 minutes | Total: 20 minutes

Bananas, chocolate, and peanuts are a trio made in heaven. Grilling the bananas in the peels creates a natural bowl, like the skin of a baked potato, perfect for scooping up bites of the sweet, warm banana.

8 ripe bananas, peeled

Vanilla ice cream

2 cups chocolate syrup

Whipped cream (optional)

2 cups coarsely chopped peanuts

1 Open the bottom and top vents of a charcoal grill completely. Light a charcoal chimney starter filled with charcoal. When the coals are covered with gray ash, pour them onto the bottom grate of the grill. Adjust vents as needed to maintain an internal temperature of 350° to 400°F. Coat the top grate with oil; place on the grill. (If using a gas grill, preheat to medium [350° to 400°F].)

2 Slice the bananas lengthwise and place on the oiled grates, cut-side down, and grill, uncovered, until softened and blackened on one side, 3 to 4 minutes. Remove from the heat and place two halves in each of eight shallow bowls.

3 Top the bananas with a scoop of ice cream, ¼ cup of the chocolate syrup, a dollop of whipped cream, if desired, and ¼ cup of the chopped peanuts.

GRILLED S'MORES

SERVES 4

Hands-On: 10 minutes | Total: 10 minutes

I can't talk about grilling and desserts without giving up my take on the campfire classic. As a kid, I was always that guy who left his marshmallows in the fire until the last minute—making sure I could get a bit of that caramelized color and flavor. That said, these days, time is often my most precious ingredient, so now I like to streamline the process. Though this preparation might not give you charred marshmallows, it will leave you with a perfectly melted, warm dessert that's a handheld dream and a cook's best friend. Wrapping the classic trio in foil not only means you can prep the s'mores hours in advance, it also ensures they will heat gently, so you don't have to stand constant watch over the flames.

2 snack-size (about ½ ounce each) milk chocolate bars (such as Hershey's), broken in half crosswise

4 sheets honey graham crackers, each broken in half crosswise into squares

4 jumbo marshmallows

1 Open the bottom and top vents of a charcoal grill completely. Light a charcoal chimney starter filled with charcoal. When the coals are covered with gray ash, pour them onto the bottom grate of the grill, and then push to one side of the grill. Adjust the vents as needed to maintain an internal temperature of 350° to 400°F. (If using a gas grill, preheat to medium [350° to 400°F] on one side.)

2 Place a chocolate piece on each of four graham cracker squares and top with a marshmallow. Top with the remaining four graham cracker pieces. Wrap the s'mores individually in heavy-duty aluminum foil.

3 Place the wrapped s'mores on grates over the side without the coals (or on the unlit side of gas grill). Grill, covered, about 4 minutes. Turn the s'mores over and grill, covered, until the marshmallows soften and squish down easily when pressed, about 4 minutes.

GRILLED PEACH COBBLER

SERVES 6 TO 8

Hands-On: 15 minutes | Total: 40 minutes

This cobbler is delicious either hot off the grill or at room temperature. Top it with a scoop of vanilla ice cream for extra sweetness.

PEACHES

7 cups (½-inch) fresh peach slices (about 6 to 8 peaches, peeled); or 2 (20-ounce) bags frozen sliced peaches, thawed and drained

¾ cup granulated sugar

2 tablespoons all-purpose flour

1 teaspoon ground cinnamon

⅛ teaspoon ground nutmeg

¼ teaspoon kosher salt

2 tablespoons unsalted butter

BISCUIT TOPPING

1 cup all-purpose flour

¼ cup granulated sugar

1½ teaspoons baking powder

½ cup heavy cream

4 tablespoons unsalted butter, melted

1 Open the bottom vent of a charcoal grill completely. Light a charcoal chimney starter filled with charcoal. When the coals are covered with gray ash, pour them onto the bottom grate of the grill, and then push to one side of the grill. Adjust the vents as needed to maintain an internal temperature of 350° to 400°F. (If using a gas grill, preheat to medium [350° to 400°F] on one side.)

2 **For the peaches:** Place the peaches in a large bowl. Stir together the sugar, flour, cinnamon, nutmeg, and salt in a small bowl. Sprinkle the mixture over the peaches and stir gently to combine. Spoon into a buttered 10-inch cast-iron skillet. Cut the butter into small pieces and sprinkle over the peaches. Cover the skillet tightly with aluminum foil.

3 Place the skillet on the grates over the side with the coals (or on the lit side of a gas grill). Grill, covered, until bubbling and hot, about 15 minutes.

4 **For the biscuit topping:** Stir together the flour, sugar, and baking powder in a small bowl. Make a well in the center and add the cream and melted butter. Stir just until the mixture comes together.

5 Uncover the grill; discard the foil from the skillet. Dollop the dough onto the peaches. Grill, covered, until the biscuits are browned, about 15 minutes. Remove the skillet from the grill and let stand for 10 minutes before serving.

resources

Black garlic: BlackGarlicNA.com

Cajun seasoning: SlapYaMama.com

Cast-iron cookware: LodgeMfg.com

Creole seasoning: TonyChachere.com

Fish sauce: Tiparos.com

Cast-iron Kamado-style grill: GoldensCastIron.com

Jack Rudy Cocktail Co.: JackRudyCocktailCo.com

Jerry Baird's all-purpose seasoning: JerryBairds.com

Mediterranean spices and blends: LaBoiteNY.com

Mojo criollo: Goya.com

Olive oil: GeorgiaOliveFarms.com

Pig tails, rabbit legs, and other wild game: DArtagnan.com

Seasoned salt: McCormick.com/Lawrys

Tajín Clásico seasoning: Tajin.com

Tortilla press, crinkle-cut fry cutter, and other accessories: Amazon.com

Zone 1 BBQ Sauces and Rubs: contact Cadillac (wherever you can find him!)

SERIAL GRILLER

DATE DUE

PRINTED IN U.S.A.